Son
Spe .al

WHERE TO STAY
ENGLAND 1998

Where to Stay in England 1998 ***'Somewhere Special'***

Published by: **Jarrold Publishing,** Whitefriars, Norwich NR3 1TR, *in association with the* **English Tourist Board,** Thames Tower, Black's Road, Hammersmith, London W6 9EL *and* **Celsius,** St Thomas House, St Thomas Street, Winchester SO23 9HE.

Managing Editor, ETB: Jane Collinson
Design, Compilation and Production: Celsius
Editorial Contributors: Tessa Lecomber, Hugh Chevallier
Photography (excluding line entries): Birmingham Museum and Art Gallery, Britain on View, Exeter City Museums and Art Gallery, Hugh Chevallier, Faringdon Tourist Information Centre, Heart of England Tourist Board, National Trust Photographic Library (Joe Cornish, Stephen Robson), Salts Mill, Stamford Museum (Lincolnshire Museums), True North Picture Source, West Country Tourist Board
Illustrations: Ian Penney (front cover), Jeffy Salt, Mary Evans Picture Library
Cartography: Colin Earl
Typesetting: Celsius
Colour Origination: Spectrum LithoScan
Printed and bound in Great Britain

Display Advertisement Sales: Madison Bell Ltd, 3 St. Peter's Street, Islington Green, London N1 8JD. Telephone: (0171) 359 7737.

ISBN 0 7117 0995 5

Important:
The information contained in this guide has been published in good faith on the basis of information submitted to the English Tourist Board by the proprietors of the premises listed, who have paid for their entries to appear. Jarrold Publishing, the English Tourist Board and Celsius cannot guarantee the accuracy of the information in this guide and accept no responsibility for any error or misrepresentation. All liability for loss, disappointment, negligence or other damage caused by reliance on this guide, or in the event of bankruptcy, or liquidation, or cessation of trade of any company, individual or firm mentioned, is hereby excluded. Please check carefully all prices and other details before confirming a reservation.

The English Tourist Board
The Board is a statutory body created by the Development of Tourism Act 1969 to develop and market England's tourism. Its main objectives are to provide a welcome for people visiting England to take their holidays there; to encourage the provision of tourist amenities and facilities in England. The Board has a statutory duty to advise the Government on tourism matters relating to England and, with Government approval and support, administers the national classification and grading schemes for tourist accommodation in England.

Front cover: Marsh Hall Country House Hotel (page 126)
Back cover: New House Farm (page 19), Danesfield House (page 175)

Contents

Welcome to the guide

Somewhere Special is the guide for the discerning traveller, featuring over four hundred hotels, guesthouses, B&Bs and inns all offering their guests that little bit extra. The format is easy to use, with attractive, detailed entries cross-referenced to full-colour maps, plus articles and features as well as helpful hints. Whatever your budget, and whether you want a short get-away or a longer break, ***Somewhere Special*** offers a choice of accommodation that promises a warm welcome and a stay that's special.

Your sure sign of where to stay

As in other English Tourist Board *Where to Stay* accommodation guides, all accommodation included in this invaluable title has been classified under the Board's quality grading and classification scheme (see page 6). In *Somewhere Special*, however, you are promised something extra, for every single entry has achieved a top quality grading of ***Highly Commended*** or ***De Luxe*** (see page 8). This means that whatever range of facilities are on offer, they are presented with exceptional care, individuality and quality of service.

Quality first

Whether you're looking for no-holds-barred luxury on a grand scale, a short break in a small hotel with character or an intimate bed and breakfast that gives personal attention to perhaps only three or four guests, you're looking in the right guide. The criterion for inclusion in *Somewhere Special* is excellence rather than the range of facilities available – though of course you'll be able to see at a glance exactly what's on offer.

How to choose

To help you choose somewhere to stay, each entry is illustrated by both a colour photograph and a detailed description. Also displayed are its quality grading, Crown classification and estimated 1998 prices. Facilities are indicated by clear, at-a-glance symbols – see the back flap for a key. You'll also find important details such as meal times, number of bedrooms, parking spaces and which credit/debit cards are accepted, together with address, telephone and fax numbers.

Regional divisions

To make finding somewhere special even easier, the guide is divided into four sections, each with its own map: England's North Country, England's Heartland, England's West Country and South and South East England. At the start of each section is a regional introduction followed by a detailed map, cross-referenced to the geographical list of accommodation. Features on topics as varied as Elgar and the annual Three Choirs Festival, and the remarkable and complex geology of the Isle of Wight are interspersed throughout the entries to make perusal even more absorbing.

Highly Commended and De Luxe

Those establishments awarded a ***Highly Commended*** or ***De Luxe*** grading represent only a small percentage of all Tourist Board quality-graded accommodation. So whether you're looking for somewhere large or small, you can expect to find accommodation of the very highest standard, accompanied by those personal touches which can transform a guesthouse, B&B, inn or hotel into *somewhere really special.*

Crown classifications and quality gradings

The English Tourist Board's accommodation rating scheme has become recognised as the authoritative indicator of the level of service you can expect to find at your selected guesthouse, B&B, inn or hotel. Our team of inspectors has visited over 11,000 establishments throughout England to carry out objective assessments of the facilities and services offered and their overall quality standard.

The Crown system explained

A system of Crown classifications may be applied to any type of establishment offering 'serviced' accommodation – hotels, guesthouses, inns, B&Bs and farmhouses. The number of Crowns is an indication of the range of facilities and services on offer – quite simply, the more Crowns, the wider the range of facilities available. There are six classification bands starting at ***Listed***, and then increasing in line with the facilities from ***One*** to ***Five Crown***. The Tourist Board lays down strict rules about how these Crown classifications are applied, stipulating, for example, that every classified establishment meets standards for the size of bed, type of bed linen and even the extent of illumination in each room. Assessment for higher bands of classification includes the provision of tourist information, the number – and location – of colour televisions, the use of 13-amp power outlets, the availability of room service and much, much more.

Crown classifications – a quick guide

Listed You can be sure that the accommodation will be clean and comfortable, but the range of facilities and services may be limited.

♛ You will find additional facilities, including washbasin and chair in your bedroom and you will have use of a telephone.

♛♛ There will be a colour TV in your bedroom (or in a lounge) and you can enjoy morning tea/coffee in your bedroom. At least some of the bedrooms will have a private bath (or shower) and WC.

♛♛♛ At least half of the bedrooms will have private bath (or shower) en-suite. You will also be able to order a hot evening meal.

♛♛♛♛ Your bedroom will have a colour TV, radio and telephone, there will be lounge service until midnight and evening meals can be ordered up to 2030 hours. At least 90% of the bedrooms will have private bath and/or shower and WC en-suite.

♛♛♛♛♛ Every bedroom will have a private bath, fixed shower and WC en-suite. The restaurant will be open for breakfast, lunch and dinner (or you can take meals in your room from breakfast until midnight) and you will benefit from an all-night lounge service. A night porter will also be on duty.

Quality gradings

A separate quality grading indicates the overall standard of services and facilities. In order to determine which of the four quality grades (APPROVED, COMMENDED, HIGHLY COMMENDED and DE LUXE) should be awarded, a highly-trained Tourist Board inspector assesses every aspect of the accommodation. Those establishments awarded a ***Highly Commended*** or ***De Luxe*** grading represent only a small, select percentage of all Tourist Board quality-graded accommodation.

The rigorous and objective annual English Tourist Board inspection takes into account such factors as warmth of welcome, atmosphere, efficiency, as well as the quality of furnishings and equipment, and the standard of meals and their presentation. Consideration is also given to the style and nature of the accommodation. This means that all types of establishment, whatever their Crown classification, can achieve a high quality grade if the facilities and services they provide, even if limited in scope, are to a very high standard. You will therefore find that *Somewhere Special* features accommodation, from ***Listed*** to ***Five Crown***, that has all been awarded a top quality grading of ***Highly Commended*** or ***De Luxe***. Since only a small percentage of establishments are awarded these top two gradings, you know that if your chosen accommodation is in this guide, it is clearly somewhere very special indeed.

An inspector calls

Before a quality grading is awarded, one of over 55 Tourist Board inspectors visits the guesthouse, B&B, farmhouse, inn or hotel for an assessment. The inspector books in advance, but does not reveal his or her identity on arrival. Sadly for those contemplating a career move, the inspector does not have a lazy time; he or she is busy noting the standard of decor, the state of the grounds, the quality of the food and the courtesy of the staff. Once the bill has been paid the next morning, the inspector announces his or her identity to the management and tours the building. At the end of the tour, they discuss the conclusions, with the inspector making suggestions where helpful. Only after the visit does the inspector arrive at a conclusion for the quality grade – so the assessment is 100 per cent independent and reliable.

Accessibility

It's all very well deciding exactly where you'd like to stay, but if you find difficulty in walking or are a wheelchair user, then you also need to know how accessible a particular establishment is. If you book your accommodation at an establishment displaying the Accessible symbol, there's no longer any guesswork involved. The National Accessibility Scheme forms part of the *Tourism for All* campaign that is being promoted by all three National Tourist Boards. The Tourist Boards recognise three categories of accessibility, based upon what are considered to be the practical needs of wheelchair users:

Category 1: accessible to all wheelchair users including those travelling independently

Category 2: accessible to a wheelchair user with assistance

Category 3: accessible to a wheelchair user able to walk short distances and up at least three steps

Additional help and guidance for those with special needs can be obtained from: Holiday Care Service, 2nd Floor, Imperial Buildings, Victoria Road, Horley, Surrey RH6 7PZ. Telephone (01293) 774535, Fax (01293) 784647, Minicom (01293) 776943.

How to use this *guide*

Somewhere Special will enable you to find that special place to stay in – whichever part of the country you are planning to visit. Even if you only have a rough idea of where you wish to go, you can easily use this guide to locate a quality place to stay.

The guide is divided into four distinct sections: England's North Country, England's Heartland, England's West Country, and South and South East England. On page 12 you will find a comprehensive break-down of which county is in which region, together with an accompanying 'England-at-a-Glance' map. At the start of each section is a full-colour regional map which clearly plots by number the location of all the *Somewhere Special* entries, as well as the positions of major roads, towns, stations and airports. If you know the area you want to visit, first locate the possible establishments on the regional map and then turn to the appropriate pages in the regional section. The entries are listed by their geographical position, so you'll find that the places you're interested in are usually close to each other in the listing.

Each entry provides detailed information on the nature of the establishment together with the facilities provided and a colour photograph so that you can easily determine whether the place meets the criteria you have in mind. It also lists 1998 estimated prices, so you immediately know whether the entry falls within your price range.

The entries in more detail

The entries are designed to convey as much information as possible in a clear, attractive and easy-to-read format. The first line contains the name of the inn, hotel, guesthouse or B&B, together with its Crown classification and quality grading. In *Somewhere Special,* of course, every entry will have a quality grading of either ***Highly Commended*** or **De Luxe**. Below these come the full address and telephone number of the establishment and, where applicable, its fax number.

Each entry features a full-colour photograph of the establishment and a short description of its main attractions. These details have been supplied by the proprietors themselves and although this information has been checked for accuracy, you are advised to confirm all relevant details at the time of booking. At the foot of each entry comes the all-important practical information:

- A guide to 1998 prices for bed & breakfast and for half board, for both single and double rooms. Prices can sometimes change after the guide has gone to press, so please check when making a booking.
- Mealtimes for both lunch and evening meal, when available.
- The numbers of bedrooms and bathrooms, and whether the latter are en-suite, private or shared.
- The number of parking spaces.
- The range of any credit and charge cards accepted.

In the bottom right-hand corner of the entry is a list of symbols representing in greater detail the range of facilities and services offered. The key explaining exactly what these mean is conveniently located on the back of the cover flap, which can be kept open while you're browsing through the entries. The symbols cover everything from the provision of private shooting rights to whether or not there's a sauna for guests' use. Most importantly, they allow you to see at a glance whether any special requirements you may have can be met.

Other features of the guide

As well as the entries – over 430 in all – you'll find many features on a wide variety of subjects scattered throughout the book. The four informative introductions to the regions appear on pages 13, 63, 117 and 167. At the back of the book (pages 201–205) you will find more detailed information about booking accommodation. You are strongly recommended to read this before committing yourself to any firm arrangements, bearing in mind the fact that all details have been supplied by proprietors themselves.

In this guide, England is divided into four main sections. A map of the area, showing each entry and its nearest town or city, as well as nearby major roads or motorways, can be found after the regional introduction.

England at a glance

England's North Country
Cumbria, Durham, Northumberland, Tees Valley, Tyne & Wear, Cheshire, Greater Manchester, Lancashire, Merseyside, East Riding of Yorkshire, North, South & West Yorkshire and North & North East Lincolnshire.

England's Heartland
Gloucestershire, Hereford & Worcester, Shropshire, Staffordshire, Warwickshire, West Midlands, Derbyshire, Rutland, Leicestershire, Nottinghamshire, Northamptonshire, Bedfordshire, Cambridgeshire, Essex, Hertfordshire, Lincolnshire, Norfolk and Suffolk.

England's West Country
Bath & North East Somerset, Bristol, Cornwall, Devon, North Somerset, Somerset, South Gloucestershire, Western Dorset, Wiltshire and the Isles of Scilly.

South and South East England
London, Berkshire, Buckinghamshire, Eastern Dorset, Hampshire, Isle of Wight, Oxfordshire, East & West Sussex, Kent and Surrey.

England's North Country

THE PENNINES – running the length of the North Country from the Peak District right up to the Cheviots straddling the Scottish border – dominate the landscape of most of England's northerly counties, giving an upland flavour to the whole region. Wherever you are, the Pennines are easily accessible, little more than an hour by car even from further-flung corners such as Spurn Head at the mouth of the River Humber or the Wirral jutting out into Liverpool Bay. Rising to 1,500ft (450m) or more at regular intervals, England's mountainous spine is home to some of the most glorious scenery in the land and each year provides recreation for millions of visitors.

Beyond even the northernmost extremity of the Pennines lies Berwick-upon-Tweed, a most attractive town known both for its geographical position and for a string of stranger claims to fame. The architectural historian Sir Alec Clifton-Taylor believed it to be one of the most intriguing towns in the land, and there is much to explore. Not far south are some of England's few east-coast islands, the Farnes. Current residents include large numbers of Arctic terns, puffins and grey seals – all best seen in May or June – but in the last century the Farne Islands were synonymous with the heroic feats of Grace Darling. Inland lies the picturesque village of

Abbeys of the Dales and Moors

When Cistercian monks from Normandy established the foundations of Rievaulx, Fountains, Jervaulx and Byland, they were given some of the poorest tracts of wasteland to farm by the Norman lords. But, by recruiting large numbers of lay-brethren and using efficient farming methods, they turned moorland into a productive asset.

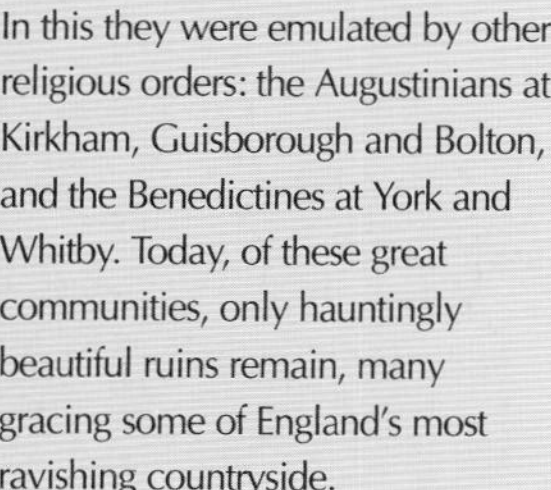

In this they were emulated by other religious orders: the Augustinians at Kirkham, Guisborough and Bolton, and the Benedictines at York and Whitby. Today, of these great communities, only hauntingly beautiful ruins remain, many gracing some of England's most ravishing countryside.

Lawnmowers on display

The British Lawnmower Museum (tel: 01704 501336) is based in the seaside resort of Southport, Merseyside. Prized exhibits include some of the first machines dating from the early 19th century, mowers once belonging to Nicholas Parsons and to Prince Charles, another capable of cutting a 2-inch (5cm) wide strip, and what is believed to be the only hand-powered rotary lawnmower in existence. Also on view is the world's largest collection of toy mowers and one of the oldest surviving racing lawnmowers (built by the curator).

Chillingham, home to a medieval castle (recently opened to the public) and a unique herd of cattle. These shy, white, crescent-horned animals are probably similar to the oxen with which the ancient Britons tilled the fields in the days before Emperor Hadrian left his mark upon the landscape.

Following Hadrian's Wall west over the Pennines and through the vastness of the Northumberland National Park leads you towards the Lake District, England's second largest upland area. The highlights of this most beautiful landscape are, of course, the endless combinations of high fell, shimmering blue-black lake, splashing stream and whitewashed farmhouse, while the ever-changing weather ensures that you never see the same canvas twice. And there are attractions other than scenery: Cumbrian sports, craft fairs, a rare chance to see the native red squirrel, the Stan Laurel Museum in Ulverston, the *Gondola* plying up and down Coniston Water, Tullie House in Carlisle, Penrith and Brougham Castles are but a few in and beyond the Lakes. Should you be especially keen to get away from it all you could try the little-known Cumbrian coast: St Bees Head if bird-watching appeals, Great Urswick (near Ulverston) if quiet, unassuming village hospitality is more to your taste.

At about this latitude the Pennines are better known as the Yorkshire Dales. Not quite matching the Lake District in terms of altitude, the flat-topped hills of the Dales are every bit as characterful. Three that typify the limestone features of the region are Ingleborough, Whernside and Pen-y-ghent, collectively known as the Three Peaks and the venue for a race that demands deep reserves of Yorkshire grit. In this terrain, a potholer's paradise, rivers disappear and reappear again and the strange phenomenon of the limestone pavement, comprising 'clints' (lumps) and 'grikes' (fissures) is commonplace. Wensleydale and Swaledale are perhaps the best known and most dramatic of the Dales, but for quiet walking where Swaledale sheep, the emblem of the Dales National Park, are your only companions it's worth heading for the Howgills north of Sedbergh, or the Forest of Bowland, south-east of Lancaster.

Solace has long been sought in this part of the world for there is a concentration of ruined abbeys on the eastern edge of the Dales and the western edge of the North York Moors. The Moors, characterised by a heathery plateau cut with narrow, steep-sided valleys, have remained largely undeveloped and unspoilt. Unlike the other national parks of the North, the Moors extend to the coast where small fishing villages of improbable beauty seem to tumble headlong into the North Sea. Staithes, Runswick Bay and Robin Hood's Bay are all ideal meandering territory – but beware the cliffs, for at Boulby, just north of Staithes, are England's highest vertical cliffs at around 700ft (220m). The coastline here is constantly being pummelled by a relentless sea and south of Flamborough Head the East Riding of Yorkshire is diminishing by up to 6ft (2m) a year; whole communities have been swept out to sea over the centuries. Only the palaeontologist, searching for ammonites and belemnites dislodged by the latest storm, benefits from the destructive power of the waves.

The Pennine valleys of West Yorkshire and south-east Lancashire are only now being appreciated for their particular mixture of natural beauty and industrial heritage, but they often provide interest that matches many of England's better-known attractions. Calderdale, south-west of Leeds, makes a good place to begin an exploration. Much-underrated Halifax, Heptonstall and Hebden Bridge, all in the dale's upper reaches, are also surrounded by fine walking country. In Saltaire, the factory village built just north of Bradford by liberal industrialist Titus Salt, lies a vast mill. The huge building no longer hums with the sound of clacking looms but with the appreciative murmur of visitors admiring the Hockneys lining its walls. Further down the Calder the local agriculture takes on a distinctive flavour for here, at Wakefield and Pontefract, farmers eschew wheat and barley for the cultivation of rhubarb.

Though the defining characteristic of the North Country may be its uplands, it has no shortage of historic towns and cities. York, Durham, Lancaster and, in the south-western corner of the region, Chester cram in more history than seems possible for such compact city-centres. Leaving Chester bound for the Victorian port of Liverpool, with its incomparable river frontage, you unwittingly enter the Botany Bay of the Middle Ages. The Wirral peninsula, bounded by sea on three sides, was the enforced home of medieval felons and undesirables. Nowadays people come here of their own volition, perhaps to visit Port Sunlight, to bird-watch on the Dee estuary or to walk the sands of West Kirby to the little, thrift-covered Hilbre Island.

Gondola

Gondola is the National Trust's only steam yacht, and plies up and down Coniston Water in the Lake District for around seven months each year. Described as 'a perfect combination of the Venetian Gondola and the English Steam Yacht', she was launched at Coniston in 1859, remaining in service until 1937, when her hull became a houseboat and her boiler was used for the cutting of timber in a saw mill. In 1977 she was bought by the National Trust, and, restored to former glory, once more ferries visitors the length of the lake.

Left: Whitby Harbour, North Yorkshire; inset: Buttermere, Cumbria

Berwick-upon-Tweed

Berwick-upon-Tweed, though still in England, is further north than much of the Hebridean island of Islay. Oddly, it is cut off from the county which bears its name, for Berwickshire lies in Scotland. Not surprisingly, Berwick's history is intractably bound up with the struggle between the English and the Scots; between 1147 and 1482, the town changed hands 13 times. The 16th century saw the town walls comprehensively fortified against a Scots-French attack which never materialised, hence their amazing state of preservation. A two-mile (3km) walk around these ramparts gives spectacular views of the historic town.

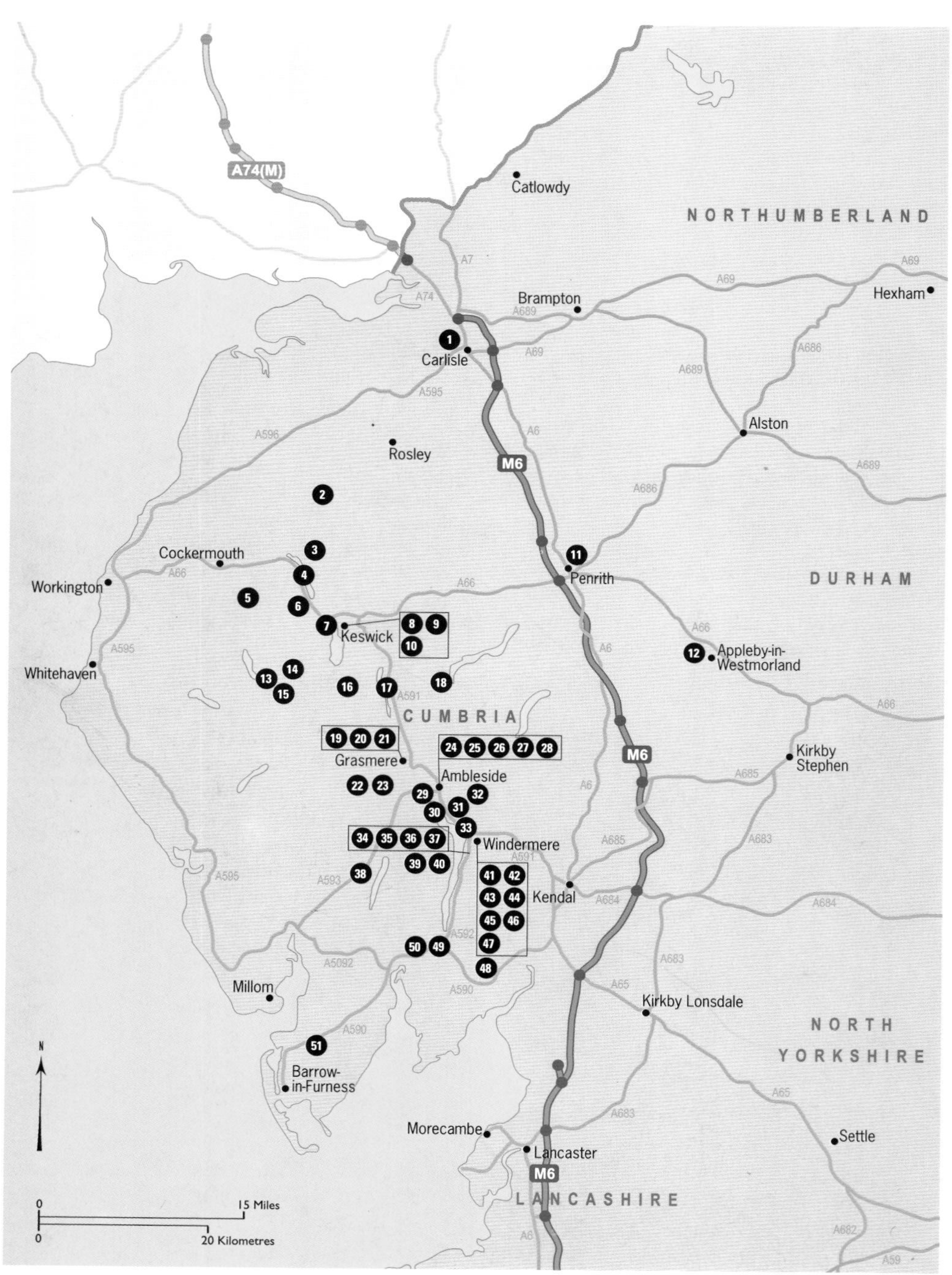
A74(M)
Catlowdy
NORTHUMBERLAND
A7
A69
A74
Brampton
A689
Hexham
1
Carlisle
A69
A686
A689
A595
A6
Alston
A596
Rosley
M6
A689
A686
2
3
Cockermouth
11
A66
4
Penrith
DURHAM
Workington
A66
5
6
7
8
9
Keswick
10
A66
12
Appleby-in-Westmorland
A595
A6
Whitehaven
14
13
15
16
17
18
A591
CUMBRIA
A66
19
20
21
24
25
26
27
28
M6
Kirkby Stephen
Grasmere
22
23
Ambleside
A685
A6
29
32
30
31
33
34
35
36
37
Windermere
A685
A683
A591
A595
A593
38
39
40
41
42
43
44
Kendal
A684
A684
45
46
A592
47
50
49
A5092
48
A683
A65
Millom
A590
Kirkby Lonsdale
NORTH YORKSHIRE
A590
51
N
Barrow-in-Furness
A65
A683
Morecambe
Settle
Lancaster
M6
LANCASHIRE
0
15 Miles
0
20 Kilometres
A6
A682
A59

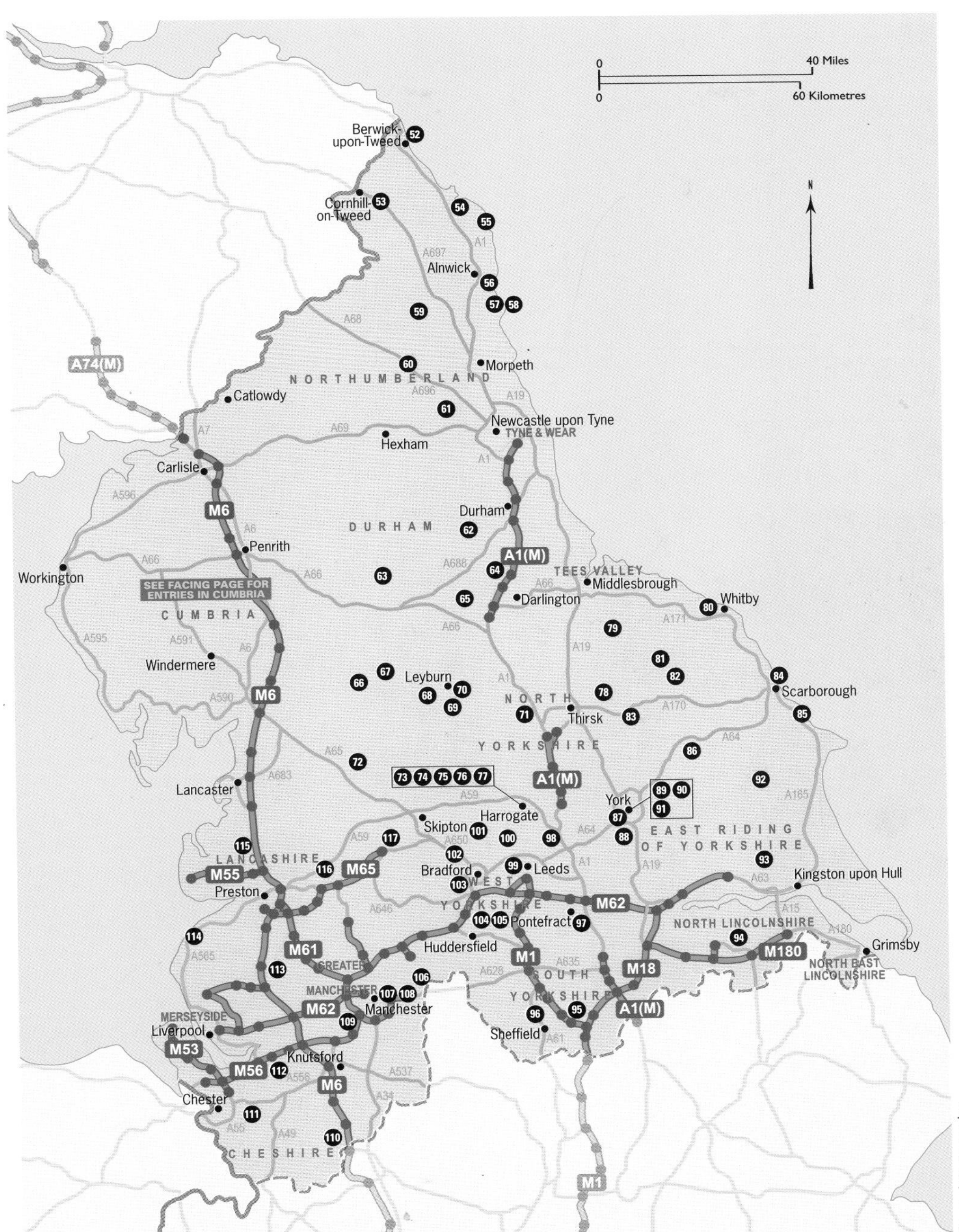
0
40 Miles
0
60 Kilometres
N
Berwick-upon-Tweed
52
Cornhill-on-Tweed
53
54
55
A697
A1
Alnwick
56
57
58
A68
59
A74(M)
60
Morpeth
NORTHUMBERLAND
A696
A19
Catlowdy
61
Newcastle upon Tyne
TYNE & WEAR
A7
A69
Hexham
A1
Carlisle
A596
M6
Durham
DURHAM
62
A6
Penrith
A1(M)
Workington
A66
A688
64
TEES VALLEY
Middlesbrough
A66
63
A66
SEE FACING PAGE FOR ENTRIES IN CUMBRIA
Darlington
65
80
Whitby
CUMBRIA
A171
A66
79
A595
A591
A6
A19
Windermere
81
82
84
Scarborough
67
66
Leyburn
70
68
69
A1
78
A590
M6
NORTH
Thirsk
A170
71
83
85
YORKSHIRE
A64
86
A65
72
73
74
75
76
77
A1(M)
92
A683
Lancaster
89
90
91
A59
York
Harrogate
87
A165
EAST RIDING OF YORKSHIRE
Skipton
101
100
98
A64
88
A59
117
A650
115
102
LANCASHIRE
116
M65
99
Leeds
93
M55
Bradford
A1
A19
Preston
103
WEST
A63
Kingston upon Hull
YORKSHIRE
M62
A646
A15
104
105
Pontefract
97
NORTH LINCOLNSHIRE
114
M61
Huddersfield
94
M180
A180
Grimsby
A565
M1
A635
NORTH EAST LINCOLNSHIRE
113
GREATER MANCHESTER
A628
SOUTH
M18
106
107
108
Manchester
YORKSHIRE
MERSEYSIDE
M62
96
95
A1(M)
Liverpool
109
Sheffield
A61
M53
Knutsford
M56
112
A556
A537
Chester
M6
A34
111
A55
A49
110
CHESHIRE
M1
M6
Colin Earl Cartography

1 NUMBER THIRTY ONE

DE LUXE

31 Howard Place, Carlisle, Cumbria CA1 1HR Tel (01228) 597080 Fax (01228) 597080

This elegant city-centre town house has been restored by Philip and Judith into an interesting and comfortable home. All rooms provide private bath, shower and toilet. Philip holds cookery courses and serves imaginative traditional and vegetarian meals. He is an enthusiastic fell walker and guide, game fisherman and water colourist. His knowledge of the Lakes, Carlisle, Hadrian's Wall and other interesting places to visit, all add to the pleasure of a stay here.

Bed & Breakfast per night: single room from £35.00–£55.00; double room from £50.00–£80.00
Half board per person: £50.00–£75.00 daily; £350.00–£525.00 weekly
Evening meal 1800 (last orders 2100)

Bedrooms: 1 single, 2 double
Bathrooms: 3 en-suite
Open: March–November

2 WOODLANDS COUNTRY HOUSE

HIGHLY COMMENDED

Ireby, Cumbria CA5 1EX Tel (016973) 71791 Fax (016973) 71482

Woodlands is an elegant Victorian house enjoying magnificent open views over the tranquil northern fells. Ireby, a truly unspoilt Cumbrian village, is an ideal base for exploring northern Lakeland. All our rooms are charmingly and comfortably appointed, and we offer freshly-prepared home cooking. John and Helen Payne offer a personal and caring service and a warm welcome. Residential licence. Non-smoking. Vegetarian alternatives. Open fires. Suitable for wheelchair users. CATEGORY 2

Bed & Breakfast per night: double room from £55.00–£60.00
Half board per person: £40.00–£43.00 daily; maximum £240.00 weekly
Evening meal 1900 (last bookings 1600)

Bedrooms: 3 double, 2 twin, 2 triple
Bathrooms: 7 en-suite
Parking for 12
Open: March–October and Christmas
Cards accepted: Mastercard, Visa, Amex, Switch/Delta

5

3 RAVENSTONE LODGE

HIGHLY COMMENDED

Bassenthwaite, Keswick, Cumbria CA12 4QG Tel (017687) 76629 or (017687) 76638 Fax (017687) 76629

A warm and friendly welcome awaits you at Ravenstone Lodge, our 19th-century stone-built property nestling at the foot of Ullock Pike, just four miles north of Keswick on the A591. The lodge is set in five acres of spectacular countryside with a private terrace, a large walled garden and ample off-the-road parking space. Enjoy the relaxed atmosphere of our stable dining room, bar and large Victorian-style conservatory.

Bed & Breakfast per night: single occupancy from £30.50–£32.50; double room from £57.00–£61.00
Half board per person: £43.50–£47.50 daily; £284.55–£309.75 weekly
Evening meal 1900 (last bookings 1800)

Bedrooms: 6 double, 2 twin, 1 family room
Bathrooms: 9 en-suite
Parking for 12
Cards accepted: Mastercard, Visa, Switch/Delta

8

Entries are cross referenced by number to the maps on pages 16–17

4 PHEASANT INN

HIGHLY COMMENDED

Bassenthwaite Lake, Cockermouth, Cumbria CA13 9YE Tel (017687) 76234 Fax (017687) 76002

A tranquil, traditional, north Lake District inn, adjacent to Bassenthwaite Lake, and surrounded by gardens and woodland providing a wealth of wildlife. Three lounges feature antiques, beams, open fires and fresh flowers. Commended by major guides for high quality English food and service, Pheasant Inn also has twenty individually-decorated bedrooms with private facilities. Dogs welcome – kennels available. CATEGORY 3

Bed & Breakfast per night: single room from £67.00–£70.00; double room from £110.00–£120.00
Half board per person: £420.00–£500.00 weekly
Lunch available: 1230–1400
Evening meal 1900 (last orders 2030)

Bedrooms: 5 single, 8 double, 7 twin
Bathrooms: 20 en-suite
Parking for 80
Cards accepted: Mastercard, Visa

5 NEW HOUSE FARM

HIGHLY COMMENDED

Lorton, Cockermouth, Cumbria CA13 9UU Tel (01900) 85404 Fax (01900) 85404

The Lorton Vale is a spectacular 'Fell and Valley' setting for this carefully restored 17th-century Lakeland stone farmhouse, which has fine views from every room. The Lorton Vale is the 'real' Lake District without the crowds, and the Vale remains quiet even throughout the summer months. New House Farm has 15 acres of open fields, woods, streams and ponds which guests (and dogs) may wander at will. Comfortable accommodation and a cosy dining room with fine traditional cooking complete the picture of this very special country guesthouse. This is a non-smoking establishment.

Bed & Breakfast per night: single occupancy from £35.00–£40.00; double room from £60.00–£80.00
Half board per person: £50.00–£60.00 daily; £356.00–£420.00 weekly
Evening meal 1900 (last bookings 1900)

Bedrooms: 3 double
Bathrooms: 3 en-suite
Parking for 20

12 S SP T

6 THWAITE HOWE HOTEL

HIGHLY COMMENDED

Thornthwaite, Keswick, Cumbria CA12 5SA Tel (017687) 78281 Fax (017687) 78529

Situated in its own grounds, with superb views across the Derwent Valley to the Skiddaw range, our hotel is in a very peaceful position, but in easy reach of all the Lake District's attractions. Mary's delicious, award-winning home cooking is complemented by fine wines, or followed by one of Harry's cask-strength malt whiskies. Red squirrels feed in the garden daily and, together with guests, enjoy the friendly informal atmosphere.

Half board per person: £44.00–£49.50 daily; £308.00–£322.00 weekly
Evening meal 1900 (last orders 1900)

Bedrooms: 5 double, 3 twin
Bathrooms: 8 en-suite
Parking for 12
Open: March–October
Cards accepted: Mastercard, Visa, Switch/Delta

7 DERWENT COTTAGE

HIGHLY COMMENDED

Portinscale, Keswick, Cumbria CA12 5RF Tel (017687) 74838

Gleaming silver, cut glass, spacious en-suite bedrooms and elegant furnishings are all to be found at Derwent Cottage. This Lakeland house, dating from the 18th century, stands in an acre of secluded gardens in the quiet village of Portinscale, one mile from Keswick. A four-course, candle light table d'hôte is served at 1900 each evening with classical music in the background. A residential licence is held and drinks and wine are available throughout the evening. We are a totally non-smoking establishment.

Bed & Breakfast per night: double room from £62.00–£74.00
Half board per person: £45.00–£50.00 daily; £266.00–£294.00 weekly
Evening meal 1900 (last orders 1900)

Bedrooms: 4 double, 2 twin
Bathrooms: 6 en-suite
Parking for 10
Open: March–October
Cards accepted: Mastercard, Visa

12

---

8 SKIDDAW HOTEL

HIGHLY COMMENDED

Market Square, Keswick, Cumbria CA12 5BN Tel (017687) 72071 Fax (017687) 74850

Situated in the heart of Keswick, northern Lakeland's leading market town, the Skiddaw Hotel provides the perfect setting for that special break away from it all. Romantic packages are available which include lake-cruise picnics, Bucks Fizz breakfasts, candle-lit dinners and our lovely new four-poster bedroom. Free facilities exclusive to our residents include in-house saunas, mid-week golf and a leisure club with fully equipped gym and swimming pool. Special breaks are always available.

Bed & Breakfast per night: single room from £32.50–£39.00; double room from £65.00–£74.00
Half board per person: £42.50–£47.00 daily; £264.00–£294.00 weekly
Lunch available: 1200–1430

Evening meal 1800 (last orders 2200)
Bedrooms: 7 single, 14 double, 11 twin, 8 triple
Bathrooms: 40 en-suite
Parking for 13
Cards accepted: Mastercard, Visa, Amex, Switch/Delta

---

9 THE GRANGE COUNTRY HOUSE HOTEL

HIGHLY COMMENDED

Manor Brow, Ambleside Road, Keswick, Cumbria CA12 4BA Tel (017687) 72500

The Grange Country House Hotel is set in its own grounds overlooking Keswick-on-Derwentwater and the surrounding mountains. An elegant Lakeland house built in the 1840s, The Grange is proudly owned by Duncan and Jane Miller. The hotel offers quality and comfort in a warm relaxing atmosphere, holds various awards and is featured in many of the leading guides. Lovely bedrooms, log fires and freshly prepared food. Unforgettable.

Bed & Breakfast per night: double room from £64.00–£76.00
Half board per person: £46.50–£53.50 daily; £325.00–£339.00 weekly
Evening meal 1930

Bedrooms: 7 double, 3 twin
Bathrooms: 10 en-suite, 1 public
Parking for 13
Open: March–November
Cards accepted: Mastercard, Visa

7

Entries are cross referenced by number to the maps on pages 16–17

10 CRAGLANDS

HIGHLY COMMENDED

Penrith Road, Keswick, Cumbria CA12 4LJ Tel (017687) 74406

An excellent Victorian house situated in a quiet location on the outskirts of Keswick overlooking the town, it offers splendid views of both Grisdale and Causey Pike to the front of the house and Latrigg to the rear. You will receive a warm welcome in a relaxing and friendly atmosphere, together with a beautifully furnished and decorated interior. The dining room offers the very best of British cuisine using fresh local produce.

Bed & Breakfast per night: single room £30.00; double room from £46.00–£50.00
Half board per person: £42.50–£44.50 daily; £240.00–£250.00 weekly
Evening meal 1900 (last orders 2000)

Bedrooms: 1 single, 3 double, 1 twin
Bathrooms: 5 en-suite
Parking for 5

8 UL S SP

11 HORNBY HALL COUNTRY HOUSE

Listed HIGHLY COMMENDED

Brougham, Penrith, Cumbria CA10 2AR Tel (01768) 891114 Fax (01768) 891114

Hornby Hall is a 16th-century farmhouse still with its original tower and spiral staircase. The house has been restored to provide comfortable accommodation and quiet country house atmosphere. Meals are served in the Great Hall, using fresh local food. We are ideally situated for trips to the Lakes, Dales, Hadrian's Wall and Carlisle which has an interesting castle and a superb museum. Ride on the famous Carlisle–Settle railway or fish quietly on Hornby's own stretch of water.

Bed & Breakfast per night: single room from £23.50–£25.00; double room from £55.00–£66.00
Half board per person: £35.00–£51.00 daily
Evening meal 1900 (last orders 2100)

Bedrooms: 1 single, 2 double, 4 twin
Bathrooms: 2 en-suite, 3 public
Parking for 10
Cards accepted: Mastercard, Visa

S TV SP

12 APPLEBY MANOR COUNTRY HOUSE HOTEL

HIGHLY COMMENDED

Roman Road, Appleby-in-Westmorland, Cumbria CA16 6JB Tel (017683) 51571 Fax (017683) 52888 E-mail 100043.1561@compuserve.com

Probably the most relaxing and friendly hotel you'll ever stay at! Set amidst breathtaking beauty, you'll find spotlessly clean accommodation; satellite television and video films; a splendid indoor leisure club that has a small swimming pool, jacuzzi, steam-room, sauna and sunbed; magnificent lounges, and great food in the award-winning restaurant – all in a genuine country house. Golf, squash, horse-riding and all the delights of the Lake District and Yorkshire Dales are close by.

Bed & Breakfast per night: single occupancy from £69.00–£76.00; double room from £98.00–£112.00
Half board per person: £54.50–£66.00 daily; £327.00–£396.00 weekly
Lunch available: 1200–1400

Evening meal 1900 (last orders 2100)
Bedrooms: 14 double, 8 twin, 1 triple, 7 family rooms
Bathrooms: 30 en-suite Parking for 50
Cards accepted: Mastercard, Visa, Diners, Amex, Switch/Delta

S SP T

At-a-glance symbols are explained on the flap inside the back cover

13 BRIDGE HOTEL

HIGHLY COMMENDED

Buttermere, Cockermouth, Cumbria CA13 9UZ Tel (017687) 70252 Fax (017687) 70252

An 18th-century coaching inn, beautifully situated between two lakes in Lakeland's loveliest valley. Superb unrestricted walking country and breathtaking scenery. Complimentary afternoon tea is served near the log fire in our very comfortable residents' lounge. Two well-stocked bars serve expertly-kept real ales. Four-poster beds. Dogs welcome. Special breaks offered throughout the year.

Bed & Breakfast per night: single room from £38.00–£43.00; double room from £76.00–£86.00
Half board per person: £54.00–£62.00 daily; from £340.00 weekly
Lunch available: 1200–1430

Evening meal 1900 (last orders 2030)
Bedrooms: 2 single, 8 double, 12 twin
Bathrooms: 21 en-suite, 2 private
Parking for 60
Cards accepted: Mastercard, Visa, Switch/Delta

S SP

Lady Anne Clifford and her monuments

'THEY THAT SHALL BE OF THEE shall build the old waste places' reads the quotation (from Isaiah 58:12) above the door of Outhgill church near Kirkby Stephen. The message, carved at the instigation of Lady Anne Clifford who restored the church in the 17th century, was one which she took to heart. When at the age of 60 she inherited lands in Cumberland, Westmorland and Yorkshire, she embarked upon a frenzy of building, repairs and restoration with a near-religious zeal.

Her enthusiasm was engendered by long years of frustration. She was just 15 in 1605 when her father died and, as his only surviving child, she confidently expected to inherit his extensive northern estates. Instead she found they had been left to his brother and nephew, and she immediately began a long and fruitless campaign to regain her inheritance. In 1643, however, her cousin Henry died without heir and the estates, at long last, passed to her, his only legitimate successor.

Neglect and the Civil War had taken their toll on her many castles. Those of Appleby, Skipton, Brough, Brougham (shown here), Pendragon and Barden Tower had all fallen into decay, but during the next two decades Lady Anne restored them to their original splendour. She also repaired churches at Skipton, Brough, Brougham and Appleby and built almshouses and monuments, a display of wealth not altogether wise in the puritan atmosphere of Commonwealth England.

To celebrate the restoration of her inheritance Lady Anne commissioned a remarkable painting – depicting herself and all the major characters from her eventful life. Known as the Great Picture, this now hangs in the keep of Appleby Castle (tel: 017683 51402). Also in the town, she built the St Anne's almshouses and the white pillars at either end of the main street, while her tomb and that of her beloved mother, Margaret, Countess of Cumberland, lie in St Lawrence's church. On the road to Brougham is the Countess Pillar marking the spot where Lady Anne last saw her mother alive.

Skipton Castle, lovingly restored by Lady Anne, remains one of the most complete and best preserved medieval castles in England (tel: 01756 792442). But, despite all her efforts Barden Tower and the castles of Pendragon, Brough and Brougham are all ruins once more. (Details from Kirkby Stephen Tourist Information Office, tel: 017683 71199). A 100-mile (161km) walk, Lady Anne's Way, takes in all the buildings and monuments associated with this redoubtable lady.

Entries are cross referenced by number to the maps on pages 16–17

14 SWINSIDE LODGE

DE LUXE

Newlands, Keswick, Cumbria CA12 5UE Tel (017687) 72948 Fax (017687) 72948

Swinside Lodge is a delightful Victorian house in a beautiful and tranquil corner of the Lake District, just beneath Cat Bells and a five-minute stroll from the shores of Derwent Water. Relax in this most comfortable and elegantly furnished house where you can enjoy superb award-winning food served by friendly staff in the candle-lit dining room. The hotel, which is personally run, is totally no smoking and is unlicensed but please bring your own favourite wines. A warm welcome awaits you.

Bed & Breakfast per night: single occupancy from £47.00–£60.00; double room from £78.00–£105.00
Half board per person: £64.00–£80.00 daily
Evening meal 1930 (last orders 2000)

Bedrooms: 5 double, 2 twin
Bathrooms: 7 en-suite
Open: February–November and Christmas

10 UL SP T

15 PICKETT HOWE

DE LUXE

Buttermere Valley, Cockermouth, Cumbria CA13 9UY Tel (01900) 85444 Fax (01900) 85209

Winner of the prestigious English Tourist Board 'England for Excellence' award (1994). Nestling peacefully beneath rugged Lakeland peaks, this 17th-century former farmhouse offers just eight non-smoking guests a unique holiday experience. Slate floors, oak beams and mullioned windows are enhanced by quality furnishings and antiques, the cosy bedrooms have whirlpool baths and Victorian brass iron beds. The exceptional breakfast menu and well-balanced, beautifully presented dinners combined with caring, relaxed hospitality make Pickett Howe a perfect holiday base.

Bed & Breakfast per night: double room £74.00
Half board per person: £59.00 daily; £399.00 weekly
Evening meal 1915

Bedrooms: 3 double, 1 twin
Bathrooms: 4 en-suite
Parking for 6
Open: April–November
Cards accepted: Mastercard, Visa

10 S T

16 HAZEL BANK

HIGHLY COMMENDED

Rosthwaite, Borrowdale, Keswick, Cumbria CA12 5XB Tel (017687) 77248 Fax (017678) 77373

Standing on an elevated site overlooking the village of Rosthwaite, there are unsurpassed views of the Borrowdale Valley and central Lakeland peaks. The peaceful location makes Hazel Bank an ideal base for walkers, birdwatchers and lovers of the countryside, with direct access to many mountain and valley walks. The Victorian residence has been carefully and sympathetically converted to provide quality country house accommodation. Come and discover how enjoyable a stay in Borrowdale can be. Non-smokers only, please.

Half board per person: maximum £46.00 daily; maximum £287.00 weekly
Evening meal 1900 (last orders 1900)

Bedrooms: 1 single, 2 double, 3 twin
Bathrooms: 6 en-suite
Parking for 12
Open: April–October
Cards accepted: Mastercard, Visa, Switch/Delta

6 SP

17 DALE HEAD HALL LAKESIDE HOTEL

HIGHLY COMMENDED

Thirlmere, Keswick, Cumbria CA12 4TN Tel (017687) 72478 or 0800 454166 Fax (017687) 71070 E-mail daleheadho@aol.com

With Helvellyn rising majestically behind, the hotel stands alone on the shores of Lake Thirlmere. At Dale Head Hall we offer a friendly home, a place of relaxation and beauty, set apart from the increasing pace of the modern world. Little can compare to a delicious dinner, prepared with love and care, particularly when wholesome ingredients come from the hotel's walled garden.

Bed & Breakfast per night: double room from £60.00–£90.00
Half board per person: £57.50–£82.50 daily; £350.00–£476.00 weekly
Evening meal 1930 (last orders 2030)

Bedrooms: 6 double, 2 twin, 1 triple
Bathrooms: 9 en-suite
Parking for 20
Cards accepted: Mastercard, Visa, Amex, Switch/Delta

18 GLENRIDDING HOTEL

HIGHLY COMMENDED

Glenridding, Penrith, Cumbria CA11 0PB Tel (017684) 82228 Fax (017684) 82555

Friendly, family-run hotel set overlooking Lake Ullswater, surrounded by mountains, in the heart of the 'real' Lake District. Indoor swimming pool with sauna and spa bath scheduled to open in December 1997. The dining room offers award-winning cuisine, and our alternative restaurant specialises in char-grills, pastas and pizzas. Two bars, including a traditional Cumbrian pub with garden, a coffee house, library with sun lounge, and a billiards room. Come and sample our good food, real ales and log fires – you'll be glad you did.

Bed & Breakfast per night: single room from £66.00–£68.00; double room from £90.00–£94.00
Half board per person: £59.50–£65.00 daily; £357.00–£390.00 weekly
Lunch available: all day

Evening meal 1900 (last orders 2030)
Bedrooms: 3 single, 22 double, 11 twin, 4 family rooms
Bathrooms: 40 en-suite Parking for 30
Cards accepted: Mastercard, Visa, Diners, Amex, Switch/Delta

19 THE GRASMERE HOTEL

HIGHLY COMMENDED

Grasmere, Ambleside, Cumbria LA22 9TA Tel (015394) 35277 Fax (015394) 35277

An elegant Victorian Lakeland stone-built country house set in the quiet location of Grasmere village, in an acre of secluded natural gardens bordered by the River Rothay. Renowned for our cuisine, our beautiful restaurant offers a four-course dinner with a varied choice of culinary delights that are imaginatively presented with only fresh produce used. A place for all seasons, The Grasmere Hotel extends a warm welcome and all the comfort you could wish for.

Bed & Breakfast per night: single room from £30.00–£55.00; double room from £50.00–£80.00
Half board per person: £40.00–£55.00 daily; £224.00–£315.00 weekly
Evening meal 1930 (last orders 2030)

Bedrooms: 1 single, 9 double, 2 twin
Bathrooms: 12 en-suite
Parking for 16
Open: February–December
Cards accepted: Mastercard, Visa, Amex, Switch/Delta

Entries are cross referenced by number to the maps on pages 16–17

20 Rothay Garden Hotel

HIGHLY COMMENDED

Broadgate, Grasmere, Ambleside, Cumbria LA22 9RJ Tel (015394) 35334 Fax (015394) 35723

A privately-operated Lakeland hotel, delightfully situated in two acres of riverside gardens and nestling amongst the fells. The elegant conservatory restaurant offers award-winning cuisine under the personal supervision of the proprietor, with an excellent wine list. All bedrooms offer en-suite facilities, welcome tray, satellite TV and other modern requirements. Superior rooms also have whirlpool baths, settees, bathrobes and trouser presses, and some feature four-poster beds.

Bed & Breakfast per night: single room from £35.00–£59.50; double room from £75.00–£120.00
Half board per person: £49.50–£85.00 daily; £285.00–£500.00 weekly
Lunch available: 1200–1345

Evening meal 1930 (last orders 2100)
Bedrooms: 2 single, 19 double, 3 twin, 2 triple
Bathrooms: 26 en-suite
Parking for 35
Cards accepted: Mastercard, Visa, Switch/Delta

21 Woodland Crag Guest House

HIGHLY COMMENDED

Howe Head Lane, Grasmere, Ambleside, Cumbria LA22 9SG Tel (015394) 35351

A warm welcome and an informal atmosphere are found in this delightful house, situated on the edge of Grasmere near Dove Cottage. Secluded but with easy access to all facilities, the accommodation has fine tastefully-decorated bedrooms, all with individual character and wonderful views of the lake, fells or gardens. Ideal for walking and centrally placed for the motorist (enclosed parking). All major outdoor activities are catered for nearby, including sailing, fishing, wind surfing and pony trekking. Totally non-smoking.

Bed & Breakfast per night: single room from £24.00–£26.00; double room from £52.00–£56.00

Bedrooms: 2 single, 2 double, 1 twin
Bathrooms: 3 en-suite, 1 public
Parking for 5

12

22 New Dungeon Ghyll Hotel

HIGHLY COMMENDED

Great Langdale, Ambleside, Cumbria LA22 9JY Tel (015394) 37213 Fax (015394) 37666

Set amidst dramatic Lakeland fells at the head of the Langdale valley. Your relaxed enjoyment of Lakeland's stunning beauty and tranquillity is our ambition, whilst you indulge in the simple, yet rewarding, pastime of fine food and wine in pleasant company at the end of each memorable day. We provide the home, Lakeland provides its best – enjoy.

Bed & Breakfast per night: single occupancy from £32.50–£35.00; double room from £65.00–£70.00
Half board per person: £48.00–£52.50 daily; £275.00–£300.00 weekly
Evening meal 1900 (last orders 2030)

Bedrooms: 11 double, 5 twin
Bathrooms: 16 en-suite
Parking for 18
Cards accepted: Mastercard, Visa, Amex, Switch/Delta

At-a-glance symbols are explained on the flap inside the back cover

23 LANGDALE HOTEL & COUNTRY CLUB

HIGHLY COMMENDED

Great Langdale, Ambleside, Cumbria LA22 9JD Tel Freephone 0500 051197 or (015394) 37302 Fax (015394) 37694

The Langdale Estate is a haven of peace and tranquillity, an ideal touring base to discover and enjoy all that the Lake District has to offer. Founded on the site of an abandoned 19th-century gunpowder works, it is dotted with massive millstones and other carefully preserved reminders of its history. The hotel has two restaurants, a traditional Lakeland pub and leisure facilities. So much to do and so much to remember... the scenery, the comfort, the good food and the warm and friendly service.

Bed & Breakfast per night: double room from £70.00–£90.00
Half board per person: £85.00–£110.00 daily
Evening meal 1900 (last orders 2200)

Bedrooms: 41 double, 24 twin
Bathrooms: 65 en-suite
Parking for 120
Cards accepted: Mastercard, Visa, Diners, Amex, Switch/Delta

SP T

24 BORRANS PARK HOTEL

HIGHLY COMMENDED

Borrans Road, Ambleside, Cumbria LA22 0EN Tel (015394) 33454 Fax (015394) 33003

Peacefully situated in the heart of Lakeland, Borrans Park is the place to enjoy award-winning traditional home cooking and experience a truly memorable sweet trolley. Choose a fine wine from the extensive personally-selected wine list and relax by the log fire or in the comfort of one of the four-poster bedrooms each with an en-suite spa bathroom. Special breaks are available all year. Complimentary membership of an exclusive nearby leisure club. CATEGORY 3

Bed & Breakfast per night: single occupancy from £30.00–£50.00; double room from £60.00–£80.00
Half board per person: £47.50–£57.50 daily; £255.00–£330.00 weekly
Evening meal 1900 (last bookings 1800)

Bedrooms: 9 double, 3 twin
Bathrooms: 12 en-suite
Parking for 20
Cards accepted: Mastercard, Visa, Switch/Delta

SP

25 LAUREL VILLA

HIGHLY COMMENDED

Lake Road, Ambleside, Cumbria LA22 0DB Tel (015394) 33240

Centrally situated in the heart of the Lake District, this elegant Victorian house, once visited by Beatrix Potter, is now personally run by resident proprietors, and is within easy walking distance of the village of Ambleside and Lake Windermere. Spacious, luxurious rooms decorated in William Morris style, and all the bedrooms overlook the fells. Private car park.

22-50

Bed & Breakfast per night: single occupancy £50.00; double room from £60.00–£80.00
Evening meal 1900 (last bookings 1700)

Bedrooms: 7 double, 1 twin
Bathrooms: 8 en-suite
Parking for 10
Cards accepted: Mastercard, Visa, Amex

SC SP T

Entries are cross referenced by number to the maps on pages 16–17

26 ROWANFIELD COUNTRY GUESTHOUSE

HIGHLY COMMENDED

Kirkstone Road, Ambleside, Cumbria LA22 9ET Tel (015394) 33686 Fax (015394) 31569

Set in idyllic tranquil countryside, three quarters of a mile from Ambleside, Rowanfield enjoys fabulous panoramic lake and mountain views. This delightful period house with its country house decor is warm and welcoming. All bedrooms are en-suite, individually and tastefully furnished, with a special de luxe room available at a supplementary rate. The chef/patron, Philip Butcher, creates exciting evening meals from the finest fresh produce. Unlicensed, but own wine welcome. Superb central location for exploring the whole Lake District area. No smoking.

CATEGORY 3

Bed & Breakfast per night: double room from £56.00–£60.00
Half board per person: £46.50–£48.50 daily; £289.00–£298.00 weekly
Evening meal 1900 (last bookings 1700)

Bedrooms: 5 double, 1 twin, 1 triple
Bathrooms: 7 en-suite
Parking for 8
Open: March–December
Cards accepted: Mastercard, Visa, Switch/Delta

8 UL S SP

27 THE SALUTATION HOTEL

HIGHLY COMMENDED

Lake Road, Ambleside, Cumbria LA22 9BX Tel (015394) 32244 Fax (015394) 34157

Being situated in the centre of Ambleside makes us the ideal base for exploring the Lake District. We offer newly refurbished en-suite rooms, a superb new lounge, and a restaurant serving à la carte and table d'hôte meals. We're proud of our friendly, efficient service and good food. Our Tavern Inn is popular with lovers of real ale. Whilst staying, take advantage of free membership of a nearby luxury leisure club to make your holiday complete.

Bed & Breakfast per night: single room from £34.00–£47.00; double room from £68.00–£94.00
Half board per person: £47.00–£60.00 daily; £292.00–£360.00 weekly
Evening meal 1900 (last orders 2100)

Bedrooms: 3 single, 21 double, 8 twin, 4 triple
Bathrooms: 36 en-suite
Parking for 40
Cards accepted: Mastercard, Visa, Amex, Switch/Delta

S SP T

28 ROTHAY MANOR HOTEL

HIGHLY COMMENDED

Rothay Bridge, Ambleside, Cumbria LA22 0EH Tel (015394) 33605 Fax (015394) 33607

Rothay Manor, an elegant Regency house run by the Nixon family for over 25 years, stands in its own grounds a quarter mile from the head of Lake Windermere. The drawing rooms and candle-lit dining room still retain the relaxed atmosphere of a private house. Care, consideration and comfort are evident throughout. The menu is varied and meals are prepared and served with flair and imagination to the highest of standards, complemented by a comprehensive wine list. Residents have free use of a nearby Leisure Centre, with swimming pool, sauna, steam room and jacuzzi, and free fishing permits are also available.

Bed & Breakfast per night: single room maximum £79.00; double room from £122.00–£137.00
Half board per person: £86.00–£93.00 daily; £546.00–£588.00 weekly
Lunch available: 1230–1400 (1245–1330 on Sundays)

Evening meal 1945 (last orders 2100)
Bedrooms: 2 single, 5 double, 3 twin, 5 triple, 3 family rooms
Bathrooms: 18 en-suite
Parking for 50 Open: February–December
Cards accepted: Mastercard, Visa, Diners, Amex

S SP T

29 NANNY BROW COUNTRY HOUSE HOTEL

HIGHLY COMMENDED

Clappersgate, Ambleside, Cumbria LA22 9NF Tel (015394) 32036 Fax (015394) 32450

This elegant country house sits peacefully under Loughrigg Fell in five acres of gardens and woodland, with access onto the fell, and also enjoys spectacular views of the River Brathay. The hotel is noted for its award-winning restaurant with a warm and friendly atmosphere. There are log fires on chilly evenings and fresh flowers are attended to daily. Bedrooms are individually designed and furnished in traditional quality. Croquet, fishing, spa bath, solarium, leisure club facilities, dogs accepted. Personally managed by the resident owners Michael and Carol Fletcher.

Bed & Breakfast per night: single occupancy from £55.00–£75.00; double room from £110.00–£140.00
Half board per person: £65.00–£120.00 daily; £412.00–£756.00 weekly
Evening meal 1930 (last orders 2030)

Bedrooms: 11 double, 4 twin, 3 triple
Bathrooms: 18 en-suite
Parking for 22
Cards accepted: Mastercard, Visa, Diners, Amex, Switch/Delta

30 WATEREDGE HOTEL

HIGHLY COMMENDED

Waterhead Bay, Ambleside, Cumbria LA22 0EP Tel (015394) 32332 Fax (015394) 31878

Wateredge is a delightfully situated family-run hotel on the shores of Windermere, with gardens leading to the lake edge. It was developed from two 17th-century fishermen's cottages which are still part of the charm of the whole building. Relax in comfortable lounges overlooking the lake, or on our lakeside patio where teas and light lunches are served. In the evening, dine under oak beams and enjoy exquisitely cooked food. Cosy bar, pretty bedrooms and relaxed friendly service.

Bed & Breakfast per night: single room from £45.00–£64.00; double room from £70.00–£148.00
Half board per person: £55.00–£94.00 daily; £375.00–£630.00 weekly
Lunch available: 1200–1400

Evening meal 1900 (last orders 2030)
Bedrooms: 3 single, 11 double, 8 twin
Bathrooms: 22 en-suite
Parking for 25 Open: February–December
Cards accepted: Mastercard, Visa, Amex, Switch/Delta

31 THE REGENT HOTEL

HIGHLY COMMENDED

Waterhead Bay, Ambleside, Cumbria LA22 0ES Tel (015394) 32254 Fax (015394) 31474

The family-run hotel at peaceful Waterhead Bay, on the shores of Lake Windermere, is highly commended for standards of comfort and cuisine. The Regent also has its own heated indoor swimming pool. The flower-drenched courtyard is spectacular in summer and not to be missed. Four-posters, garden suites with spa baths, and the Sail Loft with a panoramic view, are available for that extra special visit to this beautiful area.

Bed & Breakfast per night: single room from £59.00–£71.50; double room from £98.00–£123.00
Half board per person: £63.50–£76.00 daily; £329.00–£466.50 weekly
Lunch available: 1130–1400

Evening meal 1900 (last orders 2030)
Bedrooms: 3 single, 9 double, 7 twin, 3 triple
Bathrooms: 22 en-suite
Cards accepted: Mastercard, Visa, Switch/Delta

Entries are cross referenced by number to the maps on pages 16–17

32 BROADOAKS COUNTRY HOUSE

Listed HIGHLY COMMENDED

Bridge Lane, Troutbeck, Windermere, Cumbria LA23 1LA Tel (015394) 45566 Fax (015394) 88766

A Victorian mansion house set in acres of its own grounds, surrounded by open countryside and with magnificent views of the lake and fells. Decorated in true Victorian fashion with many antiques as well as modern luxury features. Victorian bedrooms with four-poster beds, en-suite jacuzzis and whirlpool spas. Delicious food and wine with a choice of à la carte or table d'hôte menus. Licensed for civil wedding ceremonies. Our award-winning country house is simply somewhere special!

Bed & Breakfast per night: single occupancy from £52.50–£120.00; double room from £90.00–£150.00
Half board per person: £75.00–£105.00 daily
Evening meal 1900 (last orders 2000)

Bedrooms: 8 double, 1 twin, 1 family room
Bathrooms: 10 en-suite
Parking for 40
Cards accepted: Mastercard, Visa

5 S TV SP T

33 QUARRY GARTH COUNTRY HOUSE HOTEL AND RESTAURANT

HIGHLY COMMENDED

Troutbeck Bridge, Windermere, Cumbria LA23 1LF Tel (015394) 88282 or (015394) 443761 Fax (015394) 46584

This gracious and mellow country house hotel, set in eight acres of mature gardens near Lake Windermere, combines high standards of food and service in both its Edwardian dining room and its à la carte Le Louvre restaurant. The bar lounge and residents' lounge are both comfortable and unpretentious. Fresh flowers, antiques, books, magazines and guide books are dotted around the hotel. Quarry Garth is a true home from home in every sense of the word, with log fires and oak panelling underlining the true country house ambience.

Bed & Breakfast per night: single room from £55.00–£65.00; double room from £90.00–£130.00
Half board per person: £70.00–£80.00 daily; £300.00–£350.00 weekly
Lunch available: 1200–1400

Evening meal 1830 (last orders 2115)
Bedrooms: 1 single, 9 double, 1 twin, 1 triple
Bathrooms: 11 en-suite, 2 private, 1 public
Parking for 40
Cards accepted: Mastercard, Visa, Amex, Switch/Delta

SP

34 LINDETH HOWE COUNTRY HOUSE HOTEL

HIGHLY COMMENDED

Longtail Hill, Bowness-on-Windermere, Windermere, Cumbria LA23 3JF Tel (015394) 45759 Fax (015394) 46368 E-mail lindeth.howe@dialin.net

'A little gem hidden away' – set in six beautiful acres overlooking Lake Windermere, we are 'Somewhere Special' for people looking for peace and tranquillity within comfortable surroundings with excellent food and fine wines. Every bedroom is en-suite, some have four-poster beds and jacuzzi baths and many have beautiful lake views. Leisure facilities are provided free to all residents at the exclusive Spinnaker Club in Windermere Marina just opposite the hotel grounds.

Bed & Breakfast per night: single occupancy from £48.50–£66.00; double room from £68.00–£108.00
Half board per person: £51.50–£71.50 daily; £325.00–£450.00 weekly
Evening meal 1900 (last orders 2030)

Bedrooms: 9 double, 2 twin, 3 triple
Bathrooms: 14 en-suite
Parking for 30
Cards accepted: Mastercard, Visa, Switch/Delta

S SP T

35 BLENHEIM LODGE

HIGHLY COMMENDED

Brantfell Road, Bowness-on-Windermere, Windermere, Cumbria LA23 3AE Tel (015394) 43440 Fax (015394) 43440

Set amongst idyllic countryside yet close to local attractions, our beautiful hotel makes a perfect base for a holiday in the Lake District. Situated in a quiet cul-de-sac, overlooking Old Bowness, with superb lake views and breathtaking scenery in every direction. Visitors may expect an extra treat however, as we specialise in the best traditional English cooking from our award-winning cookbook *Recipes from the Past*. Write or telephone for our free brochure, or our cookbook at £2.00 including P&P.

Bed & Breakfast per night: single room from £30.00–£35.00; double room from £52.00–£80.00
Half board per person: £44.00–£60.00 daily; £290.00–£406.00 weekly
Evening meal 1900

Bedrooms: 3 single, 5 double, 2 twin, 1 family room
Bathrooms: 11 en-suite
Parking for 14
Cards accepted: Mastercard, Visa, Amex, Switch/Delta

6 TV SP T

36 BEECHWOOD PRIVATE HOTEL

HIGHLY COMMENDED

South Craig, Beresford Road, Bowness-on-Windermere, Windermere, Cumbria LA23 2JG Tel (015394) 43403 Fax (015394) 43403

Beechwood is superbly situated with all bedrooms overlooking delightful rose gardens, with splendid mountain and fell views. Some also overlook the lake. We offer a charming variety of bedrooms – from standard en-suites with king-size beds, pretty canopies and cosy sofas, to spacious de luxe king-size four posters. Special occasions, complimentary bubbly and arrangements can be made for chocolates or flowers for your arrival. Four minutes' stroll to bistros and lake. Large private car park. A hugely popular small hotel.

Bed & Breakfast per night: double room from £46.00–£70.00

Bedrooms: 6 double
Bathrooms: 5 en-suite, 2 private
Parking for 7
Cards accepted: Mastercard, Visa, Switch/Delta

10 UL

37 LINTHWAITE HOUSE HOTEL

DE LUXE

Crook Road, Windermere, Cumbria LA23 3JA Tel (015394) 88600 Fax (015394) 88601 E-mail admin@linhotel.u-net.com

Country house hotel, twenty minutes from the M6, situated in fourteen acres of peaceful hilltop grounds, overlooking Lake Windermere and with breathtaking sunsets. The eighteen rooms have en-suite bathrooms, satellite television, radio, telephone and tea/coffee-making facilities. The restaurant serves modern British food using local produce complemented by fine wines. There is a tarn for fly-fishing, croquet, golf practice hole and free use of nearby leisure spa. Romantic breaks feature a king-size double bed with canopy, champagne, chocolates and flowers. English Tourist Board 'Hotel of the Year' 1994. CATEGORY 3

Bed & Breakfast per night: single room from £90.00–£100.00; double room from £100.00–£230.00
Half board per person: £49.00–£139.00 daily; £309.00–£876.00 weekly
Lunch available: 1230–1330 Monday –Saturday; 1230–1300 Sunday
Evening meal 1915 (last orders 2045)
Bedrooms: 1 single, 13 double, 4 twin
Bathrooms: 18 en-suite Parking for 30
Cards accepted: Mastercard, Visa, Amex, Switch/Delta

SP T

Entries are cross referenced by number to the maps on pages 16–17

38 WHEELGATE COUNTRY HOUSE

HIGHLY COMMENDED

Little Arrow, Coniston, Cumbria LA21 8AU Tel (015394) 41418

A delightful 17th-century country house with a warm, relaxed atmosphere in a peaceful rural location, close to the heart of Lakeland. The house features exquisite individually-styled bedrooms and an enchanting oak-beamed lounge with log fire. Breakfasts are delicious, comprising an extensive buffet of cereals/fruits followed by a hearty grill. Free leisure club facilities are provided. Quality service is guaranteed - a perfect and unforgettable experience. Smoking restricted to the bar.

Bed & Breakfast per night: single room from £23.00–£30.00; double room from £46.00–£60.00

Bedrooms: 2 single, 3 double
Bathrooms: 5 en-suite
Parking for 5
Open: March–November
Cards accepted: Mastercard, Visa

39 EES WYKE COUNTRY HOUSE

HIGHLY COMMENDED

Sawrey, Ambleside, Cumbria LA22 0JZ Tel (015394) 36393 Fax (015394) 36393

This Georgian house, with its idyllic setting, is a perfect choice for that special break away. Most of our spacious bedrooms have a wonderful view of Esthwaite Water – all have the comfort you would expect from a hotel with a well-established reputation. Beatrix Potter made Ees Wyke her holiday home, the surrounding scenery providing the inspiration for the illustrations in her books. Our delicious dinners and hearty breakfasts are served in our delightful restaurant overlooking the lake.

Bed & Breakfast per night: single occupancy from £44.00–£54.00; double room £88.00
Half board per person: £56.00–£66.00 daily; maximum £372.00 weekly
Evening meal 1900 (last orders 1930)

Bedrooms: 5 double, 3 twin
Bathrooms: 6 en-suite, 2 private, 1 public
Parking for 10
Open: March–December

8

40 SAWREY HOUSE COUNTRY HOTEL

HIGHLY COMMENDED

Near Sawrey, Ambleside, Cumbria LA22 0LF Tel (015394) 36387 Fax (015394) 36010

Situated in three acres of grounds in the centre of the Lake District National Park, this family-run hotel offers a very special combination of elegance and comfort. It directly overlooks both Grizedale Forest and Esthwaite Water, nestling in the conservation hamlet which won the heart of Beatrix Potter, whose house 'Hilltop' lies nearby. We place special emphasis on our delicious five-course dinners, complemented with a well-stocked cellar offering reasonably priced wines.

Bed & Breakfast per night: single room from £40.00–£45.00; double room from £60.00–£100.00
Half board per person: £45.00–£65.00 daily; £280.00–£410.00 weekly
Evening meal 1930 (last orders 2000)

Bedrooms: 1 single, 6 double, 2 twin, 2 triple
Bathrooms: 11 en-suite
Parking for 20
Open: February–December
Cards accepted: Mastercard, Visa

At-a-glance symbols are explained on the flap inside the back cover

41 HOLBECK GHYLL COUNTRY HOUSE HOTEL DE LUXE

Holbeck Lane, Windermere, Cumbria LA23 1LU Tel (015394) 32375 Fax (015394) 34743

Peacefully located in seven acres of grounds with breathtaking views across Lake Windermere. 19th-century hunting lodge, former home of Lord Lonsdale, with log fires and intimate candle-lit oak-panelled restaurant. Luxurious bedrooms with vases of fresh flowers, decanters of sherry and fluffy bathrobes. Young, caring staff offering genuine hospitality. Holbeck Ghyll is 'Something Special' for that eagerly-awaited important anniversary or birthday celebration. Rated by all guide books in their highest category. Central Lakes location. Luxury health spa and tennis court.

Half board per person: £70.00–£120.00 daily
Lunch available: 1200–1400
Evening meal 1900 (last orders 2045)

Bedrooms: 10 double, 3 twin, 1 triple
Bathrooms: 14 en-suite
Parking for 22
Cards accepted: Mastercard, Visa, Diners, Amex

S SP T

42 GILPIN LODGE COUNTRY HOUSE HOTEL AND RESTAURANT DE LUXE

Crook Road, Windermere, Cumbria LA23 3NE Tel (015394) 88818 Fax (015394) 88058

A friendly, elegant, relaxing hotel in twenty acres of woodlands, moors and delightful country gardens. Twelve miles from the M6, two miles from Lake Windermere and almost opposite the golf course. Sumptuous bedrooms – five brand new, many with jacuzzi baths, split-level sitting areas and four-poster beds. Exquisite cuisine. Attentive service. Guests have free use of nearby leisure club. Year-round breaks.

Bed & Breakfast per night: single occupancy from £75.00–£100.00; double room from £90.00–£140.00
Half board per person: £65.00–£90.00 daily; £395.00–£570.00 weekly
Lunch available: 1200–1430

Evening meal 1900 (last orders 2045)
Bedrooms: 11 double, 3 twin
Bathrooms: 14 en-suite
Parking for 40
Cards accepted: Mastercard, Visa, Diners, Amex, Switch/Delta

7 S SP T

43 LINDETH FELL COUNTRY HOUSE HOTEL HIGHLY COMMENDED

Bowness-on-Windermere, Cumbria LA23 3JP Tel (015394) 43286 or 44287 Fax (015394) 47455

'One of the most beautifully situated hotels in Lakeland'. In a magnificent garden setting above Lake Windermere, Lindeth Fell offers brilliant lake views, peaceful surroundings and superb modern English cooking – at highly competitive prices. Lawns are laid for tennis, croquet and putting, and Windermere Golf Club is one mile away. Good fishing is available free and interesting walks start from the door. Call for a brochure from the resident owners.

Bed & Breakfast per night: single room £50.00–£75.00; double room £100.00–£165.00
Half board per person: £60.00–£90.00 daily; from £399.00 weekly
Lunch available: 1230–1330; Sunday lunch 1300

Evening meal 1930 (last orders 2030)
Bedrooms: 2 single, 5 double, 5 twin, 2 triple
Bathrooms: 14 en-suite
Parking for 20
Cards accepted: Mastercard, Visa

7 S SP T

Entries are cross referenced by number to the maps on pages 16–17

44 THE BEAUMONT HOTEL

HIGHLY COMMENDED

Holly Road, Windermere, Cumbria LA23 2AF Tel (015394) 47075 Fax (015394) 47075 E-mail thebeaumonthotel@btinternet.com

The Beaumont is an elegant Victorian villa occupying an enviable position and is an ideal base from which to explore Lakeland. The highest standards prevail and the lovely en-suite bedrooms (with three superb four-poster rooms) are immaculate, offering all modern comforts. Freshly-cooked hearty breakfasts are served in the delightful dining room, and the charming sitting room is a restful place to relax with a book. Jim and Barbara Casey assure you of a warm welcome and invite you to experience quality accommodation at a realistic price. Non-smoking. Please phone or write for a full colour brochure.

Bed & Breakfast per night: single room from £28.00–£36.00; double room from £48.00–£72.00

Bedrooms: 1 single, 7 double, 1 twin, 1 triple
Bathrooms: 10 en-suite
Cards accepted: Mastercard, Visa, Amex, Switch/Delta

NEWSTEAD

HIGHLY COMMENDED

New Road, Windermere, Cumbria LA23 2EE Tel (015394) 44485

Situated between Windermere village and the lake, in large grounds with secure private parking. 'Newstead' is a unique blend of Victorian elegance with every modern comfort – beautiful polished woodwork, antiques, original fireplaces and fittings. All bedrooms are high quality en-suite. Also superb four-poster 'master' bedrooms. Lovely guests' lounge and dining room. In all, a house that is sure to delight the most discerning guest. Wide breakfast choice – vegetarian and special diets are all catered for.

Bed & Breakfast per night: double room from £44.00–£52.00

Bedrooms: 4 double, 1 twin, 1 triple, 1 family room
Bathrooms: 7 en-suite
Parking for 10

46 CEDAR MANOR HOTEL

HIGHLY COMMENDED

Ambleside Road, Windermere, Cumbria LA23 1AX Tel (015394) 43192 Fax (015394) 45970

Situated close to Windermere village and the lake, Cedar Manor Hotel is a haven for food lovers and those who enjoy the good things in life. Personally run by Lynn and Martin Hadley, the hotel has won many awards for food and service over the past twelve years. For those who like to work off the calories gained in the restaurant we have facilities at the nearby Spinnaker Club for their enjoyment.

Bed & Breakfast per night: single occupancy from £32.50–£58.00; double room from £65.00–£96.00
Half board per person: £38.00–£55.00 daily; £217.00–£357.00 weekly
Lunch available: 1230–1430, Wednesday–Sunday

Evening meal 1930 (last orders 2030)
Bedrooms: 9 double, 3 twin
Bathrooms: 12 en-suite
Parking for 16
Cards accepted: Mastercard, Visa

At-a-glance symbols are explained on the flap inside the back cover

47 Woodlands

HIGHLY COMMENDED

New Road, Windermere, Cumbria LA23 2EE Tel (015394) 43915 or (0468)596142 Fax (015394) 48558

Conveniently situated between Windermere and Bowness, the Woodlands is an excellent family-run hotel renowned for its high standard of cleanliness and comfort. All rooms are en-suite, with tea/coffee-making facilities and televisions. Guests are welcome to relax in our lounge whilst enjoying a drink from the bar. Resident proprietor Andrew Wood looks forward to welcoming you to the Woodlands.

Bed & Breakfast per night: single room from £22.00–£45.00; double room from £44.00–£90.00
Half board per person: £35.50–£58.50 daily
Evening meal 1900

Bedrooms: 2 single, 10 double, 1 twin, 1 family room
Bathrooms: 14 en-suite
Parking for 14
Cards accepted: Mastercard, Visa, Switch/Delta

48 Swan Hotel

HIGHLY COMMENDED

Newby Bridge, Ulverston, Cumbria LA12 8NB Tel (015395) 31681 Fax (015395) 31917

At the southern end of Lake Windermere, the Swan Hotel undoubtedly has one of the most picturesque locations in the whole of the Lake District, with views over the water and surrounding countryside. 36 en-suite bedrooms range from a suite, four de luxe doubles to high standard doubles, singles and twins. The public rooms are attractively decorated with comfortable bars as well as an elegant lounge which adjoins the traditional Tithe Barn Restaurant (no smoking) or less formal Mailcoach.

Bed & Breakfast per night: single room from £62.00–£70.00; double room from £100.00–£144.00
Half board per person: £62.00–£74.00 daily
Lunch available: 1145–1445
Evening meal 1900 (last orders 2130)

Bedrooms: 7 single, 13 double, 10 twin, 6 triple
Bathrooms: 36 en-suite
Parking for 106
Cards accepted: Mastercard, Visa, Diners, Amex, Switch/Delta

49 The Old Vicarage Country House Hotel

HIGHLY COMMENDED

Church Road, Witherslack, Grange-over-Sands, Cumbria LA11 6RS Tel (015395) 52381 Fax (015395) 52373 E-mail hotel@old-vic.demon.co.uk

Near to the Lakes... far from the crowds, this lovely old, family-run historic house offers the tranquil, timeless atmosphere that reflects the calm and beauty of the surrounding countryside. Use of nearby health and leisure club. Award-winning food and wine.

Bed & Breakfast per night: single occupancy from £59.00–£79.00; double room from £98.00–£138.00
Half board per person: £55.00–£85.00 daily
Lunch available: 1200–1330 (Sunday only)
Evening meal 1930–2030

Bedrooms: 9 double, 4 twin, 1 triple
Bathrooms: 14 en-suite
Cards accepted: Mastercard, Visa, Amex, Switch/Delta

Entries are cross referenced by number to the maps on pages 16–17

50 LAKESIDE HOTEL ON LAKE WINDERMERE — HIGHLY COMMENDED

Newby Bridge, Ulverston, Cumbria LA12 8AT Tel (015395) 31207 Fax (015395) 31699

Lakeside Hotel offers you a unique location on the water's edge of Lake Windermere. All the bedrooms enjoy individually-designed fabrics and colours, and many rooms offer breathtaking views of the lakes. Guests may dine in either the award-winning Lakeview Restaurant or Ruskin's Brasserie. Our location next to the Lake Cruises allows you to discover the lake from the water. Guests also enjoy free use of the Cascades Leisure Club at Newby Bridge.

Bed & Breakfast per night: single room from £80.00–£120.00; double room from £100.00–£150.00
Lunch available: 1200–1500
Evening meal 1900 (last orders 2130)

Bedrooms: 4 single, 52 double, 9 twin, 7 triple
Bathrooms: 72 en-suite
Parking for 100
Cards accepted: Mastercard, Visa, Diners, Amex, Switch/Delta

51 CLARENCE HOUSE COUNTRY HOTEL AND RESTAURANT — HIGHLY COMMENDED

Skelgate, Dalton-in-Furness, Cumbria LA15 8BQ Tel (01229) 462508 Fax (01229) 467177

Clarence House is an elegant late Victorian mansion, luxuriously furnished to the taste of its owner, set in three acres of its own grounds overlooking a beautiful wooded valley. Seventeen centrally-heated bedrooms, luxuriously decorated, offer only the finest accommodation; dine in beautiful surroundings served by our friendly welcoming staff. Our à la carte, five-course speciality and famous hors d'oeuvres table offer even the most discerning diner a superb choice. 'Quite simply the best.'

Bed & Breakfast per night: single occupancy from £50.00–£65.00; double room from £60.00–£80.00
Half board per person: £57.95–£85.00 daily; £405.65–£595.00 weekly
Lunch available: 1200–1430

Evening meal 1830 (last orders 2130)
Bedrooms: 16 double, 3 twin
Bathrooms: 19 en-suite
Parking for 40
Cards accepted: Mastercard, Visa, Amex, Switch/Delta

52 MIDDLE ORD MANOR HOUSE — DE LUXE

Middle Ord Farm, Berwick-upon-Tweed, Northumberland TD15 2XQ Tel (01289) 306323 or 0410 295004 Fax (01289) 308423

Feeling stressed, want to unwind, or are you just wanting to indulge yourselves? Either way, why not visit our award-winning home and experience the warmth and quality of gracious living in a secluded tranquil setting. Relax in our spacious en-suite rooms (four-poster if desired). Sorry, no children or pets.

Bed & Breakfast per night: single occupancy from £26.00; double room from £52.00

Bedrooms: 2 double, 1 twin
Bathrooms: 3 en-suite, 1 public
Parking for 6
Open: April–October

At-a-glance symbols are explained on the flap inside the back cover

53 THE COACH HOUSE

HIGHLY COMMENDED

Crookham, Cornhill-on-Tweed, Northumberland TD12 4TD Tel (01890) 820293 or (01890)820284 Fax (01890) 820284

The Coach House offers warm, spacious bedrooms surrounding a sunlit courtyard. The large lounge, with peach leather furniture and fine pictures, overlooks a west-facing terrace. A flock of Soay sheep graze beneath the damson trees. Food is fresh and varied, reflecting modern ideas on healthy eating, with some Mediterranean influence. Local fish, game and meat are used, organically-reared where possible. Special diets catered for. Excellent facilities for disabled guests. Lovingly renovated to a high standard.

♿ CATEGORY 1

Bed & Breakfast per night: single room from £23.00–£36.00; double room from £46.00–£72.00
Half board per person: £39.50–£52.50 daily
Evening meal 1930 (last orders 1930)

Bedrooms: 2 single, 2 double, 5 twin
Bathrooms: 7 en-suite, 2 public
Open: March–November
Cards accepted: Mastercard, Visa

54 WAREN HOUSE HOTEL

HIGHLY COMMENDED

Waren Mill, Belford, Northumberland NE70 7EE Tel (01668) 214581 Fax (01668) 214484

A traditional 18th-century country house set in six acres of well-tended, wooded grounds and a walled garden, on the edge of Budle Bay overlooking Holy Island. Anita & Peter Laverack have created a haven of peace and tranquillity for adults who enjoy good food, wine and excellent accommodation. The magnificent spacious dining room overlooks Lindisfarne, while the drawing room looks over the Cheviot Hills. The service from local staff is friendly, efficient and discreet.

Bed & Breakfast per night: single occupancy from £80.00–£100.00; double room from £110.00–£175.00
Half board per person: £98.45–£125.00 daily; £360.00–£625.00 weekly
Evening meal 1900 (last orders 2030)

Bedrooms: 5 double, 3 twin, 2 suites
Bathrooms: 10 en-suite
Parking for 15
Cards accepted: Mastercard, Visa, Diners, Amex, Switch/Delta

55 RAILSTON HOUSE

HIGHLY COMMENDED

133 Main Street, North Sunderland, Seahouses, Northumberland NE68 7TS Tel (01665) 720912 Fax (01665) 720912

This charming country house, built in 1828, has been refurbished with style and imagination to offer delightful bedrooms furnished with traditional pieces and enhanced with tasteful fabrics. They are equipped to include clock radio, tea/coffee-making facilities and CTV. The room without en-suite facilities has the sole use of a super bathroom. Downstairs the flagstone hall leads to the sunlounge and walled garden. Excellent breakfasts served in the elegant dining room. Central heating. No smoking.

Bed & Breakfast per night: single occupancy £28.00; double room £40.00

Bedrooms: 1 double, 2 twin
Bathrooms: 2 en-suite, 1 private, 1 public
Parking for 2

Entries are cross referenced by number to the maps on pages 16–17

56 DUKES RYDE

HIGHLY COMMENDED

Longhoughton Road, Lesbury, Alnwick, Northumberland NE66 3AT Tel (01665) 830855

Dukes Ryde is a detached house standing in lovely gardens on the outskirts of the peaceful village of Lesbury. It is furnished with interesting antiques, and all rooms have tea/coffee-making facilities, colour televisions and views over the gardens. One room has a four-poster bed. It is an ideal base from which to explore magnificent sandy beaches, castles, bird sanctuaries and golf courses.

Bed & Breakfast per night: double room from £42.75–£45.00

Bedrooms: 1 double, 2 twin
Bathrooms: 2 en-suite, 1 private
Parking for 6

UL S SP

Grace Darling

FEW WOMEN HAVE ATTRACTED such uninvited public adulation in their lifetimes as Grace Darling. From the day that newspapers reported her courageous exploits she became an overnight national heroine. The rest of her short life would never be the same again.

Grace was the daughter of William Darling, keeper first of Brownsman Lighthouse, then of Longstone, both situated on the wild, inhospitable Farne Islands, off the Northumberland coast. Aside from her large family (eight brothers and sisters) she met few other people.

Then, on 7 September 1838, the steamer *Forfarshire* ran aground near the Longstone light. Grace first saw the wreck at dawn from her bedroom window, and later made out survivors clinging to the rocks. Her brothers were away from home; only Grace was on hand to help her father attempt a rescue. Braving heavy seas, they launched their small, wooden rowing boat into the storm, arriving at the wreck to find nine alive and three dead.

Within days newspapers were celebrating the rescue, all emphasising and increasingly exaggerating the part played by Grace. It was soon alleged, almost certainly falsely, that she alone had insisted on putting out to sea, persuading her father to do so against his better judgement. From then on the islands were visited by a stream of people anxious to glimpse Grace; she was besieged by requests for locks of her hair and even offers of marriage; innumerable souvenirs were brought out to mark the event. Despite it all, Grace did her best to live quietly at Longstone. Three years later, in 1841, she died, probably of consumption.

Visitors to Bamburgh churchyard can see the Darling family grave in which Grace is buried, together with another elaborate memorial to her. Just opposite is the Grace Darling Museum (tel: 01668 214465), containing many items of memorabilia, including the boat in which the rescue was made. A few yards further west is the humble cottage (then her grandfather's house) in which Grace was born. Weather permitting, a boat trip around the Farne Islands is an unforgettable experience, both for the glimpses of the islands' rich wildlife, and for the insight it offers into the lonely, inhospitable life Grace endured. On Inner Farne, St Cuthbert's chapel contains another memorial to the Farnes' most famous daughter.

At-a-glance symbols are explained on the flap inside the back cover

57 20 Castle Street

 DE LUXE

Warkworth, Northumberland NE65 0UW Tel (01665) 711136

A three hundred year old cottage offering de luxe accommodation. All rooms are en-suite with four-poster beds. Situated in the centre of this beautiful unspoilt village dominated by the 12th-century castle. There are several good pubs, restaurants, antique shops and galleries within two minutes' walk. Pristine award-winning beaches are ten minutes' walk. Other walks lead through woods inhabited by red squirrels and other wildlife to a 14th-century hermitage carved from solid rock.

Bed & Breakfast per night: double room £50.00

Bedrooms: 3 double
Bathrooms: 3 en-suite
Cards accepted: Mastercard, Visa, Amex, Switch/Delta

58 North Cottage

 HIGHLY COMMENDED

Birling, Warkworth, Morpeth, Northumberland NE65 0XS Tel (01665) 711263

Situated on the outskirts of the historic coastal village of Warkworth, North Cottage is an ideal base from which to explore Northumberland with its superb beaches, castles, scenery and golf courses. Our ground floor en-suite bedrooms have colour television, hospitality trays, central heating and electric overblankets. A full breakfast is served in the dining room and there is a sitting room to relax in, or a large well-kept garden to wander around in. Weekly rates available. Totally non-smoking.

Bed & Breakfast per night: single room from £18.50–£19.00; double room from £37.00–£38.00

Bedrooms: 1 single, 2 double, 1 twin
Bathrooms: 3 en-suite, 1 public
Parking for 8

59 Farm Cottage

 HIGHLY COMMENDED

Thropton, Rothbury, Northumberland NE65 7NA Tel (01669) 620831

Farm Cottage – a deceptive name for a spacious, detached house, oozing with character – is well situated in the village of Thropton, in the heart of the Coquet Valley. Occupied by the Telford family for over 150 years, it is ideally placed for visiting Northumbria's many scenic and historic attractions. Your hosts, Joan and Allen, pride themselves on providing the warmest of welcomes and the finest of home cooking for the pleasure of their guests.

Bed & Breakfast per night: single occupancy from £26.00–£30.00; double room from £36.00–£40.00
Half board per person: £32.00–£38.00 daily; £202.00–£240.00 weekly

Bedrooms: 1 double, 1 twin
Bathrooms: 1 en-suite, 1 private
Parking for 3

Entries are cross referenced by number to the maps on pages 16–17

60 TOAD HALL

HIGHLY COMMENDED

1 Woodburn Park, West Woodburn, Hexham, Northumberland NE48 2RA Tel (01434) 270013

Beautiful, spacious bungalow situated just above the village of West Woodburn. Bright beautifully appointed en-suite rooms with colour televisions, hospitality trays and hairdryers. Comfortable visitors' lounge with large colour television and piano. Packed lunches. Over half an acre of garden with wonderful views and sunny patio. Car-parking spaces. Non-smoking. Ideal situation for walking, wildlife, Kielder Water and water sports, cycling and forestry. Near Hadrian's Wall, Roman forts, and medieval castles. 30 minutes from Newcastle airport.

Bed & Breakfast per night: single occupancy from £23.00–£27.00; double room from £36.00–£44.00

Bedrooms: 1 double, 1 twin, 1 triple
Bathrooms: 3 en-suite
Parking for 4
Open: March–October

4 UL S TV

61 HAZEL COTTAGE

HIGHLY COMMENDED

Eachwick, Dalton, Newcastle upon Tyne, Northumberland NE18 0BE Tel (01661) 852415

Situated in pretty countryside within easy reach of Hadrian's Wall, the MetroCentre, Newcastle and rural Northumberland, Hazel Cottage offers very comfortable farmhouse B &B. Enjoy your evening meal served with home-made food in a warm and friendly atmosphere. We are unlicensed but guests are welcome to bring their own wine. For your comfort, our excellently equipped en-suite bedrooms ensure a relaxing stay in Northumberland. Set in large gardens with ample private parking.

Bed & Breakfast per night: single occupancy £25.00; double room £40.00
Half board per person: £35.00 daily; £227.50 weekly
Evening meal 1900 (last bookings 1830)

Bedrooms: 1 double, 1 twin
Bathrooms: 2 en-suite
Parking for 4

3 UL TV T

62 GREENHEAD COUNTRY HOUSE HOTEL

HIGHLY COMMENDED

Fir Tree, Crook, County Durham DL15 8BL Tel (01388) 763143 Fax (01388) 763143

Greenhead Hotel is perfectly situated at the centre of rural Durham countryside at the foot of Weardale, just fifteen minutes from Durham city, surrounded by open fields and woodlands. The tranquillity of Greenhead is complemented by the fact that only residential guests are catered for (no public bars or discos). The accolades, describing why Greenhead offers something special in the way of service and accommodation, can be seen in our full colour brochure.

Bed & Breakfast per night: single room from £40.00–£45.00; double room from £50.00–£55.00
Evening meal 1800 (last bookings 1700)

Bedrooms: 1 single, 3 double, 2 twin
Bathrooms: 6 en-suite
Parking for 15
Cards accepted: Mastercard, Visa

13 TV SP T

63 GROVE LODGE

HIGHLY COMMENDED

Hude, Middleton-in-Teesdale, Barnard Castle, County Durham DL12 0QW Tel (01833) 640798

Elegant country house, set in one acre of lawned gardens with uninterrupted views. Grove Lodge is a mid-Victorian building, formerly a royal shooting lodge. Luxurious en-suite bedrooms, with TV lounge, licensed bar and private parking. All home cooking with a wide choice of menu. Ideally located on the outskirts of a market town with easy access to Northumberland and the Lake District, Barnard Castle and the renowned Bowes Museum.

Bed & Breakfast per night: single occupancy £29.50; double room £49.00
Half board per person: £37.00–£47.00 daily; £259.00–£300.00 weekly
Lunch available: 1130–1330

Evening meal 1800 (last orders 2100)
Bedrooms: 1 double, 1 twin, 1 family room
Bathrooms: 2 en-suite, 1 private
Parking for 20

64 ELDON HOUSE

HIGHLY COMMENDED

East Green, Heighington, Darlington, County Durham DL5 6PP Tel (01325) 312270

This is a 17th-century house with spacious bedrooms, overlooking the village green, with a large garden and tennis court. There is ample parking. Easy to find and convenient, it is situated six miles from Darlington railway station, twelve miles from Teesside Airport, three miles from A1(M), and three miles from Newton Aycliffe.

Bed & Breakfast per night: single occupancy from £30.00–£35.00; double room from £40.00–£50.00

Bedrooms: 3 twin
Bathrooms: 1 en-suite, 4 private
Parking for 6

65 HEADLAM HALL HOTEL

HIGHLY COMMENDED

Headlam, Gainford, Darlington, County Durham DL2 3HA Tel (01325) 730238 Fax (01325) 730790 E-mail headlam@onyxnet.co.uk

Set in four acres of formal gardens and surrounded by its own rolling farmland, Headlam Hall offers tastefully furnished en-suite bedrooms. These include two suites, three family rooms and ten four-poster bedrooms; leisure facilities available for guests include an indoor heated swimming pool, sauna, snooker room, tennis court and fishing. The restaurant serves traditional English and Continental cuisine of the highest standards. Secluded yet easily accessible from main transport links, Headlam Hall is a family business offering value and individuality.

Bed & Breakfast per night: single occupancy from £55.00–£83.00; double room from £78.00–£98.00
Lunch available: 1200–1400
Evening meal 1930 (last orders 2200)

Bedrooms: 19 double, 8 twin, 3 triple
Bathrooms: 30 en-suite
Parking for 60
Cards accepted: Mastercard, Visa, Diners, Amex, Switch/Delta

Entries are cross referenced by number to the maps on pages 16–17

66 SIMONSTONE HALL

HIGHLY COMMENDED

Hawes, North Yorkshire DL8 3LY Tel (01969) 667255 Fax (01969) 667741

A large stone-built house situated on a plateau facing south and overlooking Upper Wensleydale. With spectacular views, this country house hotel has an atmosphere of warm, relaxed friendliness, with peace, tranquillity, luxury and indulgence as its guiding principles. All eighteen bedrooms are extremely elegant, en-suite, have four-poster or French sleigh beds, and are individually furnished with antiques. Simonstone Hall is ideal for a sporting break or simply getting away from it all, shedding the cares of modern-day living, and enjoying some of the luxuries of life we can offer.

Bed & Breakfast per night: single occupancy from £45.00–£60.00; double room from £90.00–£120.00
Half board per person: £62.00–£77.00 daily; £346.50–£441.00 weekly
Lunch available: 1200–1400

Evening meal 1900 (last orders 2030)
Bedrooms: 13 double, 5 twin
Bathrooms: 18 en-suite
Cards accepted: Mastercard, Visa, Switch/Delta

Swaledale sheep

VISITORS EXPLORING the fells of the Yorkshire Dales will soon appreciate the national park's choice of emblem – the Swaledale tup, or adult male sheep. With its characteristic black face, white nose and the curly horns that are carried by both sexes of the breed it is a distinctive sight. One of Britain's most popular breeds for wool, meat and crossing with other types of sheep, the Swaledale began life in the Pennine hills, being bred to survive some of the harshest winter conditions in the country, and has since played a significant part in trimming the Dales landscape. It is sometimes seen on the fells with a newer breed, the Dalesbred, originally a cross between the Swaledale and the Scottish blackface and easily confused with the Swaledale (look at the faces: the Swaledale is black with an all-white nose, the Dalesbred has two white patches).

The Yorkshire Dales have a tradition of sheep-farming that goes back to the monastic houses of the Middle Ages. Today's sheep farmers distinguish between hardy breeds, such as the Swaledale and Dalesbred, which graze the impoverished uplands, and the more productive and weightier halfbreeds such as Mashams (distinguished by their long, crinkly fleece), raised in the lusher valleys. One characteristic of the Swaledale that farmers appreciate, apart from its ability to look after itself on the high fells, is its habit of returning to and staying on the same area of moorland (or 'heaf'), generation after generation, making it easy to shepherd. It is an active, alert sheep and the ewes have excellent mothering instincts. Swaledale wool is of medium length, light and strong, and has traditionally been used in carpets and hard-wearing worsteds. Recently, new markets have been found for the wool in clothing for polar expeditions and mountaineering. Locally, the old-established knitting industry has been revived and Swaledale Woollens at Muker (tel: 01748 886251) sells hand- and machine-knitted jumpers, ties, gloves and hats. Swaledale ewe's cheese is also back in production in the Dales.

In March and April visitors to Hazelbrow Farm, Low Row, may see lambs being born and can also try their hand at bottle-feeding – as well as holding chicks, feeding hens and watching cows being milked (tel: 01748 886224). Alternatively, to see some particularly fine specimens, visit one of the agricultural shows in the area, Reeth in late August, Muker early September, or (especially good for Swaledale sheep) the May fair at Tan Hill Inn. (Phone the Dales National Park office on 01756 752748 for details.)

67 HELM COUNTRY HOUSE

HIGHLY COMMENDED

Askrigg, Leyburn, North Yorkshire DL8 3JF Tel (01969) 650443 Fax (01969) 650443

Idyllically situated with 'the finest view in Wensleydale'. Experience the comfort, peace and quiet of our 17th-century hillside Dales farmhouse. Each charmingly furnished bedroom has en-suite facilities and many special little touches. Period furniture, oak beams and log fires create the ideal atmosphere in which to relax and share our passion for really good food. We offer a superb choice of breakfasts, home-made bread and preserves, exceptionally good dinners and an inspired selection of wines. Totally non-smoking.

Bed & Breakfast per night: double room from £56.00–£68.00
Half board per person: £44.00–£50.00 daily; £308.00–£322.00 weekly
Evening meal 1900 (last orders 1900)

Bedrooms: 2 double, 1 twin
Bathrooms: 3 en-suite
Parking for 5
Open: January–November

10

68 WENSLEYDALE HEIFER INN

HIGHLY COMMENDED

West Witton, Wensleydale, North Yorkshire DL8 4LS Tel (01969) 622322 Fax (01969) 624183

17th-century country inn located in the Yorkshire Dales National Park, amidst glorious and unspoilt countryside. Ideal for visits to historic castles, National Trust properties and Middleham Racing Stables. Superbly placed for walking in the Dales. All bedrooms recently refurbished. Log fires burn when necessary. Four-posters available for that special occasion. Rustic country cooking. Award-winning food. Pets most welcome!

Bed & Breakfast per night: single occupancy £54.00; double room from £70.00–£90.00
Half board per person: £58.50–£68.50 daily
Lunch available: 1130–1400
Evening meal 1900 (last orders 2130)

Bedrooms: 8 double, 5 twin, 1 triple, 1 family room
Bathrooms: 15 en-suite
Parking for 40
Cards accepted: Mastercard, Visa, Diners, Amex, Switch/Delta

69 MILLERS HOUSE HOTEL

HIGHLY COMMENDED

Middleham, Wensleydale, North Yorkshire DL8 4NR Tel (01969) 622630 Fax (01969) 623570

An award-winning luxury hotel set in the historic village of Middleham in the heart of Herriot's Yorkshire Dales where the owners emphasise personal care and attention to detail. The renowned restaurant uses quality local produce, including homegrown herbs and vegetables, and provides an original selection of dishes, including vegetarian choices. Elegant, individually-furnished en-suite rooms, including a luxury four-poster, are decorated in keeping with the Georgian period. Gourmet Wine Weekends, Racing Breaks, and Christmas and New Year celebrations are a must. Yorkshire & Humberside Tourist Board 'Hotel of the Year' runner-up.

Bed & Breakfast per night: single room £37.50; double room from £75.00–£90.00
Half board per person: £55.00–£62.50 daily; £360.00–£420.00 weekly
Evening meal 1900 (last orders 2030)

Bedrooms: 1 single, 3 double, 3 twin
Bathrooms: 6 en-suite, 1 private
Parking for 8
Open: February–December
Cards accepted: Mastercard, Visa, Switch/Delta

10

Entries are cross referenced by number to the maps on pages 16–17

70 Hayloft Suite

HIGHLY COMMENDED

Foal Barn, Spennithorne, Leyburn, North Yorkshire DL8 5PR Tel (01969) 622580

A two hundred year old barn, set around a picturesque garden courtyard in a tranquil village by the River Ure, this cottage suite is for the exclusive use of one party of up to four people and offers privacy, peace and comfort. Climb old stone steps to the private entrance to your own beamed lounge with an open fire. A freshly-cooked breakfast of your choice will be served. Two miles from Leyburn market town and the historical town of Middleham.

Bed & Breakfast per night: single occupancy £24.50; double room £49.00

Bedrooms: 1 double, 1 twin
Bathrooms: 2 private
Parking for 1

71 Upsland Farm

HIGHLY COMMENDED

Kirklington, Bedale, North Yorkshire DL8 2PA Tel (01845) 567709

Elegant comfortable farmhouse, two miles from A1. Ideally situated for York, Herriot and Heartbeat country, coast, moors and dales. Nearby are golf, riding and fishing facilities. There are many good pubs in the neighbourhood. All rooms have en-suite bathrooms, colour TV, hospitality tray and central heating. Comfortable, well-furnished guest drawing room with log fires. Croquet, private parking, non-smoking.

Bed & Breakfast per night: double room £40.00
Half board per person: £29.50 daily; £185.50 weekly
Evening meal 1900 (last orders 2000)

Bedrooms: 2 double, 1 twin
Bathrooms: 3 en-suite
Parking for 6

72 Husbands Barn

HIGHLY COMMENDED

Stainforth, Settle, North Yorkshire BD24 9PN Tel (01729) 822240 or (01729) 822580

Give yourself a special treat in an imaginatively converted barn, restored to a very high standard and run as part of a working farm. Three en-suite rooms with colour TVs, tea/coffee-making facilities, hair dryers, plus a lounge with open fire – all with exposed beams. The dining room has lovely views over the surrounding countryside. An ideal base for walking or touring the Yorkshire Dales. Close to the Settle–Carlisle railway, the Three Peaks and the village pub! Sorry, no children under ten, no pets and no smoking.

Bed & Breakfast per night: single occupancy from £25.00–£30.00; double room from £44.00–£55.00

Bedrooms: 2 double, 1 twin
Bathrooms: 3 en-suite
Parking for 5

At-a-glance symbols are explained on the flap inside the back cover

73 GRANTS HOTEL AND CHIMNEY POTS RESTAURANT — HIGHLY COMMENDED

Swan Road, Harrogate, North Yorkshire HG1 2SS Tel (01423) 560666 Fax (01423) 502550

Award-winning, privately-owned Victorian town house hotel situated in the heart of Harrogate. Affiliated to the Academy Health and Leisure Club. Chimney Pots Restaurant provides an imaginative menu in an elegant, air-conditioned atmosphere and is a firm favourite with local gourmets. Close to the Yorkshire Dales, Herriot Country, the ancient city of York and the Royal Armouries in Leeds – an ideal base for touring, with lots to see and do.

Bed & Breakfast per night: single room from £56.00–£102.00; double room from £85.00–£154.00
Half board per person: from £57.00 daily; from £255.00 weekly
Lunch available: 1200–1330

Evening meal 1830 (last orders 2130)
Bedrooms: 13 single, 10 double, 17 twin, 2 triple
Bathrooms: 42 en-suite Parking for 23
Cards accepted: Mastercard, Visa, Diners, Amex, Switch/Delta

74 DELAINE HOTEL — HIGHLY COMMENDED

17 Ripon Road, Harrogate, North Yorkshire HG1 2JL Tel (01423) 567974 Fax (01423) 561723

Set in beautiful award-winning gardens, with the convenience of the town centre and Valley Gardens only a few minutes' walk away. We offer our guests a warm welcome and take pride in ensuring you have a pleasant and enjoyable stay with the personal attention of the owners, Rupert and Marian Viner. Beautifully appointed en-suite bedrooms, including two in the Coach House and one on the ground floor.

Bed & Breakfast per night: single room from £37.00–£40.00; double room from £55.00–£60.00
Evening meal 1830 (last orders 1900)

Bedrooms: 1 single, 5 double, 2 twin, 2 triple
Bathrooms: 10 en-suite
Parking for 14
Cards accepted: Mastercard, Visa, Amex

75 BALMORAL HOTEL & HENRY'S RESTAURANT — HIGHLY COMMENDED

Franklin Mount, Harrogate, North Yorkshire HG1 5EJ Tel (01423) 508208 Fax (01423) 530652

Keith and Alison Hartwell, the owners and managers, have built a reputation for providing a rather special hotel with the most desirable accommodation in Harrogate: nine four-poster bedrooms and three suites. Henry's, the award-winning restaurant, is open to non-residents and has an extensive cellar. It is ideal for business/conference dinners as it is only a three-minute walk from the Conference and Exhibition Centre. Car park available.

Bed & Breakfast per night: single room from £65.00–£88.50; double room from £80.00–£180.00
Half board per person: £55.00–£150.00 daily
Evening meal 1900 (last orders 2100)

Bedrooms: 5 single, 12 double, 4 twin
Bathrooms: 21 en-suite
Parking for 20
Cards accepted: Mastercard, Visa, Amex, Switch/Delta

Entries are cross referenced by number to the maps on pages 16–17

76 ACACIA LODGE

HIGHLY COMMENDED

21 Ripon Road, Harrogate, North Yorkshire HG1 2JL Tel (01423) 560752 Fax (01423) 503725

Acacia Lodge is a warm, lovingly restored and charming small family-run hotel with pretty gardens in a select, central conservation area, just a short stroll from Harrogate's fashionable shops, many restaurants and attractions. It retains all of its original character, with fine furnishings, beautiful antiques and old paintings. All bedrooms are en-suite and luxuriously furnished with every comfort to accomodate the most discerning guest. Award-winning breakfasts are served in the oak-furnished dining room and guests can relax in the beautiful lounge, which has an open fire and a library of books. Private floodlit parking for all. A non-smoking establishment.

Bed & Breakfast per night: single occupancy from £38.00–£54.00; double room from £48.00–£68.00

Bedrooms: 2 double, 3 twin, 1 triple
Bathrooms: 6 en-suite
Parking for 7

77 RUSKIN HOTEL AND RESTAURANT

HIGHLY COMMENDED

1 Swan Road, Harrogate, North Yorkshire HG1 2SS Tel (01423) 502045 Fax (01423) 506131

A truly outstanding small Victorian hotel set in lovely mature gardens in a quiet conservation area, only five minutes' stroll from the town, magnificent gardens and conference/exhibition halls. Beautifully appointed and decorated, antique furnished en-suite bedrooms, including a four-poster and ground floor room. Gracious and relaxing drawing room with fine antiques, open fire and interesting books. Renowned for superb breakfasts and excellent English/French cuisine served in the delightful Victorian-style restaurant with bar. Our warmth and hospitality ensure your stay is 'something special'. Private floodlit car park.

Bed & Breakfast per night: single room from £40.00–£59.00; double room from £65.00–£95.00
Half board per person: £44.00–£73.00 daily
Evening meal 1900 (last orders 2100)

Bedrooms: 2 single, 3 double, 2 triple
Bathrooms: 7 en-suite
Parking for 10
Cards accepted: Mastercard, Visa, Amex

78 MOUNT GRACE FARM

HIGHLY COMMENDED

Cold Kirby, Thirsk, North Yorkshire YO7 2HL Tel (01845) 597389

A warm welcome awaits you in our luxury farmhouse in the North Yorkshire Moors National Park, between Thirsk and Helmsley. Beautiful open countryside in quiet village setting. Traditional farmhouse fayre is a speciality – cooked in our Aga and served in the elegant dining room. An ideal centre for touring or walking. If you feel the need to get away from the hustle and bustle of the cities and towns, come and relax in our peaceful surroundings. Contact Joyce Ashbridge on 01845 597389.

Bed & Breakfast per night: single occupancy from £27.00; double room from £45.00

Bedrooms: 2 double, 1 twin
Bathrooms: 2 en-suite, 1 private
Parking for 6

At-a-glance symbols are explained on the flap inside the back cover

79 Manor House Farm

HIGHLY COMMENDED

Ingleby Greenhow, Great Ayton, North Yorkshire TS9 6RB Tel (01642) 722384

A charming old farm (part c1760) set idyllically in 168 acres of parkland and woodland at the foot of the Cleveland Hills in the North York Moors National Park. Wildlife surrounds the farmhouse. The environment is tranquil and secluded, and the accommodation is warm and welcoming. Guests have their own entrance, dining room and lounge with library. Evening dinners are prepared meticulously and the hosts are proud of their reputation for fine food and wines.

Half board per person: £40.00–£43.00 daily; £266.00 weekly
Evening meal 1900 (last bookings 1600)

Bedrooms: 1 double, 2 twin
Bathrooms: 1 en-suite, 2 private
Parking for 66
Cards accepted: Mastercard, Visa, Switch/Delta

12 S TV

Wade's Causeway

WADE, LEGEND HAS IT, was a giant, a Saxon king who lived in Mulgrave Castle, Lythe. Legend also decrees that he lies buried near by, stretched out between two standing stones a mile or so apart, the one near Goldsborough, the other at East Barnby. His giantess wife, Bell, kept cows at Pickering Castle and so had to cross 20 miles (32km) of moorland each day to milk them. To make things easier, Wade built her a footpath. He scooped out earth, creating the Hole of Horcum near Saltersgate, and what was left over he threw across the moors, making Blakey Topping or, some say, Roseberry Topping. Bell helped in the construction work by carrying stones for the surface in her apron, dropping some now and then and leaving great mounds dotted about the moors.

Wade's Causeway is, if the truth be told, Britain's best-preserved stretch of Roman road. Under the governorship of Agricola, the Romans built a network of roads and forts north of York in about 80AD. One of these roads ran 25 miles (40km) north from Malton, entering the North York Moors at Cawthorne, north of Pickering, where four camps were built in about 100AD, and running on across to a signal station and landing point on the coast at Goldsborough. After the Romans left, the road lay uncared for on the bleak and boggy moor, with heather gradually creeping over it, until it was rediscovered in 1914. A section about 1¼ miles (2km) long was cleared.

Like any other Roman road, or stratum (from which our word 'street' derives), Wade's Causeway was constructed with a foundation of large stones that were then covered with pebbles or gravel. About 16ft (4.8m) wide, it is cambered, allowing drainage into gutters at either side. The gravel top-surface is lost, but foundation slabs, some kerb stones and a few drainage culverts at the northern end survive. Only a century ago most of our roads were unsurfaced tracks, so it is nothing but amazing, and a tribute to the engineering skills of the Romans, that a length of road constructed some 2,000 years ago should have survived in such remarkably good condition.

Wade's Causeway is on Wheeldale Moor, south-west of the village of Goathland, parallel to and west of Wheeldale Beck. It is best approached either from Goathland (it is close to Wheeldale Lodge Youth Hostel, 2 miles (3.2km) south of the village) or from the minor road between Stape and Egton Bridge at National Grid ref. SE 805 975.

Entries are cross referenced by number to the maps on pages 16–17

80 DUNSLEY HALL COUNTRY HOUSE HOTEL AND LEISURE CLUB — HIGHLY COMMENDED

Dunsley, Whitby, North Yorkshire YO21 3TL Tel (01947) 893437 Fax (01947) 893505

An elegant country hall in four acres of grounds, three miles north of Whitby in the North Yorkshire Moors National Park. Warm and relaxing, friendly service and good food. All the rooms are en-suite with toiletries, hairdryers and full central heating. There is also an indoor heated swimming pool, sauna/solarium, gym, tennis court and putting green. An ideal touring centre for the heritage coast, moors and Captain Cook country. Renowned cuisine. Full conference and wedding facilities. New Pyman bar. Riding, fishing and golf by arrangement.

Bed & Breakfast per night: single room from £54.50–£64.50; double room from £89.00–£130.00
Half board per person: £116.00–£153.00 daily
Lunch available: 1200–1400
Evening meal 1930 (last orders 2130)

Bedrooms: 2 single, 11 double, 2 twin, 1 triple, 1 family room
Bathrooms: 17 en-suite
Parking for 22
Cards accepted: Mastercard, Visa, Amex, Switch/Delta

81 SEVENFORD HOUSE — HIGHLY COMMENDED

Thorgill, Rosedale Abbey, Pickering, North Yorkshire YO18 8SE Tel (01751) 417283 Fax (01751) 417505

Originally a vicarage, and built from the stones of Rosedale Abbey, Sevenford House stands in four acres of lovely gardens in the heart of the beautiful Yorkshire Moors National Park. Three tastefully furnished en-suite bedrooms with TV, radio, and tea/coffee-making facilities, offer wonderful views of the surrounding valley and moorland. A relaxing guests' lounge/library with open fire. This is an excellent base for exploring the region. Riding and golf locally. Ruined abbeys, Roman roads, steam railways, beautiful coastline and pretty fishing towns are all within easy reach.

Bed & Breakfast per night: double room from £39.00–£42.00

Bedrooms: 2 double, 1 triple
Bathrooms: 3 en-suite

82 BURR BANK COTTAGE — HIGHLY COMMENDED

Cropton, Pickering, North Yorkshire YO18 8HL Tel (01751) 417777 Fax (01751) 417789

A quarter mile from the village and set in forty five acres, with wonderful views over Cropton Forest and Moors. Comfortable and spacious ground-floor accommodation. Noted for personal attention to detail. Will provide an interesting, peaceful holiday with easy access to the coast, Moors, Wolds, Howardian Hills and York. Much to do and see using Burr Bank as your home for a while. We hope you enjoy our part of Yorkshire as much as we do. No smoking.

Bed & Breakfast per night: single room £21.00; double room £42.00
Half board per person: £33.00 daily; £210.00 weekly
Evening meal 1900 (last orders 1900)

Bedrooms: 1 single, 1 double, 1 twin
Bathrooms: 3 en-suite
Parking for 20

83 SPROXTON HALL

HIGHLY COMMENDED

Sproxton, Helmsley, North Yorkshire YO6 5EQ Tel (01439) 770225 Fax (01439) 771373

Relax in the tranquil atmosphere and comfort of our 17th-century Grade II Listed farmhouse. Magnificent views over idyllic countryside on a 300 acre working farm, one mile south of the market town of Helmsley. Lovingly and tastefully furnished, giving the cosy elegance of a country home. Restful, oak-beamed drawing room with log fire. Enjoy a hearty breakfast in a most attractive dining room. Extremely comfortable, centrally heated double and twin bedrooms. En-suite or private bathrooms, tea-making facilities, remote control colour television. Guests' laundry facilities. Delightful country garden to relax in. No smoking.

Bed & Breakfast per night: single occupancy from £27.00–£33.00; double room from £40.00–£50.00

Bedrooms: 2 double, 2 twin
Bathrooms: 1 en-suite, 3 private

84 OX PASTURE HALL

HIGHLY COMMENDED

Lady Ediths Drive, Throxenby, Scarborough, North Yorkshire YO15 5TD Tel (01723) 365295 Fax (01723) 355156

This Grade II Listed hotel nestles peacefully in twenty acres of mature gardens and woodland, surrounded by superb National Park vistas, just three miles from Yorkshire's historic coastline. Resident owners Paul and Jennifer Cusworth have tastefully renovated this jewel with personal touches throughout. Bedrooms, many ground floor, are individual and spacious with every facility. Imaginative meals using fresh local produce and an excellent wine list complement the candle-lit restaurant. Come and sample our genuine hospitality.

Bed & Breakfast per night: single room from £31.50–£36.50; double room from £63.00–£73.00
Half board per person: £49.00–£54.00 daily; £308.70–£340.20 weekly
Evening meal 1830 (last orders 2100)

Bedrooms: 1 single, 8 double, 5 twin, 2 triple, 1 family room
Bathrooms: 17 en-suite
Parking for 40
Cards accepted: Mastercard, Visa, Switch/Delta

85 THE DOWNCLIFFE HOUSE HOTEL

HIGHLY COMMENDED

The Beach, Filey, North Yorkshire YO14 9LA Tel (01723) 513310 Fax (01723) 516141

Tastefully refurbished to recapture its former Victorian glory, but with all the comforts expected by today's discerning customer:. luxury en-suite bedrooms with panoramic sea views; attractively designed restaurant and bar overlooking Filey Bay; extensive breakfast choice and evening meals prepared from the finest produce ...and most of all, peace and quiet. If you want to get away from it all and relax, this is the place to be!

Bed & Breakfast per night: single room from £30.00–£36.00; double room from £60.00–£72.00
Half board per person: £42.00–£50.00 daily; £264.60 weekly
Lunch available: Sundays 1200–1430; bar lunches 1200–1400 daily

Evening meal 1800 (last orders 2100)
Bedrooms: 1 single, 6 double, 1 twin, 1 triple, 1 family room
Bathrooms: 10 en-suite
Open: February–December
Cards accepted: Mastercard, Visa, Switch/Delta

Entries are cross referenced by number to the maps on pages 16–17

86 Newstead Grange

HIGHLY COMMENDED

Norton, Malton, North Yorkshire YO17 9PJ Tel (01653) 692502 Fax (01653) 696951

The Grange is an elegant Georgian country house set in two and a half acres of gardens and grounds with delightful views of the North Yorkshire Moors and Wolds. The style of the house is tastefully enhanced by antique furniture, open log fires burn in cooler weather and the bedrooms are individually furnished. The proprietors personally prepare the award-winning meals with produce from the organic kitchen garden and fresh local produce to a very high standard. Totally non-smoking.

Bed & Breakfast per night: single occupancy from £37.00–£43.00; double room from £57.00–£74.00
Half board per person: £43.00–£59.00 daily; £270.00–£325.00 weekly
Evening meal 1930 (last bookings 1900)

Bedrooms: 4 double, 4 twin
Bathrooms: 8 en-suite
Parking for 15
Open: February–November
Cards accepted: Mastercard, Visa

10 S SP

87 Curzon Lodge and Stable Cottages

HIGHLY COMMENDED

23 Tadcaster Road, Dringhouses, York, YO2 2QG Tel (01904) 703157

A charming early 17th-century former farmhouse and stables in a conservation area overlooking York's Knavesmire race-course, close to the historic heart of the city. Once a home of the Terry 'chocolate' family, guests are now invited to share the relaxed atmosphere in ten comfortably furnished en-suite rooms, some with four-posters or period brass beds. Country antiques, books, magazines, maps, local information, fresh flowers and sherry in our cosy sitting room contribute to the traditional English house ambience. Friendly and informal. Delicious breakfasts. Enclosed parking within grounds. Restaurants nearby.

Bed & Breakfast per night: single room from £30.00–£42.00; double room from £45.00–£64.00

Bedrooms: 1 single, 4 double, 3 twin, 1 triple, 1 family room
Bathrooms: 10 en-suite
Parking for 16
Cards accepted: Mastercard, Visa

8 S SP

88 The Manor Country House

HIGHLY COMMENDED

Acaster Malbis, York, North Yorkshire YO2 1UL Tel (01904) 706723 Fax (01904) 706723

Family-run manor house in rural tranquillity, with private lake, set in five and a half acres of beautiful mature grounds on the banks of the River Ouse. Fish in the lake, cycle or walk. Close to race-course and only a ten-minute car journey from the city – or take the leisurely river bus from Bishopthorpe (Easter to October). Conveniently situated to take advantage of the Dales, Moors, Wolds and splendid coastline. Cosy lounge and licensed lounge bar with open fire. Conservatory dining room with Aga-cooked food.

Bed & Breakfast per night: single room from £38.00–£42.00; double room from £52.00–£64.00
Evening meal 1900 (last orders 2030)

Bedrooms: 1 single, 4 double, 2 twin, 3 triple
Bathrooms: 10 en-suite

S

89 DEAN COURT HOTEL

HIGHLY COMMENDED

Duncombe Place, York, North Yorkshire YO1 2EF Tel (01904) 625082 Fax (01904) 620305

Superbly situated in the shadow of York Minster, the hotel has an unrivalled position in the heart of York. This historic city's main attractions are within walking distance and tours to Castle Howard, the Moors and Dales can be arranged. Renowned for very friendly service, it boasts an elegant restaurant offering excellent modern food and a delightful Tea-room Conservatory as well as comfortable lounges. Secure car park with valet parking service. De luxe and superior rooms are now available.

Bed & Breakfast per night: single room from £75.00–£85.00; double room from £115.00–£145.00
Half board per person: £60.00–£72.50 daily
Lunch available: 1230–1400
Evening meal 1900 (last orders 2130)

Bedrooms: 10 single, 19 double, 8 twin, 1 triple, 2 family rooms
Bathrooms: 40 en-suite
Parking for 30
Cards accepted: Mastercard, Visa, Diners, Amex, Switch/Delta

AMBASSADOR

HIGHLY COMMENDED

123-125 The Mount, York, North Yorkshire YO2 2DA Tel (01904) 641316 Fax (01904) 640259

The Ambassador Hotel is a fine example of a Georgian town house with beautiful mature gardens – and just an easy walk from the city and the racecourse. Built in 1842, The Ambassador has been carefully created without sacrificing the building's Georgian style and elegance, and still retains the feeling of a much loved home. The award-winning Grays Restaurant strives always to create an atmosphere of peace, with imaginative cooking using the finest of local foods.

Bed & Breakfast per night: single occupancy from £98.00; double room from £118.00
Half board per person: from £63.75 daily; from £446.25 weekly
Evening meal 1830 (last orders 2130)

Bedrooms: 17 double, 8 twin
Bathrooms: 25 en-suite
Parking for 30
Cards accepted: Mastercard, Visa, Amex, Switch/Delta

91 HOLMWOOD HOUSE HOTEL

HIGHLY COMMENDED

112-114 Holgate Road, York, North Yorkshire YO2 4BB Tel (01904) 626183 Fax (01904) 670899

Close to the city walls, an elegant listed Victorian town house offering a feeling of home with a touch of luxury. All the en-suite bedrooms are different in size and decoration, some with four-poster beds and one has a spa bath; all rooms are non-smoking. Imaginative breakfasts are served to the sound of gentle classical music. The inviting sitting room, with its open fire, highlights the period style of the house. Car park. On the A59.

Bed & Breakfast per night: single occupancy from £40.00–£60.00; double room from £50.00–£70.00

Bedrooms: 8 double, 2 twin, 1 triple
Bathrooms: 11 en-suite
Parking for 9
Cards accepted: Mastercard, Visa, Amex, Switch/Delta

Entries are cross referenced by number to the maps on pages 16–17

92 THE OLD RECTORY

HIGHLY COMMENDED

Cowlam, Driffield, East Riding of Yorkshire YO25 0AD Tel (01377) 267617 Fax (01377) 267403

A Victorian rectory set in the traditional Riding of East Yorkshire. Enjoy the unspoilt market towns and historic houses, as well as the Minster cities of York and Beverley. We offer classic good food, log fires and elegant en-suite rooms in the heart of the unspoilt countryside and within easy reach of the coast. For our brochure and sample menus of our four-course dinners, please ring 01377 267617.

Bed & Breakfast per night: double room from £55.00–£59.00
Half board per person: £47.50–£49.50 daily
Evening meal 1900 (last orders 2000)

Bedrooms: 2 double, 1 twin
Bathrooms: 2 en-suite, 1 private
Parking for 12

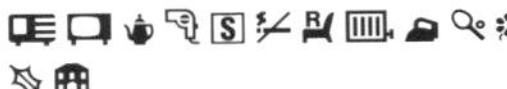

Spurn Head

THERE ARE RECORDS of a monastery being established on a peninsula between the Humber estuary and the North Sea in about 670AD, but that spit lay some way to the east of today's. Indeed, there have been several others in between, each one swept away by the North Sea, each one replaced by a ridge of sand and shingle a little to the west of its predecessor. In the 13th and 14th centuries, for instance, on one of these spits there was a town called Ravenser, which now lies beneath the waves a mile or so out to sea. An early medieval lighthouse was built on the next peninsula, washed away following a breach at the beginning of the 17th century. After that the Spurn Head we know today began to develop, formed, like its predecessors, by material washed down from the Holderness coast to the north. Sea walls at Holderness have slowed down the process of erosion and, therefore, the building up of deposits at Spurn. Only 30 years ago the spit was significantly wider than today and in places there is at high tide little dry land between the North Sea and the Humber. If the historic cycle of breach and re-growth continues, Spurn may well fall prey to a severe storm or the coincidence of a high spring tide and a strong gale. Meanwhile, the beach is stabilised with sea defences and the road that runs down the 3½ mile (5km) length of this unique peninsula is diverted around recent near-breaches.

Spurn is a Yorkshire Wildlife Trust nature reserve. Its long thin shape funnels birds on to a narrow flight path and makes it one of the best places in the country to see migrants. From July to April the tidal mudflats inside the spit are rich feeding grounds for waders – including dunlins, knots, redshanks, curlews, turnstones, oystercatchers – and wintering wildfowl such as brent geese and shelducks. Sandwich, common little and arctic tern pass through in late summer. Sea buckthorn flourishes in the sandy areas and is useful in August and September for pied and spotted flycatchers, wheatear, whinchat and redstart. In winter flocks of starlings, redwings and fieldfares feed on its orange berries. The dunes also support such flora as sea holly, sea bindweed, storksbill, yellow-wort and pyramidal orchid. Insect life is varied and abundant, with some species of moth and butterfly not found elsewhere in the region. Seals are sometimes seen. Dogs are not allowed in the nature reserve.

At-a-glance symbols are explained on the flap inside the back cover

93 MANOR HOUSE

HIGHLY COMMENDED

Newbald Road, Northlands, Walkington, Beverley, East Riding of Yorkshire HU17 8RT Tel (01482) 881645 Fax (01482) 866501

The Manor House is set amidst rolling countryside and landscaped gardens within easy reach of Beverley. Serious 'foodie' restaurant with friendly, efficient service. The area is surrounded by historic houses, local museums and many other tourist attractions, with Scarborough and York being easily accessible.

Bed & Breakfast per night: single occupancy from £70.00–£75.00; double room from £80.00–£100.00
Half board per person: £88.50–£103.00 daily
Evening meal 1930 (last orders 2115)

Bedrooms: 6 double, 1 family room
Bathrooms: 7 en-suite
Parking for 50
Cards accepted: Mastercard, Visa, Switch/Delta

94 BRIGGATE LODGE INN

HIGHLY COMMENDED

Ermine Street, Broughton, Brigg, Scunthorpe, North Lincolnshire DN20 0NQ Tel (01652) 650770 Fax (01652) 650495

Superbly located for all business and pleasure needs. Nestling amid an idyllic landscape of two hundred acres of wooded parkland, the hotel is a haven for those who enjoy being pampered. Easily accessible from the motorway system, Lincoln, Hull and York are within easy reach. International cuisine is served in the elegant Beech Tree Restaurant. Extensive table d'hôte and à la carte menus are available daily. For those who prefer more casual dining, the Buttery and Grill is open all day, every day, for drinks and bar meals. Forest Pines, a new 27-hole Championship Golf Course set in mature woodland, is now open for fantastic golfing breaks.

Bed & Breakfast per night: single occupancy from £51.70–£80.00; double room from £62.70–£88.00
Half board per person: £70.20–£90.00 daily
Lunch available: all day
Evening meal 1900 (last orders 2200)

Bedrooms: 37 double, 49 twin
Bathrooms: 86 en-suite
Parking for 300
Cards accepted: Mastercard, Visa, Diners, Amex, Switch/Delta

95 HELLABY HALL

HIGHLY COMMENDED

Old Hellaby Lane, Hellaby, Rotherham, South Yorkshire S66 8SN Tel (01709) 702701 Fax (01709) 700979

Yorkshire Tourist Board: "Hotel of the Year" for 1996, the Hall has been carefully restored to reflect its 17th-century Dutch-Colonial influence. The tastefully decorated bedrooms are of a high standard and include family rooms and a four-poster suite. A quiet corner can be found in the library or oak-panelled bar, overlooking the walled garden which has skittles, croquet and putting. The renowned Attic Restaurant is not to be missed, with a pianist who plays each Friday and Saturday evening. Nearby are Sheffield, Rotherham, the Peak District, horse racing at Doncaster, and Meadowhall (one of Europe's largest shopping malls). CATEGORY 1

Bed & Breakfast per night: single room from £55.00–£90.00; double room from £75.00–£98.00
Half board per person: £74.50–£109.50 daily; maximum £661.50 weekly
Lunch available: 1200–1400

Evening meal 1900 (last orders 2200)
Bedrooms: 15 single, 20 double, 13 twin, 4 triple
Bathrooms: 52 en-suite
Parking for 230
Cards accepted: Mastercard, Visa, Diners, Amex, Switch/Delta

Entries are cross referenced by number to the maps on pages 16–17

96 WHITLEY HALL HOTEL

HIGHLY COMMENDED

Elliott Lane, Grenoside, Sheffield, South Yorkshire S35 8NR Tel (0114) 245 4444 Fax (0114) 245 5414

Whitley Hall dates from the 16th century and is a lovely country house standing in its own thirty acres of gardens, woodland and lakes. Privately owned as a hotel for over twenty five years, we offer accommodation, food and service of the highest quality and in the best English tradition. This popular country hotel is ideally situated between the Yorkshire Dales and Derbyshire Peak District and only a few minutes from Sheffield's theatres, sports facilities and magnificent Meadowhall shopping complex.

Bed & Breakfast per night: single room from £65.00–£78.00; double room from £86.00–£103.00
Half board per person: £63.00–£98.00 daily
Lunch available: 1200–1400 (not Saturday)
Evening meal 1900 (last orders 2130)

Bedrooms: 2 single, 8 double, 7 twin, 1 family room
Bathrooms: 18 en-suite
Parking for 100
Cards accepted: Mastercard, Visa, Diners, Amex, Switch/Delta

Pontefract liquorice

'In the liquorice fields at Pontefract
My love and I did meet
And many a burdened liquorice bush
Was blooming round our feet.'

IN THE 1950s when John Betjeman wrote these lines it was still possible to stand amongst the liquorice bushes of Pontefract. Today the crop is no longer grown here, the last field being ploughed up in 1972. The liquorice heritage, however, lives on, embodied especially in the famous Pontefract (or 'Pomfret') cakes, one of several liquorice products manufactured in the town.

Liquorice grows best in the warm climes of the Mediterranean and it is surprising that it was ever sown as far north as Pontefract, though its connections with the town date back 400 years or more. In 1649 Dunhills, one of several liquorice merchants in the town, were certainly cultivating it amongst the ruins of Pontefract's old castle. Today this is one of the venues for the town's annual liquorice fair, a week-long festival of entertainment held in August. In Pontefract museum exhibits provide an insight into the liquorice industry, displaying, amongst other things, the multifarious products to which it was added, including tobacco, lipstick, boot polish, beer, fire-extinguishers and insulation board.

Liquorice is known to have been used as a sweet as early as 1614, the year of the first existing date stamp pressed into Pontefract cakes. Credit for the greatest upsurge in the popularity of liquorice sweets, occurring early this century, goes to Bassets, originally a Sheffield company but now (as Trebor Basset) based in Pontefract. The story goes that their most popular product was the accidental creation of an inebriated salesman who, in a drunken sales pitch, hopelessly mixed up his samples, but with great bravado passed them off as a new invention: 'liquorice allsorts'. Sales increased massively until the rationing of the 1940s. The industry never recovered: liquorice could never compete with costlier chocolate in the more affluent post-War marketplace. But Trebor Basset still produce allsorts, Pontefract cakes and a range of other liquorice sweets in Pontefract, all of which can be sampled straight from the production line at the factory shop.

Liquorice also flavours one of the local ales brewed in the town. Three Sieges Ale brewed at Tomlinson's Brewery is a strong stout flavoured with block liquorice. Tours of the brewery are available (for groups only – details from Wakefield Tourism, tel: 01924 305841) and the warming brew can be sampled at a number of Pontefract hostelries, including the aptly named Liquorice Bush Inn.

97 WENTBRIDGE HOUSE HOTEL

HIGHLY COMMENDED

Wentbridge, Pontefract, West Yorkshire WF8 3JJ Tel (01977) 620444 Fax (01977) 620148

Dating from 1700 and situated in twenty acres of the beautiful Went Valley among century-old trees, Wentbridge House is within easy reach of the M62 and A1. A traditional open fireplace and a fine collection of Meissen porcelain welcome you to the cocktail bar. The Fleur de Lys Restaurant, with its international ambience and Master Sommelier, attracts cosmopolitan lovers of food and wine. Individually furnished bedrooms include the Oakroom with its Mouseman four-poster bed.

Bed & Breakfast per night: single room from £52.00–£89.00; double room from £62.00–£99.00
Half board per person: £73.00–£110.00 daily; £581.00–£840.00 weekly
Lunch available: 1215–1400

Evening meal 1930 (last orders 2130)
Bedrooms: 1 single, 14 double, 4 twin
Bathrooms: 19 en-suite
Parking for 100
Cards accepted: Mastercard, Visa, Diners, Amex

98 WOOD HALL HOTEL

HIGHLY COMMENDED

Trip Lane, Linton, Wetherby, West Yorkshire LS22 4JA Tel (01937) 587271 Fax (01937) 584353

Wood Hall is an elegant Georgian house situated in 100 acres of wood and parkland, with the River Wharfe flowing through its grounds. A relaxed ambience is enhanced by staff who combine attentive service with friendliness and care. The cuisine is a delicious blend of modern and classical English cooking, creating appetising menus which are supported by an excellent wine list. Guests may use our leisure club, beauty treatment room or go fishing on the Wharfe.

Bed & Breakfast per night: single occupancy from £99.00–£155.00; double room from £109.00–£185.00
Lunch available: 1200–1400
Evening meal 1930 (last orders 2130)

Bedrooms: 27 double, 16 twin
Bathrooms: 43 en-suite
Parking for 120
Cards accepted: Mastercard, Visa, Diners, Amex, Switch/Delta

99 WEETWOOD HALL

HIGHLY COMMENDED

Otley Road, Far Headingley, Leeds, West Yorkshire LS16 5PS Tel (0113) 230 6000 Fax (0113) 230 6095

Set in impressive grounds bordering the Yorkshire Dales and close to the market towns of Ilkley and Harrogate, this luxury hotel, incorporating a manor house dating from 1625, is within easy access of Leeds with its thriving commercial and cultural centre. Accompanied by a choice of dining facilities, our own pub, the stables, and only the best in leisure and recreation provided by David Lloyd Leisure. CATEGORY 2

Bed & Breakfast per night: single room from £37.50–£80.75; double room from £65.00–£96.50
Half board per person: from £96.00 daily
Lunch available: 1200–1400
Evening meal 1900 (last orders 2130)

Bedrooms: 66 single, 22 double, 15 twin, 5 triple
Bathrooms: 108 en-suite
Parking for 150
Cards accepted: Mastercard, Visa, Diners, Amex, Switch/Delta

Entries are cross referenced by number to the maps on pages 16–17

100 CHEVIN LODGE COUNTRY PARK HOTEL

HIGHLY COMMENDED

Yorkgate, Otley, West Yorkshire LS21 3NU Tel (01943) 467818 Fax (01943) 850335

A superb hotel situated in fifty acres of woodland and lakes. The lakeside restaurant offers both English and French cuisine of the highest standard, together with an extensive wine list. The hotel is well positioned for visiting many lovely beauty spots – the Dales, Brontë country, York, Harrogate, Yorkshire Abbeys and museums. There is an excellent leisure club. A tennis court and mountain bikes are available.

Bed & Breakfast per night: single room from £60.00–£99.00; double room from £89.00–£114.00
Half board per person: £57.50–£67.50 daily
Evening meal 1930 (last orders 2130)

Bedrooms: 15 single, 26 double, 2 twin, 2 triple, 5 family rooms
Bathrooms: 50 en-suite
Parking for 100
Cards accepted: Mastercard, Visa, Amex, Switch/Delta

101 ROMBALDS HOTEL AND RESTAURANT

HIGHLY COMMENDED

West View, Wells Road, Ilkley, West Yorkshire LS29 9JG Tel (01943) 603201 Fax (01943) 816586

Located on the edge of the famous Ilkley Moor, yet within walking distance of the centre of the beautiful Victorian spa town of Ilkley. This elegant Georgian hotel is run by the resident proprietors, Jo and Colin Clarkson. The award-winning restaurant is well known for its cuisine and friendly service. The hotel is the ideal location for touring the North of England, with York, the Lakes and Peak District all approximately one hour's drive away.

Bed & Breakfast per night: single room from £52.50–£97.50; double room from £65.00–£115.00
Half board per person: £50.45–£110.45 daily; £303.00–£423.00 weekly
Lunch available: 1200–1400

Evening meal 1830 (last orders 2130)
Bedrooms: 3 single, 9 double, 2 twin, 1 triple
Bathrooms: 15 en-suite
Parking for 22
Cards accepted: Mastercard, Visa, Diners, Amex, Switch/Delta

102 FIVE RISE LOCKS HOTEL

HIGHLY COMMENDED

Beck Lane, Bingley, West Yorkshire BD16 4DD Tel (01274) 565296 Fax (01274) 568828

Built for a wealthy Victorian mill owner, the house stands in mature gardens overlooking the Aire valley, yet is only a few minutes' walk away from the Five Rise Locks and Bingley town centre. Each en-suite bedroom has a unique view and has been individually designed and furnished. Enjoy home cooking prepared with intelligence and imagination and wines from a well-chosen list in elegant, yet comfortable, surroundings. Experience Haworth – the Brontës, Esholt village, steam trains, museums and tranquil, vast open spaces.

Bed & Breakfast per night: single occupancy from £32.50–£46.00; double room from £46.00–£55.00
Half board per person: £35.50–£58.50 daily
Evening meal 1930 (last orders 2100)

Bedrooms: 7 double, 2 twin
Bathrooms: 9 en-suite
Parking for 15
Cards accepted: Mastercard, Visa, Switch/Delta

103 CEDAR COURT HOTEL BRADFORD

HIGHLY COMMENDED

Mayo Avenue (top of the M606), Off Rooley Lane, Bradford, West Yorkshire BD5 8HZ Tel (01274) 406606 Fax (01274) 406600

Cedar Court Hotel is Bradford's first purpose-built luxury hotel for more than twenty years. A gateway to the Dales and the many delights of Yorkshire, its location is ideal. Extensive leisure facilities, an international restaurant, luxury bedrooms, conference/function facilities and over 300 free parking spaces complete this ideal venue. Special weekend breaks available.

Bed & Breakfast per night: single occupancy from £55.00–£105.00; double room from £65.00–£115.00
Half board per person: £50.00–£125.00 daily
Lunch available: 1200–1400 (except Sunday)
Evening meal 1800 (last orders 2200)

Bedrooms: 87 double, 35 twin, 7 family rooms, 2 suites
Bathrooms: 131 en-suite
Parking for 320
Cards accepted: Mastercard, Visa, Diners, Amex

S SC SP T

Salts Mill

A MARVEL OF ITS AGE and pre-eminent among Bradford's textile mills until its closure in the 1980s, Salts Mill was built in 1853 by Titus Salt for his worsted manufacturing business. Now the vast Italianate-style mill is a Grade II Listed building, still surrounded by the terraced sandstone houses and community buildings of the village that the visionary Salt planned to cater for his workers' every need. In 1987 it was bought by locally-born Jonathan Silver and since then has been undergoing creative but sympathetic restoration. It is now home to several businesses (employing some 1,400 people in fields such as electronics and manufacturing) and a clutch of cultural enterprises. Of the latter, the most notable are the galleries devoted to the work of artist David Hockney, another of Bradford's sons, a schoolmate of Jonathan Silver and a regular visitor to the mill.

The 1853 Gallery, on the ground floor of the main spinning block, was the first of the three Hockney galleries to open. On its walls hang 350 original works, a permanent exhibition of cartoons, prints, paintings (including *The Other Side*, above) and computer-generated images from Hockney's childhood years to recent times. Here, too, a bookshop displays its wares not on conventional shelves but on tables, chairs and other pieces of furniture, between vases of flowers and local pottery. The mood is set for browsing with strains of Hockney's favourite pieces of music, often from opera, playing in the background. A second gallery is to be found in an old wool-sorting room, next to Salts Diner on the second floor. This is an experimental space and exhibitions change regularly: the past few years have seen pictures of Hockney's dachshunds, his opera sets, and paintings done in 1996. The third and newest gallery, above the Diner, is a more intimate space, displaying images that have a particular meaning for David Hockney personally.

Apart from the galleries, Salts Mill has some fairly upmarket shops, whose goods range from contemporary furniture and high-quality household objects to the top designer label clothes for men, women and children. The civilised, relaxed atmosphere that pervades the galleries carries through to Salts Diner, where you can pick up a newspaper to read while you enjoy good, reasonably priced food and drink.

Salts Mill (tel: 01274 531163, fax 01274 531184) is open daily 10am–6pm, admission free. Frequent trains link Saltaire with Bradford and Leeds.

Entries are cross referenced by number to the maps on pages 16–17

104 MOORFIELD HOUSE — HIGHLY COMMENDED

Oxford Road, Gomersal, Cleckheaton, West Yorkshire BD19 4HD Tel (01274) 870611 or 0850 460959 Fax (01274) 851887

An elegant Victorian residence set in secluded gardens and adjoining open farmland, yet close to the M62/M1, Leeds, Bradford, Dewsbury and Huddersfield. Joan and Bryan Webb look forward to welcoming you to their small but delightful hotel, with its warm, peaceful and friendly atmosphere. Their dining room offers home cooking of the highest standard, using fresh and home-grown produce. All bedrooms are beautifully furnished. Private car park. Jaeger Mill Shop within one mile.

Bed & Breakfast per night: single room from £38.50–£42.50; double room from £53.00–£58.00
Half board per person: £40.50–£56.50 daily; £286.00–£387.50 weekly
Evening meal 1900 (last orders 2030)

Bedrooms: 1 single, 2 double
Bathrooms: 3 en-suite
Parking for 8
Cards accepted: Mastercard, Visa

105 HEATH COTTAGE HOTEL & RESTAURANT — HIGHLY COMMENDED

Wakefield Road, Dewsbury, West Yorkshire WF12 8ET Tel (01924) 465399 Fax (01924) 459405

Heath Cottage Hotel is a substantial stone-built Victorian residence standing in approximately one acre of grounds. The renovated stable block is full of character, with original exposed roof timbers on the upper floor. These rooms are most popular for honeymoons and weekend breaks. There are twenty seven bed rooms in total, some of which are non-smoking rooms. The well-appointed restaurant provides freshly-prepared ingredients cooked with flair and imagination. Ample car parking is available.

Bed & Breakfast per night: single room £48.00; double room from £60.00–£65.00
Half board per person: £45.00–£60.95 daily
Lunch available: 1200–1400
Evening meal 1830 (last orders 2130)

Bedrooms: 10 single, 13 double, 1 twin, 3 triple
Bathrooms: 27 en-suite
Parking for 65
Cards accepted: Mastercard, Visa, Switch/Delta

106 YORK HOUSE HOTEL — HIGHLY COMMENDED

York Place, Off Richmond Street, Ashton-under-Lyne, Lancashire OL6 7TT Tel (0161) 330 9000 Fax (0161) 343 1613

Situated in a peaceful tree-lined cul-de-sac, close to the A635/A6107 junction. This very well maintained family-run hotel has thirty four well-kept en-suite bedrooms set around a courtyard and an award-winning garden. The hotel's restaurant has an excellent reputation. Keith Absolom has owned the hotel for over twenty five years and the care and attention to his guests is to be found throughout the hotel.

Bed & Breakfast per night: single room from £55.00–£59.00; double room from £66.00–£72.00
Lunch available: 1200–1400
Evening meal 1900 (last orders 2130)

Bedrooms: 9 single, 18 double, 5 twin, 2 triple
Bathrooms: 34 en-suite
Parking for 36
Cards accepted: Mastercard, Visa, Diners, Amex, Switch/Delta

At-a-glance symbols are explained on the flap inside the back cover

107 VICTORIA AND ALBERT HOTEL

HIGHLY COMMENDED

Water Street, Manchester, Greater Manchester M3 4JQ Tel (0161) 832 1188 Fax (0161) 834 2484

We are a luxury hotel situated in the city centre of Manchester. The hotel has 156 luxuriously appointed bedrooms, plus two superb but completely different restaurants. Close by are all the amenities that Manchester has on offer: shops, theatres and tourist attractions. What better place to combine pleasure with business, or indeed just have the pleasure of staying at the Victoria and Albert. ♿ CATEGORY 1

Bed & Breakfast per night: single room from £90.00–£160.95; double room from £99.00–£172.90
Lunch available: 1200–1400
Evening meal 1900 (last orders 2130)

Bedrooms: 14 single, 120 double, 22 twin
Bathrooms: 156 en-suite
Parking for 127
Cards accepted: Mastercard, Visa, Diners, Amex, Switch/Delta

SP T

Footballing history of the North-West

FOOTBALL'S SPIRITUAL HOME, many would claim, lies firmly in the North-West. In the past two or three decades no clubs from outside the area have been able to match the success of Liverpool and Manchester United. The odd trophy or two won by Everton and Blackburn Rovers has only strengthened the hold enjoyed by the region on the footballing honours of the nation. The following that these clubs possess is legendary, and spreads beyond the immediate area to other parts of the country – and abroad. To celebrate the considerable achievements and illustrious history of the club, Liverpool and Manchester United have each set up visitor centres.

The centrepiece of the Anfield attraction, which opened its doors to the public at the end of 1997, is a re-creation of the Liverpool dressing-room of the 1950s. Here is the small but distinctive frame of Bill Shankly, the manager who took Liverpool from the second to first division in the early 1960s and who laid the foundations of the team that would go on to win the European Cup. It seems appropriate that Shankly, revered by true Liverpool fans, be at the centre of this shrine to soccer. Also here, amongst the trophies and memorabilia dating back to the last century, is a scale model of the Kop, perhaps the best-known grandstand in football. Famously noisy and atmospheric, the Kop, which had standing room only, disappeared a few years ago upon the introduction of all-seater stadiums.

Visitors to Old Trafford's Museum & Tour Centre make something of an entrance for they go through the famous doors once positioned at the ground's main entrance and used by Matt Busby and hundreds of other Manchester United stars. Inside the museum you can discover that for the first 25 years of its existence the club was known as Newton Heath, and that the world-famous red and white strip was only adopted in 1902. The shirts worn by the likes of Charlton, Meredith, Edwards, Best, Robson and Cantona are all on display, as is a tribute to the 'Busby Babes', seven of whom died in 1958 in the Munich air disaster.

Both Anfield (tel: 0151 263 2361) and Old Trafford (tel: 0161 877 4002) offer the facility to view video recordings of glorious moments from the club's history – and both grounds, in common with Everton's Goodison Park (tel: 0151 330 2200) and Blackburn Rovers' Ewood Park (tel: 01254 698888), organise stadium tours. In each case it is best to phone ahead to check on availability.

Entries are cross referenced by number to the maps on pages 16–17

108 The Portland Thistle Hotel

HIGHLY COMMENDED

Portland Street, Piccadilly Gardens, Manchester, Greater Manchester M1 6DP Tel (0161) 228 3400 Fax (0161) 228 6347

In the heart of Manchester's city centre, the Portland Thistle Hotel, with its impressive Grade I Listed façade, offers the ideal location for the discerning guest. Our hotel prides itself on its comfortable and stylish accommodation, charming and friendly service, and comprehensive amenities. The acclaimed Winstons Restaurant offers excellent international cuisine and is the perfect choice to wine and dine in style. So for those visiting Manchester,The Portland is the ideal place to discover the city delights and beautiful surrounding countryside of Cheshire, the Peak and Lake District.

Bed & Breakfast per night: single room from £85.00–£133.00; double room from £95.00–£155.00
Lunch available: 1200–1400
Evening meal 1900 (last orders 2200)

Bedrooms: 107 single, 75 double, 11 twin, 12 suites
Bathrooms: 205 en-suite
Cards accepted: Mastercard, Visa, Diners, Amex, Switch/Delta

109 Cornerstones

HIGHLY COMMENDED

230 Washway Road, Sale, Cheshire M33 4RA Tel (0161) 283 6909 or (0161) 881 0901 Fax (0161) 283 6909

Cornerstones is located on the main A56 road into the city centre. The building is Victorian – built by Sir William Cunliff Brooks, a banker and Lord of the Manor. A total refurbishment was carried out in 1985, reproducing the splendour of the Victorian era. Brookland Metro station is less than five minutes' walk away, and on the fifteen minute journey into the city you will pass Manchester United Football Club, the Lancashire County Cricket Club and the G-Mex. At your journey's end you will find an abundance of shops, theatres, museums and art galleries.

Bed & Breakfast per night: single room from £23.00–£34.66; double room from £46.00–£54.05
Half board per person: £38.00–£52.28 daily; £300.49–£324.00 weekly
Evening meal 1830 (last orders 1930)

Bedrooms: 3 single, 3 double, 3 twin
Bathrooms: 5 en-suite, 4 private showers
Parking for 18
Cards accepted: Mastercard, Visa

110 Moss Cottage Farm

HIGHLY COMMENDED

Hassall Road, Winterley, Sandbach, Cheshire CW11 4RU Tel (01270) 583018

Beautiful 17th-century beamed country house, in the heart of the Cheshire countryside, with lovely secluded gardens in which guests can sit and enjoy the wonderful views. All rooms are very tastefully appointed and there is a guest lounge with television (including Sky). Afternoon tea and evening meals by prior arrangement.

Bed & Breakfast per night: single room from £19.00–£20.00; double room from £40.00–£42.00
Half board per person: from £30.00 daily
Evening meal 1700 (last orders 2000)

Bedrooms: 1 single, 1 double, 1 twin
Bathrooms: 1 en-suite, 2 public
Parking for 10

111 GROVE HOUSE

HIGHLY COMMENDED

Holme Street, Tarvin, Cheshire CH3 8EQ Tel (01829) 740893 Fax (01829) 741769

A warm welcome awaits you in a relaxing, spacious, comfortable home with a long-established Cheshire family. Ideal situation for Chester, Oulton Park, North Wales, Liverpool, the Potteries and Manchester Airport (where guests can be met by prior arrangement). Hosts happy to help with sight-seeing suggestions. Attractive walled garden, listed trees and ample off-road parking. Traditional English breakfast served in family dining room. In winter an open coal fire burns in the elegant drawing room. Excellent evening meals available within two miles. North West Tourist Board 'Place to Stay' Award and this year's runner-up for B&B of the Year.

Bed & Breakfast per night: single room from £23.00–£35.00; double room from £46.00–£56.00

Bedrooms: 1 single, 1 double, 1 twin
Bathrooms: 1 en-suite, 1 public
Parking for 6

12 UL S TV

Port Sunlight

'IT IS MY HOPE... to build houses in which our work-people will be able to live and be comfortable – semi-detached houses, with gardens back and front.' So said Lord Leverhulme on 3 March 1888 at the opening of Port Sunlight – 3 miles (4.8km) south-east of Birkenhead on the Wirral peninsula. The name the soap manufacturer chose for his garden village was appropriate; Sunlight Soap was Lever Brothers' leading brand, while the opportunity for all workers to live their lives away from the dark and shady back-to-backs so prevalent in Victorian Britain was central to his beliefs.

As well as providing quality houses for his workers, Leverhulme paid generously for shorter hours. A late-19th-century working man would have considered himself most fortunate to receive a wage of 25 shillings (£1.25) for a 48-hour week. There was a small rent to pay, but the maintenance of the garden village was funded by Lever Brothers' profits – and few other workers could have afforded such comfortable accommodation. A reasonable wage, secure job and subsidised housing were important to the industrialist, but Leverhulme felt there was more to life than simply work and the home. He ran several educational initiatives, built a cottage hospital and encouraged a range of clubs and societies that fostered an appreciation of music, science and the arts. By the time the hospital was finished in 1907, the benefits for the 3,600 population were clear: those living in Port Sunlight enjoyed an average death rate and a level of infant mortality half that in nearby Liverpool.

Very much a family man, Lord Leverhulme (born William Hesketh Lever in 1851) was devastated at the

death of his wife, Lady Lever, in 1913. She had shared his vision of a just and equitable society and his love of the arts, and so in her memory he created the Lady Lever Art Gallery in which to exhibit their extensive collection. Perhaps the main focus of a visit to Port Sunlight is the gallery's magnificent works of art. Foremost are the pre-Raphaelite paintings of Burne-Jones, Lord Leighton and Sargent, but also on display are canvases by Turner, Constable, Gainsborough and Reynolds – as well as notable collections of English furniture and Wedgwood china. Equally fascinating is to wander through the garden village itself, with its varying architectural styles. Leverhulme took a personal interest in the development and amongst the 30 or so architects he employed was a young Edwin Lutyens (17–23 Corniche Road). Further details about all aspects of Port Sunlight are available from the Heritage Centre (95 Greendale Road, Port Sunlight, tel: 0151 644 6466).

Entries are cross referenced by number to the maps on pages 16–17

112 THE PARK ROYAL INTERNATIONAL HOTEL, HEALTH AND LEISURE SPA — HIGHLY COMMENDED

Stretton Road, Stretton, Cheshire WA4 4NS Tel (01925) 730706 Fax (01925) 730740

Ideally situated with easy access to historic Chester, Manchester, Granada Studios, Liverpool's Albert Dock and set in its own breathtaking gardens. The hotel has 114 de luxe bedrooms and the Harlequin Restaurant, renowned in the locality for its food and comfortable lounges, will enhance your break in Cheshire. Our superb Health and Leisure Spa excels in holistic and beauty treatments. CATEGORY 3

Bed & Breakfast per night: single room from £73.00–£106.50; double room from £93.00–£116.50
Half board per person: £90.00–£123.50 daily
Lunch available: 1200–1430
Evening meal 1900 (last orders 2200)

Bedrooms: 2 single, 73 double, 35 twin, 2 triple, 2 family rooms
Bathrooms: 114 en-suite
Cards accepted: Mastercard, Visa, Diners, Amex, Switch/Delta

113 KILHEY COURT HOTEL — HIGHLY COMMENDED

Chorley Road, Standish, Wigan, Greater Manchester WN1 2XN Tel (01257) 472100 Fax (01257) 422401 E-mail Reservations@kilhey.co.uk

Kilhey Court, set amidst its own ten-acre gardens, is a striking Victorian-style hotel offering the highest standards of service and accommodation. We have 62 en-suite bedrooms, all designed with the guest in mind, offering direct-dial telephone, trouser press etc. The Laureate Restaurant, with its splendid Victorian conservatory, offers a choice of tempting cuisine. A perfect venue for special occasions.

Bed & Breakfast per night: single occupancy from £90.00–£115.00; double room from £100.00–£135.00
Lunch available: 1200–1430 (1200–1400 on Sunday)
Evening meal 1900 (last orders 2200)

Bedrooms: 33 double, 29 twin
Bathrooms: 62 en-suite, 2 public
Parking for 500
Cards accepted: Mastercard, Visa, Diners, Amex, Switch/Delta

114 STUTELEA HOTEL AND LEISURE CLUB — HIGHLY COMMENDED

Alexandra Road, Southport, Merseyside PR9 0NB Tel (01704) 544220 Fax (01704) 500232 E-mail Stutelea@mail.cybase.co.uk

A charming hotel offering excellent cuisine and hospitality, refurbished to a high standard and some rooms now have balconies overlooking gardens. Extensive leisure facilities including swimming pool, jacuzzi, sauna, steam room, gymnasium, solariums, treatment room and games room. Two licensed bars, restaurant, lift, gardens, and car park. 'Lets Go' special short breaks: £90.00 per person DB&B any two days, sharing twin or double room.

Bed & Breakfast per night: single occupancy £50.00; double room from £80.00–£85.00
Lunch available: light snacks served in Garden Bar all day
Evening meal 1900 (last orders 2100)

Bedrooms: 8 double, 9 twin, 3 triple
Bathrooms: 20 en-suite, 4 public
Cards accepted: Mastercard, Visa, Diners, Amex, Switch/Delta

115 OLDE DUNCOMBE HOUSE

HIGHLY COMMENDED

Garstang Road, Bilsborrow, Preston, Lancashire PR3 0RE Tel (01995) 640336 Fax (01995) 640336

A traditional, family-run, cottage-styled bed and breakfast offering a high standard of accommodation with all the rooms en-suite, plus many extra facilities and ideal for business people and tourists. Situated alongside the tranquil Lancaster Waterway, you can enjoy the picturesque scenery on our exclusive charter boat with a full bar for a simple cruise or a champagne buffet party (maximum 12 people). Charter boat not included in bed and breakfast price. All rooms can be used for single occupancy.

Bed & Breakfast per night: single room from £32.50–£39.50; double room from £45.00–£49.50
Evening meal 1800 (last orders 2030)

Bedrooms: 2 single, 4 double, 2 twin, 1 triple
Bathrooms: 9 en-suite
Parking for 12
Cards accepted: Mastercard, Visa, Amex

116 NORTHCOTE MANOR HOTEL

HIGHLY COMMENDED

Northcote Road, Langho, Blackburn, Lancashire BB6 8BE Tel (01254) 240555 Fax (01254) 246568

Northcote Manor is a small, privately owned and managed hotel with fourteen en-suite bedrooms. Lovingly cared for, it is situated in the Ribble Valley, one of the least known and most beautiful parts of the country. The manor is best known for its excellent restaurant which has won many awards. Gourmet One-Night Breaks are available all year round and include champagne aperitif and a five-course gourmet meal, prepared individually for each guest.

Bed & Breakfast per night: single occupancy from £80.00–£100.00; double room from £100.00–£120.00
Half board per person: £120.00–£150.00 daily
Lunch available: 1200–1330
Evening meal 1900 (last orders 2130)

Bedrooms: 10 double, 4 twin
Bathrooms: 14 en-suite
Parking for 50
Cards accepted: Mastercard, Visa, Diners, Amex, Switch/Delta

117 REEDYMOOR FARM

Listed HIGHLY COMMENDED

Reedymoor Lane, Foulridge, Colne, Lancashire BB8 7LJ Tel (01282) 865074

16th-century Reedymoor, set in large gardens by the side of Lake Burwain, offers a warm welcome with excellent accommodation. Just 15 minutes' walk to the village and canalside. Home-cooked evening and vegetarian meals on request. We have three rooms, all with complimentary tea/coffee-making facilities and colour TV. Fridge for guests' use. Non-smoking. Open all year.

Bed & Breakfast per night: single room from £18.00–£25.00; double room from £40.00–£60.00
Half board per person: £32.00–£40.00 daily; £200.00–£250.00 weekly
Evening meal 1830 (last orders 1900)

Bedrooms: 1 single, 1 twin, 1 double/triple
Bathrooms: 1 en-suite, 2 public
Parking for 10

Entries are cross referenced by number to the maps on pages 16–17

England's Heartland

ENGLAND IS the proverbial land of contrasts, containing within a relatively small area towns and countryside of sharply differing character. The same applies to this region, England's Heartland. To the east is the fertile, low-lying arable land of East Anglia; to the north the upland drama of the Peak District; to the west are the quiet by-ways of the Welsh Marches; to the south the busier and elegant thoroughfares of the Home Counties and southern Midlands. And in the midst of it all is the birthplace of the Industrial Revolution over two centuries ago, yet still preserving hidden corners of peace and beauty. Each area, in its individual style, manages to offer countless diversions and attractions to the curious visitor.

What East Anglia, the Fens and Lincolnshire lack by way of hills and mountains is easily offset by the dry climate, the unspoilt coastline and the range of superlative architecture. Come here and the chances that you will avoid rain are greater than anywhere else. Come here and discover mile after mile of uncluttered beach – from Aldeburgh (not far from Ipswich) to Hunstanton (on the Wash) are a hundred or so miles (160km) of almost unbroken sands. Come here to discover what some claim are the most beautiful city (Cambridge), cathedral (Ely), village (Kersey), parish church (Long Melford) and architectural style (pargeting). But what there is here,

Slimbridge

When the naturalist and painter Peter Scott founded the Wildfowl & Wetlands Trust at Slimbridge, Gloucestershire, in 1946, he operated from two derelict cottages and used wartime pill-boxes as hides. Today the organisation is internationally recognised for its research into wetland conservation, and, at Slimbridge, offers visitors a superb opportunity to watch a vast range of birds. In winter up to 8,000 migrants fly in to the 800-acre (323-hectare) reserve, forming possibly the world's largest collection of ducks, geese and swans. Slimbridge is also the only place in Europe where all six species of flamingo can be seen!

Dunmow Flitch

The once-common phrase 'to eat Dunmow bacon' means to live in conjugal bliss, and refers to an ancient custom still practised in Great Dunmow, near Bishop's Stortford in Essex. In order to win a flitch (or side) of bacon, a couple must prove that in the first twelve months and a day of their marriage they have not exchanged a word of anger, and certainly never repented of the day they wed. The trial, held every four years before a bewigged judge, is conducted with the utmost (mock) seriousness.

greater abundance than anywhere else in the land, is space. Stand, f example, beside the River Great Ouse near Downham Market and the s seems impossibly large. Sixteen miles (26km) dista the medieval octagon of Ely Cathedral stands out l a lighthouse in a rippling sea of corn. If you have taste for the particular beauty of this lowland wor indulge yourself in Wicken Fen, six miles (10k south of Ely, one of the last remnants of the marshla elsewhere drained by 18th-century Dutch enginee In 1899 it became the country's first wildl reserve. If characterful towns of unself-conscious cha are more your thing, then three to choose from are Coggeshall (Essex), Lou (Lincolnshire) and Framlingham (Suffolk).

The difference between the plains of the east and the hills of the north England's Heartland could hardly be clearer, but in between there lie the gen rolling and wooded slopes that form the northern reaches of Sherwood Fore Around Worksop these hills are known as the Dukeries, a reference to t area's vast estates, owned either by a duke (Kingston, Newcastle, Norfolk a Portland) or an earl (Byron, Manvers and Savile). By way of contrast, Works is home to one of the National Trust's more modest (but hugely fascinatir properties, an early 20th-century 'semi' called Mr Straw's House. Dominati the scenery to the west is the Peak District. Britain's oldest national park nee little introduction, offering the cities of the north a playground of spectacu beauty. The mountains hide some intriguing secrets, for near Castleton is t only place in the world where Blue John, a semiprecious stone, can be foun The towns, too, have their own appeal, with the spa of Buxton perhaps bei the urbane cultural capital. Staffordshire remains off the beaten track for man and so offers relatively undiscovered highlights away from the Peak District; o to try is the Churnet Valley ten miles (16km) east of Stoke-on-Trent, with t attractive old market town of Cheadle a good base.

The area around Kettering and Northampton is about as far from the co as you can reach in England, yet surprisingly it's something of a boati centre. Sailors can choose from several reservoirs, the Grand Union Canal the River Nene on which to make their wate progress. The Nene flows through any number tranquil, stone-built villages, one of whic Fotheringhay, has a sad and not-so-tranquil story tell. In 1587 the now-demolished castle witnessed t execution, after 19 years' incarceration, of Ma Queen of Scots. The castle fabric was plundered f use in the construction of some of the village's fin cottages. Naturalists may head for Bedfordshire, t next county south, for here are Sandy (home of t Royal Society for the Protection of Birds), Woburn (home to many speci of deer, including Père David's, now extinct in the wild) and Whipsnade Z (home to countless exotic creatures). After negotiating a narrow gap in t Chiltern Ridge, those who have sailed south on the Grand Union Canal m disembark at Berkhamsted, one of a host of handsome Hertfordshire tow of which St Albans is perhaps the finest.

or many the perennially popular Cotswolds epitomise what England does so vell – villages of an improbable perfection surrounded by rolling hills of fertile asturelandand golden wheatfields. But there is so much more to this area: n unlimited supply of inns for the pub enthusiast; a range of prehistoric emains (such as the neolithic tomb at Notgrove); and a choice of magnificent ardens. Hidcote Manor and Kiftsgate Court cater for the plantsman while Vestonbirt's trees are an arboriculturist's dream. Crossing the Severn from the otswolds takes you into a little piece of often forgotten England. In more han one sense the Forest of Dean, celebrated most famously by Dennis Potter, s a place apart, somewhere that does not readily give up its secrets. The wild plands of the Welsh Marches were once sufficient barrier to keep the Welsh nd Saxons apart, though the 8th-century Mercian King Offa took the recaution of adding a huge earthwork running from Severn to Dee. Much of the remains can be seen from Offa's Dyke Path, a long-distance ootpath that crosses and re-crosses the border on its journey north. Views are frequently spectacular and – with a little licence – take in ome of the most fascinating of English towns and cities. Tewkesbury, Gloucester, Hereford, Worcester, Malvern, Ludlow, Bridgnorth and Shrewsbury are reason enough to spend weeks here, let alone the little natter of majestic countryside and widely respected musical events (the Three Choirs and Malvern Festivals).

And in the middle of all this are Birmingham and the Midlands. Two world-class art galleries (the Garman Ryan Collection of 20th-century art and the Birmingham Art Gallery's superb Pre-Raphaelite canvases), a range of hills nudging over 1,000ft (300m) (the Clent Hills) and a mysterious example of the topiarist's art (Packwood House) are all within a few miles of the heart of England's second city. Add the City of Birmingham Symphony Orchestra and Sadler's Wells – both resident in the city – and the intriguing industrial past of Ironbridge, and the breadth of opportunities for the visitor is clear.

Left: Bridge End, Warwickshire; inset: Bircham Windmill, Norfolk

Garman Ryan Collection

Ask where you can see works by Van Gogh, Turner, Picasso, Constable, Cézanne, Gainsborough, Titian, Reynolds and Gauguin outside London, and few would suggest Walsall. But the Garman Ryan collection at the Walsall Museum and Art Gallery boasts some 353 works by these and other artists. Their presence here is due to Kathleen Garman, wife of the renowned English sculptor, Sir Jacob Epstein, who, together with American sculptress Sally Ryan, Epstein's lifelong admirer, amassed this superb collection. After Ryan's death, Garman, who was born at Wednesbury, near Walsall, donated the collection to the town.

Bakewell puddings

The story of Bakewell's famous puddings is one of triumph over adversity. In 1860 a cook at the White Horse Inn (now the Rutland Arms) preparing a strawberry tart for some dignitaries mistakenly placed egg mixture intended for the pastry base on top of the jam. The resulting 'disaster' was nevertheless cooked up and promptly declared a culinary masterpiece. The puddings (those in the know never call them 'tarts') have been served in the town ever since.

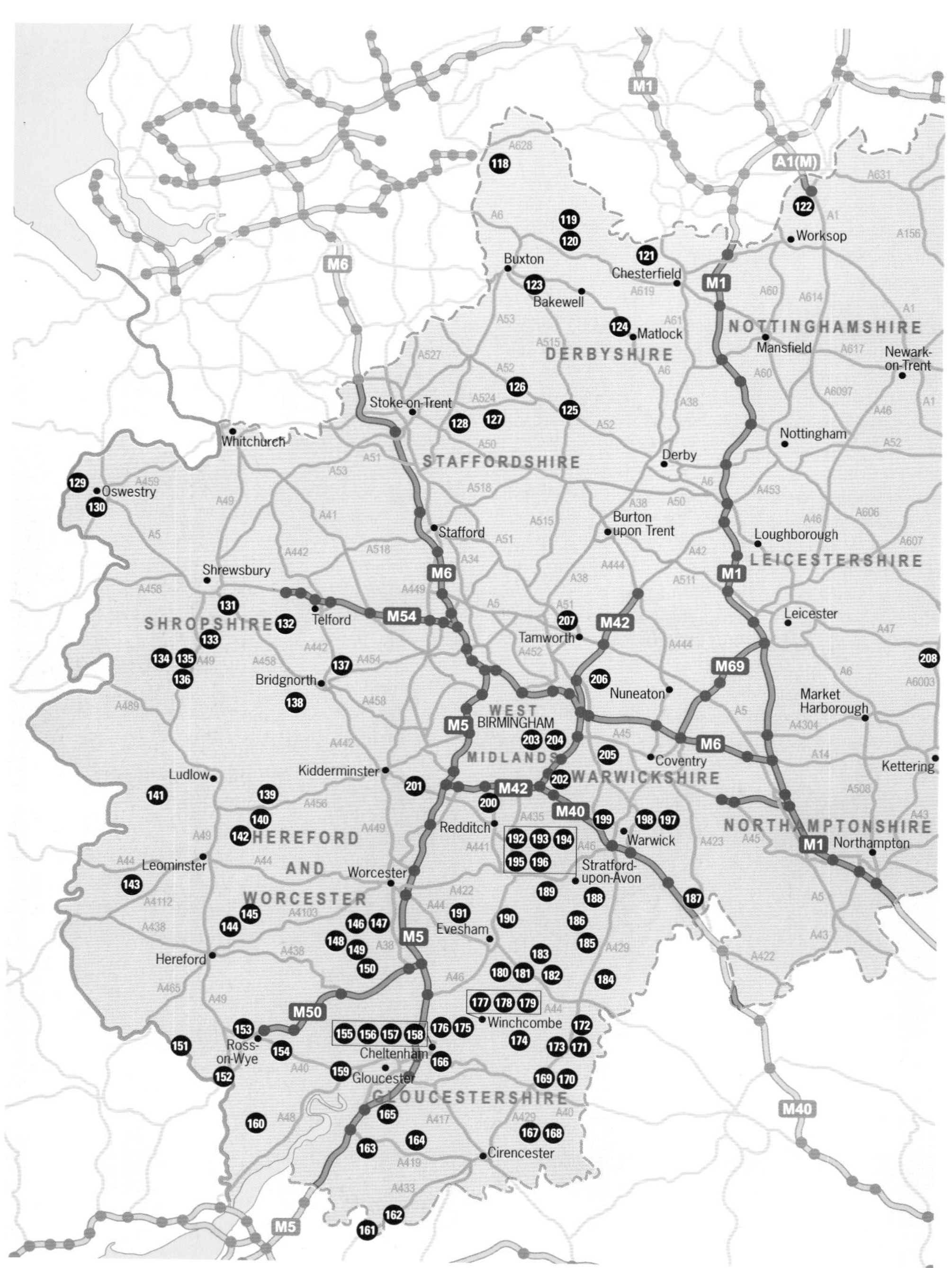
DERBYSHIRE
NOTTINGHAMSHIRE
STAFFORDSHIRE
LEICESTERSHIRE
SHROPSHIRE
WEST MIDLANDS
WARWICKSHIRE
NORTHAMPTONSHIRE
HEREFORD AND WORCESTER
GLOUCESTERSHIRE
Buxton
Chesterfield
Worksop
Bakewell
Matlock
Mansfield
Newark-on-Trent
Stoke-on-Trent
Nottingham
Whitchurch
Derby
Oswestry
Stafford
Burton upon Trent
Loughborough
Shrewsbury
Telford
Tamworth
Leicester
Bridgnorth
Nuneaton
Market Harborough
BIRMINGHAM
Coventry
Kettering
Ludlow
Kidderminster
Redditch
Warwick
Northampton
Leominster
Worcester
Stratford-upon-Avon
Evesham
Hereford
Winchcombe
Ross-on-Wye
Cheltenham
Gloucester
Cirencester
M1
M6
M5
M54
M42
M69
M40
M50
A1(M)

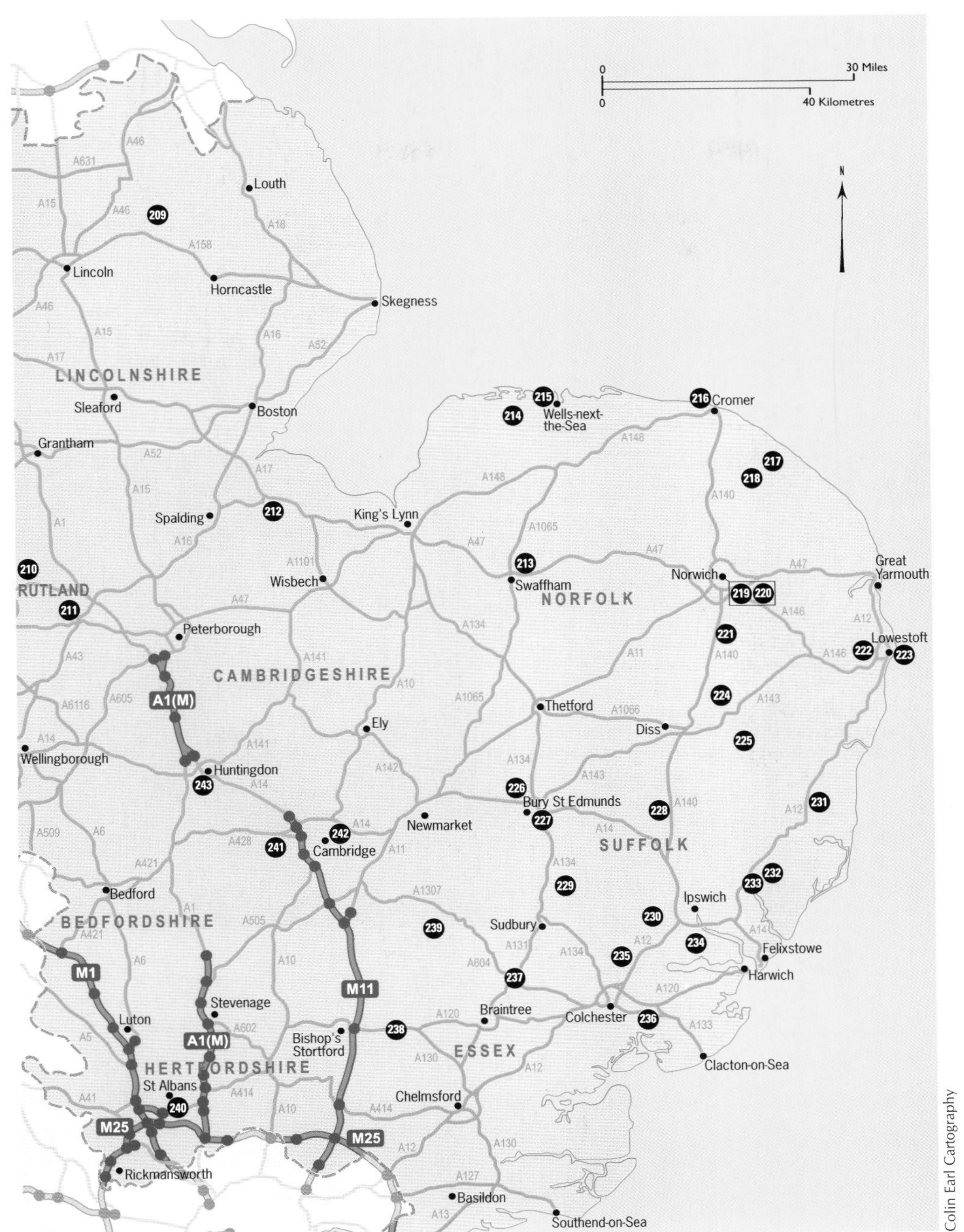

Colin Earl Cartography

118 WIND IN THE WILLOWS HOTEL

HIGHLY COMMENDED

Derbyshire Level, off Sheffield Road (A57), Glossop, Derbyshire SK13 9PT Tel (01457) 868001 Fax (01457) 853354

"Not so much an hotel, more a delightful experience" as someone said. A delightful combination of antiques, wood panelling, log fires and homely atmosphere, but with true professionalism. All rooms are individual and have en-suite facilities of the highest standard. Some half-tester beds, four-poster and brass beds, all of which are antiques. The dining room offers fine English food, all freshly prepared.

Bed & Breakfast per night: single occupancy from £65.00–£85.00; double room from £80.00–£105.00
Evening meal 1930 (last bookings 1600)

Bedrooms: 9 double, 3 twin
Bathrooms: 12 en-suite
Parking for 20
Cards accepted: Mastercard, Visa, Diners, Amex

Blue John

THE DERBYSHIRE TOWN of Castleton lies in the White Peak, a rolling limestone plateau carved into steep gorges and valleys by the last ice age. As glaciers melted they forced tremendous volumes of water downwards through joints in the limestone to form turbulent underground rivers, gouging out the rock into an impressive network of caverns. Castleton boasts four separate cave systems in its immediate vicinity.

Two of these, Treak Cliff Cavern and Blue John Cavern, contain deposits of Britain's rarest mineral, a beautifully veined fluorspar known as blue john, found nowhere else in the world. The origin of its name is uncertain, but it may derive from the French bleu-jaune (blue-yellow), two of the mineral's predominant colours (much of the stone found its way to French workshops). Its use for ornamental purposes may date back to Roman times, but it was not until the 18th century that blue john was commercially mined and worked on a large scale. The architect Robert Adam used the mineral to decorate fireplaces in the music room at Kedleston Hall (tel: 01332 842191) in 1762, and also created the famous Chatsworth Tazza, the largest bowl ever constructed from a single piece of blue john (Chatsworth House, tel: 01246 582204).

The caverns provided useful access to many of the deposits of the valuable mineral. Extracting it, however, was no easy matter. Blue john occurs in two distinct formations, either as cylindrical nodules completely buried by clay, or as flat veins sandwiched between hard layers of limestone. In the past, the deposits were extensive; the mines yielded over 20 tons annually at their peak of production, and the size of individual formations was correspondingly impressive; some nodules measured more than a foot (30cm) in diameter. Today only about half a ton is produced and few large formations are ever found. Consequently most is used for small items of jewellery, cutlery handles and small bowls, on sale in Castleton's souvenir shops.

Guided tours of Blue John Cavern (tel: 01433 620638) and Treak Cliff Cavern (tel: 01433 620571) provide a fascinating insight into a unique Peak District industry, while the massive scale of the caves and the superb formations of stalactites cannot fail to impress by their sheer natural grandeur.

Entries are cross referenced by number to the maps on pages 66–67

119 UNDERLEIGH HOUSE

HIGHLY COMMENDED

Edale Road, Hope, Hope Valley, Derbyshire S33 6RF Tel (01433) 621372 Fax (01433) 621324

A 19th-century, farmhouse-styled home with countryside views, privately situated one and a half miles from the village centre. Stone-flagged floors and oak beams, along with quality furnishings, create the ambience, and each excellent en-suite room has many extras including a resident teddy bear. Renowned for hearty breakfasts and gourmet houseparty dinners cooked by the owner/chef. Winner of national garden competition. Underleigh is ideally situated for exploring the area on foot or by car. No children under 12 yrs. Sorry, no pets – we have our own!!

Bed & Breakfast per night: double room from £60.00–£66.00
Half board per person: £44.00–£48.00 daily; from £290.00 weekly
Evening meal 1930 (last bookings 1200)

Bedrooms: 4 double, 2 twin/double
Bathrooms: 6 en-suite
Parking for 6
Cards accepted: Mastercard, Visa, Switch/Delta

120 MAYNARD ARMS HOTEL

HIGHLY COMMENDED

Main Road, Grindleford, Derbyshire S32 2HE Tel (01433) 630321 Fax (01433) 630445

Established in 1898 in the heart of the Peak National Park, the Maynard Arms is an idyllic location for pleasure or business. Superior bedrooms have views over the Derwent Valley. The best local produce is served for both lunch (1200–1400) and dinner (1900–2130) accompanied by our extensive wine list, in the Padley Restaurant overlooking the hotel gardens. The Longshaw Bar satisfies the heartiest of appetites between 1200–1400 and 1900–2130, also serving traditional hand-pulled beers.

Bed & Breakfast per night: single occupancy from £59.00–£79.00; double room from £69.00–£89.00
Lunch available: 1200–1400
Evening meal 1900 (last orders 2130)

Bedrooms: 8 double, 2 twin
Bathrooms: 10 en-suite
Parking for 80
Cards accepted: Mastercard, Visa, Amex, Switch/Delta

121 SPRINGWOOD HOUSE

HIGHLY COMMENDED

Cowley Lane, Holmesfield, Derbyshire S18 7SD Tel (0114) 289 0253 or 0831 398373 Fax (0114) 289 1365

Situated in five acres with beautiful open views of the surrounding countryside in a peaceful location. On the edge of the Peak District National Park, yet within easy reach of Sheffield, Chesterfield, and the M1. Golf course, horse riding and trout fishing are easily accessible and a wide variety of local hostelries serve excellent food. Springwood is furnished to a high standard and a warm, friendly welcome awaits all guests.

Bed & Breakfast per night: single occupancy from £20.00–£25.00; double room from £40.00–£45.00

Bedrooms: 1 double, 1 twin
Bathrooms: 1 en-suite, 2 private
Parking for 12

At-a-glance symbols are explained on the flap inside the back cover

122 THE CHARNWOOD HOTEL

HIGHLY COMMENDED

Sheffield Road, Blyth, Worksop, Nottinghamshire S81 8HF Tel (01909) 591610 Fax (01909) 591429

Centrally placed near to the heart of England, The Charnwood Hotel is set in extensive landscaped gardens and offers an ideal choice for both business and pleasure. Whether your requirements are for a wedding reception, business conference, relaxing accommodation, a bar snack from our extensive menu, a meal in our renowned Lantern Restaurant or just a drink from the bar, you can be assured of a warm welcome from this family-owned and managed hotel.

Bed & Breakfast per night: single room from £60.00–£70.00; double room from £75.00–£85.00
Lunch available: 1200–1400
Evening meal 1900 (last orders 2145)

Bedrooms: 2 single, 23 double, 9 twin
Bathrooms: 34 en-suite
Parking for 75
Cards accepted: Mastercard, Visa, Diners, Amex, Switch/Delta

123 SHALLOW GRANGE

HIGHLY COMMENDED

Chelmorton, Buxton, Derbyshire SK17 9SG Tel (01298) 23578 Fax (01298) 78242

Shallow Grange is part of a working dairy farm which is set in the heart of the Peak District National Park. Luxurious accommodation with extensively equipped bedrooms, all with en-suite bathrooms. Spectacular views and numerous unspoilt walks. Chatsworth stately home, and the towns of Buxton and Bakewell are all within a short drive. This striking 18th-century farmhouse is an ideal base to enjoy peace and quiet, with all home comforts catered for.

Bed & Breakfast per night: single occupancy from £30.00–£45.00; double room from £42.00–£50.00

Bedrooms: 3 double
Bathrooms: 3 en-suite
Parking for 10

124 RIBER HALL

HIGHLY COMMENDED

Matlock, Derbyshire DE4 5JU Tel (01629) 582795 Fax (01629) 580475

Relax in this tranquil, historic Derbyshire country house, enjoy excellent cuisine and stroll in the old walled garden and orchard which is full of bird life and bird song. Recently nominated as "one of the most romantic hotels in Britain". Recommended by all major hotel and restaurant guides.

Bed & Breakfast per night: single occupancy from £87.50–£101.50; double room from £108.00–£153.00
Half board per person: £119.50–£135.50 daily
Lunch available: 1200–1330
Evening meal 1900 (last orders 2130)

Bedrooms: 12 double, 2 twin
Bathrooms: 14 en-suite
Parking for 50
Cards accepted: Mastercard, Visa, Diners, Amex, Switch/Delta

Entries are cross referenced by number to the maps on pages 66–67

125 STANSHOPE HALL

♛♛ HIGHLY COMMENDED

Stanshope, Ashbourne, Derbyshire DE6 2AD Tel (01335) 310278 Fax (01335) 310470

Between Dovedale and the Manifold Valley in the southern Peak District, Stanshope Hall offers peace and quiet, comfortable licensed en-suite accommodation and home cooking. The rooms have been decorated by theatre artists and the result is a mixture of the theatrical, the humorous and the indulgent. Fruit and vegetables served at dinner are, whenever possible, from our own kitchen garden.

Bed & Breakfast per night: single occupancy from £25.00–£35.00; double room from £50.00–£70.00
Half board per person: £43.00–£53.00 daily; £274.00–£334.00 weekly
Evening meal 1900 (last orders 2000)

Bedrooms: 2 double, 1 twin
Bathrooms: 3 en-suite
Parking for 3

126 LEE HOUSE FARM

♛♛ HIGHLY COMMENDED

Leek Road, Waterhouses, Stoke-on-Trent ST10 3HW Tel (01538) 308439

A charming 18th-century house in the centre of a picturesque village in the Peak District National Park. Lee House is full of character: all bedrooms are non-smoking, centrally heated and en-suite, with colour TV and tea/coffee-making facilities. Ideally situated for walking and cycling in the Manifold Valley, visiting stately homes, touring the Staffordshire moorlands, the Peak District and the famous Potteries. Waterhouses is midway between Leek and Ashbourne on the A523. 6 miles from Alton Towers.

Bed & Breakfast per night: double room from £40.00–£50.00

Bedrooms: 2 double, 1 twin
Bathrooms: 3 en-suite
Parking for 4
Open: All year except Christmas

127 BANK HOUSE

♛♛ HIGHLY COMMENDED

Farley Road, Oakamoor, Stoke-on-Trent, Staffordshire ST10 3BD Tel (01538) 702810 Fax (01538) 702810

A luxurious, elegant and peaceful licensed country home offering the highest standards of food and comfort, a third of a mile south of the village. Each en-suite or private-bath bedroom has a beautiful view of the picturesque Churnet Valley, England's little Rhineland. Within the Staffordshire Moorlands, next to the National Park, one mile from Alton Towers, and amidst superb countryside for walking, it is also convenient for visiting the Potteries, Derbyshire Dales, numerous great houses, gardens and other attractions. Heart of England Tourist Board nominee for 'England for Excellence' Award 1994.

Bed & Breakfast per night: single room from £40.00–£50.00; double room from £54.00–£74.00
Half board per person: £47.00–£60.00 daily; £285.00–£345.00 weekly
Evening meal 1930 (last orders 2130)

Bedrooms: 1 single, 1 double, 1 twin
Bathrooms: 2 en-suite, 1 private
Parking for 8
Cards accepted: Mastercard, Visa

128 CAVERSWALL CASTLE

HIGHLY COMMENDED

Caverswall, Staffordshire ST11 9EA Tel (01782) 393239 Fax (01782) 394590

Grade I Listed, family-run, 13th-century stone castle with a moat, gatehouse and battlements. Bed and breakfast in an oak-panelled Cromwellian mansion, with four-poster bedrooms and magnificently carved dining and reception rooms. Play on a full-size table in the billiards room. Extensive grounds, swimming pool (seasonal) and trout fishing. Close to Alton Towers, Potteries and Peak District. Children welcome.

Bed & Breakfast per night: single occupancy from £55.00; double room from £65.00–£85.00

Bedrooms: 3 double
Bathrooms: 3 en-suite
Parking for 6
Open: February–October

129 PEN-Y-DYFFRYN COUNTRY HOTEL

HIGHLY COMMENDED

Rhyd-y-Croesau, Oswestry, Shropshire SY10 7DT Tel (01691) 653700 Fax (01691) 653700

Once a Georgian rectory, now an award-winning country hotel in the most peaceful of situations in the lovely Shropshire Hills, midway between Shrewsbury and Chester. Full of character with a delightfully informal atmosphere, the hotel has eight bedrooms (including one on the ground floor), all with lovely hill views and en-suite bathrooms. Our renowned restaurant, which is fully licensed, utilises the best local produce. Guests return again and again.

Bed & Breakfast per night: single room from £46.00–£49.00; double room from £68.00–£73.00
Half board per person: £50.00–£52.50 daily; £280.00–£312.00 weekly
Evening meal 1900 (last orders 2100)

Bedrooms: 1 single, 3 double, 3 twin, 1 triple
Bathrooms: 8 en-suite
Parking for 38
Cards accepted: Mastercard, Visa, Amex, Switch/Delta

130 PANT-HIR

HIGHLY COMMENDED

Croesaubach, Oswestry, Shropshire SY10 9BH Tel (01691) 791457

Just outside Oswestry (3 miles), and only 500 yards from the Welsh border, lies our pretty farmhouse surrounded by 26 acres which are grazed by our miniature ponies. The house is spacious and very comfortable, with attractive en-suite bedrooms, each with a TV. The view is truly beautiful and the rural tranquillity very relaxing. An ideal centre for exploring Wales and Shropshire. Within easy reach of Shrewsbury, Chester and several National Trust properties. Special breaks. Pets welcome. Proprietor: Mrs S A Werry.

Bed & Breakfast per night: double room maximum £36.00
Half board per person: maximum £27.00 daily; maximum £175.00 weekly

Bedrooms: 1 double, 1 twin, 1 triple
Bathrooms: 3 en-suite
Parking for 10
Open: January–November

Entries are cross referenced by number to the maps on pages 66–67

131 UPPER BROMPTON FARM

HIGHLY COMMENDED

Brompton, Cross Houses, Shrewsbury, Shropshire SY5 6LE Tel (01743) 761629 Fax (01743) 761679

Our delightful Georgian farmhouse with extensive lawns and gardens is a haven of peace, comfort and elegance. Five minutes from Shrewsbury – 'England's finest Tudor town' – and fifteen minutes from Ironbridge – 'the birthplace of industry' – we are ideally situated for exploring Housman's Shropshire. Our three guest bedrooms have en-suite facilities and are furnished to the highest standard with many welcoming touches. The two double rooms have four-poster beds and wonderful views to the Shropshire Hills. Breakfast in the sun-filled dining room. Relax in front of an open fire.

Bed & Breakfast per night: double room from £50.00–£60.00

Bedrooms: 2 double, 1 twin
Bathrooms: 3 en-suite
Parking for 10
Open: All year except Christmas

132 BRIDGE HOUSE

HIGHLY COMMENDED

Buildwas, Telford, Shropshire TF8 7BN Tel (01952) 432105

A charming 17th-century Grade II Listed period residence, set close to the beautiful Ironbridge Gorge. Our character home offers guests a comfortable relaxing stay with a breakfast to be remembered. A perfect place to stay in order to discover the wonders that Shropshire has to offer.

Bed & Breakfast per night: single occupancy from £30.00–£35.00; double room from £48.00–£56.00

Bedrooms: 2 double, 1 twin, 1 triple
Bathrooms: 3 en-suite, 1 private
Parking for 12

133 ASHTON LEES

HIGHLY COMMENDED

Dorrington, Shrewsbury, Shropshire SY5 7JW Tel (01743) 718378

For many years we have welcomed guests to our family home. On cold winter evenings, open roaring fires entice you to curl up and read a book with a drink purchased from our small licensed bar. In the summer we serve afternoon teas in the tree-shaded garden. A place of relaxation and tranquillity.

Bed & Breakfast per night: single occupancy from £18.00–£21.00; double room from £36.00–£42.00
Half board per person: £26.50–£29.50 daily; £172.00–£191.00 weekly
Evening meal 1830 (last bookings 0900)

Bedrooms: 2 double, 1 twin
Bathrooms: 1 en-suite, 1 public
Parking for 6

At-a-glance symbols are explained on the flap inside the back cover

134 INWOOD FARM

 DE LUXE

All Stretton, Church Stretton, Shropshire SY6 6LA Tel (01694) 724046

A superbly located country house, set amidst the Stretton Hills on the south-facing slopes of the Long Mynd, with stunning views of the rolling countryside. Surrounded by twelve acres of gardens, fields and terraces, with its own area of parkland and immediate access to 6,000 acres of National Trust land. Enjoy the atmosphere of country elegance with the highest standards of service and accommodation. Inwood is perfectly situated for the exploration of the Strettons and the Welsh Marches.

Bed & Breakfast per night: single room from £30.00–£40.00; double room from £45.00–£55.00
Half board per person: £38.00–£45.00 daily
Evening meal 1900

Bedrooms: 1 single, 2 double
Bathrooms: 3 en-suite
Parking for 10
Open: March–November

12

135 JINLYE

HIGHLY COMMENDED

Castle Hill, All Stretton, Church Stretton, Shropshire SY6 6JP Tel (01694) 723243 Fax (01694) 723243

Winner of Heart of England Tourist Board 'Bed & Breakfast of the Year' 1997. A beautifully situated country guest house set in the lovely Shropshire Highlands. A stroll from the house can provide some of the most stunning views in England. Delightfully furnished in period decor, offering luxurious and peaceful accommodation. Inglenook fireplaces and comfortable lounges. All of our spacious en-suite rooms have magnificent views. For a romantic interlude, our Wedding Suite is furnished around a splendidly carved 17th-century French wedding bed. Ground floor rooms. Excellent home cooking. Licensed. Traditional Christmas breaks. Colour brochure. CATEGORY 3

Bed & Breakfast per night: single occupancy from £43.00–£52.00; double room from £46.00–£64.00
Half board per person: £40.50–£49.50 daily; £255.00–£312.00 weekly
Evening meal 1900 (last bookings 1200)

Bedrooms: 4 double, 4 twin
Bathrooms: 8 en-suite
Parking for 10

12

136 MYND HOUSE HOTEL

HIGHLY COMMENDED

Little Stretton, Church Stretton, Shropshire SY6 6RB Tel (01694) 722212 Fax (01694) 724180

Set in an idyllic rural hamlet with thatched church, hills and walks in all directions. Ludlow, Shrewsbury and Ironbridge are within a half-hour's drive. Visit romantic monasteries, castles and churches. Interesting range of themed breaks available. Small informal hotel and restaurant, all bedrooms en-suite, two suites available, one with four-poster bed. Four-course à la carte dinners featuring cuisine of the Marches and the best of rural Italy and France. Outstanding cellar offering over three hundred wines in bottles and over two hundred in halves.

Bed & Breakfast per night: single room from £40.00–£45.00; double room from £70.00–£90.00
Half board per person: £45.00–£85.00 daily
Evening meal 1930 (last orders 2115)

Bedrooms: 1 single, 3 double, 3 twin
Bathrooms: 7 en-suite
Parking for 16
Open: February–December
Cards accepted: Mastercard, Visa, Amex, Switch/Delta

Entries are cross referenced by number to the maps on pages 66–67

137 OLD VICARAGE HOTEL

♛♛♛♛ DE LUXE

Worfield, Bridgnorth, Shropshire WV15 5JZ Tel (01746) 716497 Fax (01746) 716552

An Edwardian vicarage set in two acres of grounds on the edge of a conservation village in glorious Shropshire countryside, close to Ironbridge Gorge, Severn Valley Railway and Welsh border towns. With an award-winning dining room and cellar, the Old Vicarage is personally run by Peter and Christine Iles. Two-night leisure breaks available at any time of the year which include free passport tickets to the Ironbridge Gorge museums. CATEGORY 2

Bed & Breakfast per night: single occupancy from £70.00–£95.00; double room from £107.50–£152.50
Half board per person: £95.00–£108.75 daily; £490.00–£647.50 weekly
Lunch available: Wednesday and Sunday only 1200–1400

Evening meal 1930 (last orders 2130)
Bedrooms: 8 double, 5 twin, 1 triple
Bathrooms: 14 en-suite
Parking for 30
Cards accepted: Mastercard, Visa, Diners, Amex

138 MIDDLETON LODGE

♛♛ HIGHLY COMMENDED

Middleton Priors, Bridgnorth, Shropshire WV16 6UR Tel (01746) 712228 Fax (01746) 712675

An imposing stone building in a one-acre garden with spacious bedrooms overlooking Brown Clee Hill, Middleton Lodge is within easy reach of many places of interest, including Severn Valley Railway, Ironbridge, and the historic towns of Ludlow, Shrewsbury, Much Wenlock, Bridgnorth and Church Stretton.

Bed & Breakfast per night: single occupancy from £30.00–£35.00; double room from £45.00–£50.00

Bedrooms: 2 double, 1 twin
Bathrooms: 2 en-suite, 1 private
Parking for 4

12

139 PEACOCK INN

♛♛♛ HIGHLY COMMENDED

Boraston, Tenbury Wells, Worcestershire WR15 8LL Tel (01584) 810506 or (01584) 811236 Fax (01584) 811236

Nestling in the Teme valley, a mile and a quarter from Tenbury Wells and thirteen miles from Ludlow – a 14th-century inn on three borders: Worcestershire, Shropshire and Herefordshire. The inn has a wealth of old timbers, oak panelling and open log fires in the winter. Highly acclaimed cuisine in the lounge or bistro, cask conditioned ales and fine wines. The inn has three en-suite bedrooms (non-smoking), with hand-crafted polished furniture, which all have their own entrance.

Bed & Breakfast per night: single occupancy £40.00; double room £50.00
Lunch available: 1130–1415
Evening meal 1900 (last orders 2130)

Bedrooms: 3 double
Bathrooms: 3 en-suite
Parking for 30
Cards accepted: Mastercard, Visa, Switch/Delta

At-a-glance symbols are explained on the flap inside the back cover

140 THE WHITE HOUSE

HIGHLY COMMENDED

White House Lane, Kyrewood, Tenbury Wells, Worcestershire WR15 8SQ Tel (01584) 810694

The White House is a large Georgian country house set in an acre of gardens, surrounded by orchards and open countryside on the Worcestershire/Shropshire border. Three spacious luxury bedrooms with en-suite bathrooms. Four-poster room available. Large elegant drawing room, where a coal fire burns in the winter. Local inns nearby serve excellent cuisine. Perfectly situated for touring Worcestershire, Herefordshire, Mid-Wales, The Marches and historic Ludlow. Golf, swimming, horse riding nearby. Non-smoking.

Bed & Breakfast per night: single occupancy from £25.00–£30.00; double room from £44.00–£50.00

Bedrooms: 2 double, 1 twin
Bathrooms: 3 en-suite
Parking for 6
Open: April–December

10

Cruck-framed houses

THE MIDLANDS ARE PARTICULARLY rich in timber-framed or, to use the popular term, half-timbered buildings – 'half-timbered' being a reference to the early medieval period when the timbers were formed by cutting logs in half. These buildings are classified as either box-frame construction or cruck construction. By far the more common type was box-frame, where jointed horizontal and vertical timbers formed a wall and either the panels were infilled or the whole wall was covered with some sort of cladding. In the cruck construction, the structure was supported by pairs of inclined, slightly curved timbers that normally met at the ridge of the roof and were tied by a collar or tie-beam, making an A shape. These timbers, called crucks or blades, were spaced at regular intervals along the building to take the weight of the roof and often of the walls too. Wherever possible crucks were cut from the trunk of one tree split along its length to get a symmetrical arch. Alternatively, they were taken from trees with a natural curve in the trunk and blades matched as closely as possible.

There were various forms of cruck construction, the most important being full cruck, base or truncated cruck, raised cruck and jointed cruck. Full crucks extend from ground level to the apex. Base or truncated begin on the ground but stop below the apex and are joined by a tie-beam or collar that supports the roof. Raised crucks start a few feet off the ground in a solid wall, and in jointed cruck construction the curving blade is jointed to a vertical post that begins on the ground.

Many crucks have been incorporated into larger buildings, hidden behind a cladding of stone or brick or plastered over, but where they are visible as the gable end they are an attractive and striking feature. Cruck-framing is particularly prevalent in the Midlands, the North and West (and is more or less entirely absent in East Anglia and the South-East, where box-framing predominates), and it is in Hereford & Worcester that the greatest concentration of cruck buildings is to be found. There are some fine examples in Weobley, unsurpassed for its black-and-white buildings. Explore its streets and you cannot fail to admire the skills of the 15th-, 16th- and 17th-century craftsmen. Other towns in the county worth visiting for their half-timbering are Eardisley, Eardisland, Pembridge and Dilwyn. Some excellent examples of cruck-framed buildings have been reconstructed at the Avoncroft Museum of Historic Buildings in Bromsgrove (tel: 01527 831886).

141 THE BRAKES

HIGHLY COMMENDED

Downton, Ludlow, Shropshire SY8 2LF Tel (01584) 856485 Fax (01584) 856485

In the heart of beautiful rolling countryside, only five miles from the historic town of Ludlow, The Brakes offers delightful accommodation with excellent cuisine. A period farmhouse, tastefully furnished, with central heating throughout, standing in three acres of grounds with a beautiful garden. Bedrooms are en-suite, with TV, and there is a charming lounge with a log fire for chilly evenings. Excellent walking country, including Offa's Dyke and the Long Mynd. Golf, riding and fishing available. Steeped in history, with many places of interest nearby.

Bed & Breakfast per night: single occupancy from £30.00; double room from £50.00

Bedrooms: 1 double, 2 twin
Bathrooms: 3 en-suite
Parking for 8
Open: all year except Christmas and New Year

13

142 THE HILLS FARM

HIGHLY COMMENDED

Leysters, Leominster, Herefordshire HR6 0HP Tel (01568) 750205 Fax (01568) 750205

We offer stunning views, scrumptious food and charming bedrooms. The Hills stands on high ground amidst 120 arable acres, complete with a two-mile farm walk. Three of our bedrooms are in lovingly converted barns, each completely self-contained and so offering the ultimate in seclusion and privacy. To round the day off – delicious home-cooked dinners complete with a vegetarian choice if required. No smoking. Brochure available.

Bed & Breakfast per night: double room from £46.00–£50.00
Half board per person: £39.00–£41.00 daily
Evening meal 1900 (last bookings 1700)

Bedrooms: 3 double, 2 twin
Bathrooms: 4 en-suite, 1 private
Parking for 5
Open: March–October
Cards accepted: Mastercard, Visa, Switch/Delta

143 BROXWOOD COURT

HIGHLY COMMENDED

Broxwood, Leominster, Herefordshire HR6 9JJ Tel (01544) 340245 Fax (01544) 340573

This beautiful home, with its sweeping lawns where peacocks roam, magnificent trees and lake, and uninterrupted views of the Black Mountains, offers an atmosphere of peace and tranquillity. Relax in the cosy library, enjoy the views from the drawing room, play tennis on the all-weather court, swim in the pool, or walk in the lovely thirty-acre garden. Mike and Anne are a relaxed and well-travelled couple who will give you a very warm welcome.

Bed & Breakfast per night: single occupancy £40.00; double room from £60.00–£70.00
Half board per person: £48.00–£58.00 daily; £336.00–£406.00 weekly
Evening meal 1900 (last orders 2100)

Bedrooms: 1 double, 2 twin
Bathrooms: 2 en-suite, 2 private
Parking for 15
Open: January and March–December
Cards accepted: Mastercard, Visa

At-a-glance symbols are explained on the flap inside the back cover

144 FELTON HOUSE

HIGHLY COMMENDED

Felton, Hereford HR1 3PH Tel (01432) 820366

Marjorie and Brian Roby extend a warm welcome to their romantic and homely old stone former rectory. With three acres of beautiful gardens, you can enjoy the tranquil setting and period atmosphere of four-poster, half-tester and brass beds, a well-stocked library, drawing and garden rooms, all centrally heated. In the superb dining room, select from a full English or vegetarian breakfast menu; excellent evening meals available at local inns. Just off the A417, eight miles from Hereford, Leominster and Bromyard.

Bed & Breakfast per night: single room £21.00; double room £42.00

Bedrooms: 1 single, 2 double, 1 twin
Bathrooms: 2 en-suite, 2 private, 1 public
Parking for 6

145 THE STEPPES

HIGHLY COMMENDED

Ullingswick, Hereford HR1 3JG Tel (01432) 820424 Fax (01432) 820042

This award-winning country-house hotel with an intimate atmosphere abounds in antique furniture, inglenook fireplaces, oak beams and flag-stoned floors. The old dairy now houses a magnificent cobbled bar with Dickensian atmosphere, and a restored timber-framed barn and converted stable accommodate six large luxury en-suite bedrooms. Outstanding cordon bleu cuisine is served by candle light, and highly praised breakfasts come with an imaginative selection.

Bed & Breakfast per night: single occupancy from £40.00–£60.00; double room from £80.00–£90.00
Half board per person: £55.00–£70.00 daily; £365.00–£390.00 weekly
Evening meal 1930 (last orders 2030)

Bedrooms: 4 double, 2 twin
Bathrooms: 6 en-suite
Parking for 8
Open: February–December
Cards accepted: Mastercard, Visa, Amex, Switch/Delta

146 WYCHE KEEP COUNTRY HOUSE

HIGHLY COMMENDED

22 Wyche Road, Malvern, Worcestershire WR14 4EG Tel (01684) 567018 Fax (01684) 892304

Wyche Keep is a mock castle perched high on the Malvern Hills. Built by the family of Prime Minister Sir Stanley Baldwin, it has a long history of entertaining house guests. All luxury suites enjoy spectacular sixty-mile views, and magical rhododendron gardens lead to hill ridge walks. Guests are treated to personal attention and can savour memorable English four-course candle-lit dinners. We specialise in tour holidays with the resident historian host, through Wales and the Cotswolds. A no smoking establishment. Fully licensed.

Bed & Breakfast per night: single occupancy from £35.00–£40.00; double room from £50.00–£60.00
Half board per person: £43.00–£48.00 daily; £301.00–£336.00 weekly
Evening meal 1930 (last orders 2000)

Bedrooms: 1 double, 2 twin
Bathrooms: 3 en-suite
Parking for 6

Entries are cross referenced by number to the maps on pages 66–67

147 COWLEIGH PARK FARM

HIGHLY COMMENDED

Cowleigh Road, Malvern, Worcestershire WR13 5HJ Tel (01684) 566750

Cowleigh Park Farm is a delightful 17th-century timber-framed farmhouse which is Grade II Listed. This beautifully restored home is peacefully situated at the foot of the Malvern Hills, creating a tranquil setting for a relaxing and friendly stay. Period furnishings throughout, and a choice of three comfortable rooms all with en-suite facilities. Guests are welcome to enjoy the two and a half acres of landscaped gardens before exploring some of Britain's finest scenery and walks. Plenty of parking within the grounds.

Bed & Breakfast per night: single occupancy from £30.00; double room from £44.00–£48.00
Evening meal 1830 (last bookings 1000)

Bedrooms: 1 double, 2 twin
Bathrooms: 3 en-suite
Parking for 6

Elgar and the Three Choirs Festival

NO ONE ACTUALLY KNOWS when the tradition of annual music-making involving the three cities of Hereford, Worcester and Gloucester, now known as the Three Choirs Festival, began. It is probable that it was well established by the end of the 17th century, making it the oldest musical festival of its type in Europe. From the start it revolved around the three great cathedrals (Gloucester Cathedral shown below) and consisted of a couple of days' performances of religious music each year in a different city. Even at this early stage, much informal music-making probably went on 'out of hours' and, by the mid-18th century, secular concerts had become an established part of the event.

Over the years the meetings expanded, becoming by the 1830s the 'festival' in existence today, with large-scale choral works held in the cathedral and secular and orchestral performances in various venues around the city, spread over a period of a week in August. During the 20th century the festival has played an important rôle in fostering new British composers, seeing the world premieres of works now well established in the musical repertoire by composers such as Parry, Vaughan Williams, Holst, Delius, Walton, Bliss and Britten. Of all those associated with the festival, the most famous is Edward Elgar, whose music is inextricably linked with the Three Choirs and its history.

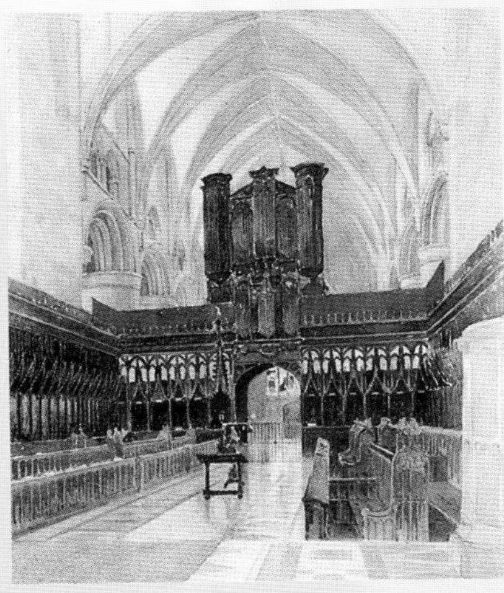

Elgar was born at Broadheath, 3 miles west of Worcester, and his birthplace is now open as a museum (tel: 01905 333224). His early career was not promising, and when his overture *Froissart* was first accepted by the festival committee in 1890 he, at 32, had not yet made a name for himself. It was the start of a more productive period however, and by the time his great *Dream of Gerontius* was premiered at the festival in 1902 his reputation was firmly established. From the end of the First World War until his death in 1934, Elgar made frequent appearances at the festival, a grand old man, knighted, frequently wearing his court dress, and often conducting his own works. Though his fame inevitably took him to London, he never lost touch with his beloved Malverns, taking homes in the area, cycling around its lanes and drawing inspiration from its calm English beauty. A detailed Elgar route is available from tourist offices, taking in sites associated with the composer. Elgar's music continues to be heard at the Three Choirs Festival and also at Malvern's Elgar festival held in late May and early June.

148 COLWALL PARK HOTEL

HIGHLY COMMENDED

Colwall, Malvern, Worcestershire WR13 6QG Tel (01684) 540206 or (01684) 541033 Fax (01684) 540847

Situated on the western slopes of the Malvern Hills, the hotel provides an ideal setting for a relaxing break with the care and comfort required. The award-winning Edwardian Restaurant offers English menus at their most enjoyable, with local fresh produce being used where possible. A wonderful centre from which to appreciate some of England's still unspoilt countryside.

Bed & Breakfast per night: single room from £59.50–£69.50; double room from £89.50–£135.00
Half board per person: £59.50–£89.50 daily; £416.50–£626.50 weekly
Lunch available: 1200–1400

Evening meal 1930 (last orders 2100)
Bedrooms: 3 single, 9 double, 7 twin, 2 triple, 2 family rooms
Bathrooms: 23 en-suite
Parking for 40
Cards accepted: Mastercard, Visa, Diners, Amex, Switch/Delta

149 THE COTTAGE IN THE WOOD HOTEL

HIGHLY COMMENDED

Holywell Road, Malvern Wells, Malvern, Worcestershire WR14 4LG Tel (01684) 575859 Fax (01684) 560662

Stunningly set high on the Malvern Hills, looking across thirty miles of the Severn Plain to the horizon formed by the Cotswold Hills. Owned and run by the Pattin family for ten years, the aim is to provide a relaxing and peaceful base from which to tour this area of outstanding natural beauty. The restaurant provides exceptional food backed by an extensive wine list of over four hundred bins. The daily half board price is based on a minimum two-night stay, and the weekly price offers seven nights for the price of six. Special breaks are available all week, all year.

Bed & Breakfast per night: single occupancy from £69.00–£79.00; double room from £89.50–£140.00
Half board per person: £52.00–£70.00 daily; £312.00–£420.00 weekly
Lunch available: 1230–1400

Evening meal 1900 (last orders 2100)
Bedrooms: 16 double, 4 twin
Bathrooms: 20 en-suite
Parking for 40
Cards accepted: Mastercard, Visa, Amex, Switch/Delta

150 HOLDFAST COTTAGE HOTEL

HIGHLY COMMENDED

Marlbank Road, Little Malvern, Malvern, Worcestershire WR13 6NA Tel (01684) 310288 Fax (01684) 311117

Pretty wisteria-covered country house hotel, set in two acres of gardens and private woodland, tucked into the foot of the Malvern Hills. Highly recommended for its freshly-prepared menu which changes daily and uses the best local and seasonal produce. Delightful dining room and bar. Cosy lounge with log fire. Enchanting en-suite bedrooms are individually furnished. A personal welcome plus care and attention throughout your stay is assured by the resident proprietors, Stephen and Jane Knowles.

Bed & Breakfast per night: single room from £42.00–£44.00; double room from £84.00–£85.00
Half board per person: £56.00–£58.00 daily; £336.00–£348.00 weekly
Evening meal 1900 (last orders 2100)

Bedrooms: 1 single, 5 double, 2 twin
Bathrooms: 8 en-suite, 1 public
Parking for 20
Cards accepted: Mastercard, Visa, Switch/Delta

Entries are cross referenced by number to the maps on pages 66–67

151 THE OLD RECTORY

HIGHLY COMMENDED

Garway, Hereford HR2 8RH Tel (01600) 750363 Fax (01600) 750364

Our home is Victorian, with a wonderfully welcoming atmosphere – the tick of the grandfather clock, the smell of log fires, arrangements of flowers and Aga cooking all combine to make you feel at home. The Blue Room has a double four-poster and the Pink Room has twin beds; both have handbasins and beautiful views of the countryside looking towards Wales. Private sitting room with colour TV. Peaceful garden with many birds.

Bed & Breakfast per night: single occupancy from £23.00–£25.00; double room from £36.00–£40.00
Half board per person: £34.00–£36.00 daily; £214.20–£226.80 weekly
Evening meal 1900 (last orders 2030)

Bedrooms: 1 double, 1 twin
Bathrooms: 2 public
Parking for 4
Open: March–November
Cards accepted: Mastercard, Visa

8 UL TV

152 NORTON HOUSE

HIGHLY COMMENDED

Whitchurch, Ross-on-Wye, Herefordshire HR9 6DJ Tel (01600) 890046 Fax (01600) 890045 E-mail jackson@osconwhi.source.co.uk

A 17th-century Grade II Listed former farmhouse, which has been beautifully renovated with pine shutters and doors, oak beams, flagstone floors and inglenook fireplaces. It oozes old fashioned charm but offers all the modern comfort our guests could wish for. Delicious Aga-cooked meals served by candle light make for a romantic escape. Situated in the beautiful Wye Valley, a short walk from the River Wye and five minutes' drive from Yat Rock, making it an ideal touring centre.

Bed & Breakfast per night: single occupancy from £25.00–£30.00; double room from £40.00–£44.00
Half board per person: £29.50–£39.50 daily
Evening meal 1930

Bedrooms: 3 double
Bathrooms: 3 en-suite
Parking for 3

UL S TV SP

153 THE CHASE HOTEL

HIGHLY COMMENDED

Gloucester Road, Ross-on-Wye, Herefordshire HR9 5LH Tel (01989) 763161 Fax (01989) 768330

A country house hotel set in 11 acres of gardens and grounds yet close to the town centre. All rooms have en-suite facilities, hair dryers, colour satellite televisions, radios and hospitality trays. The award-winning restaurant provides excellence in food, service and cuisine. All public rooms look over the gardens and, with ample parking, this hotel offers an ideal situation to enjoy a relaxing time while touring the area.

Bed & Breakfast per night: single occupancy £70.00; double room £85.00
Half board per person: from £95.00 daily; from £300.00 weekly
Evening meal 1900 (last orders 2145)

Bedrooms: 17 double, 21 twin, 1 triple
Bathrooms: 39 en-suite
Parking for 200
Cards accepted: Mastercard, Visa, Diners, Amex, Switch/Delta

S TV

154 BOLLITREE LAWNS

 HIGHLY COMMENDED

Weston under Penyard, Ross-on-Wye, Herefordshire HR9 7PF Tel (01989) 768129

Relax in our elegant Victorian country home which is set in 19 acres of peaceful garden and pastureland, with fine views. We pay close attention to detail to ensure complete enjoyment during your stay. Our recently-restored house is furnished in comfort and style and both guest bedrooms, a double and a twin, have luxury en-suite bathrooms. As food lovers and keen gardeners, we are restoring and enhancing the Victorian/Edwardian garden. Open March to November. No smoking. Brochure available.

Bed & Breakfast per night: single occupancy from £34.00–£39.00; double room from £50.00–£60.00

Bedrooms: 1 double, 1 twin
Bathrooms: 2 en-suite
Parking for 2
Open: March–November

155 STRETTON LODGE HOTEL

HIGHLY COMMENDED

Western Road, Cheltenham, Gloucestershire GL50 3RN Tel (01242) 570771 Fax (01242) 528724

The Victorian Stretton Lodge Townhouse is now a family-managed hotel nestling in the heart of Cheltenham, yet located in a quiet area with its own garden and parking. Each en-suite bedroom is individually decorated, whilst the elegant sitting and dining rooms reflect a past age of gracious living. Light meals and snacks are served throughout the day and home-cooked meals each evening. Please contact Carol and Christopher Tallis for further assistance and to make your reservation.

Bed & Breakfast per night: single room from £35.00–£50.00; double room from £52.00–£72.00
Half board per person: £40.00–£48.00 daily; £260.00–£290.00 weekly
Lunch available: all day

Evening meal 1700 (last orders 1930)
Bedrooms: 1 single, 2 double, 1 twin, 1 triple
Bathrooms: 5 en-suite
Parking for 6
Cards accepted: Mastercard, Visa, Amex, Switch/Delta

156 WYASTONE HOTEL

HIGHLY COMMENDED

Parabola Road, Cheltenham, Gloucestershire GL50 3BG Tel (01242) 245549 Fax (01242) 522659

Centrally situated in a quiet, tree-lined road in elegant Montpellier, and just five minutes' walk to the Promenade shops. A charming Victorian town hotel with the feel of a well-run private house. Period furniture and decoration help create a blend of comfort and character, which is combined with friendly and attentive service from the resident Anglo-French owners and their staff. Secluded patio garden. Free colour brochure upon request.

Bed & Breakfast per night: single room £51.00; double room £71.00
Evening meal 1830 (last orders 2030)

Bedrooms: 5 single, 6 double/twin, 2 triple
Bathrooms: 13 en-suite
Parking for 14
Cards accepted: Mastercard, Visa, Amex, Switch/Delta

Entries are cross referenced by number to the maps on pages 66–67

157 Hotel on the Park

DE LUXE

Evesham Road, Cheltenham GL52 2AH Tel (01242) 518898 Fax (01242) 511526 E-mail hotel@epinet.co.uk/www.i2i.net/hotelonthepark.him

This exclusive town house hotel is set within a classic example of a Regency villa and successfully combines the highest standards of traditional hotel-keeping with the charm and character of a period house. The twelve individually-designed bedrooms and suites and the elegant, candle-lit public rooms complement a restaurant serving some of the best modern British cooking on offer today. Situated opposite Pittville Park and five minutes from the race-course and the town centre.

Bed & Breakfast per night: single occupancy from £80.50–£140.50; double room from £101.50–£161.50
Half board per person: from £65.78–£92.78 daily
Lunch available: 1200–1400
Evening meal 1900 (last orders 2130)

Bedrooms: 8 double, 4 twin
Bathrooms: 12 en-suite
Parking for 10
Cards accepted: Mastercard, Visa, Diners, Amex, Switch/Delta

158 Deerhurst House

HIGHLY COMMENDED

Deerhurst, Gloucester, Gloucestershire GL19 4BX Tel (01684) 292135 or 0850 520051 Fax (01684) 296535

Deerhurst House is a beautiful, classically-proportioned, period country house of mellow brick, adorned by a stone portico, standing in three acres in the ancient riverside village of Deerhurst (containing the oldest dated church in England), three miles south of Tewkesbury. Guest rooms are generous and comfortable with en-suite facilities and glorious views across unspoilt countryside to the Malvern Hills. A perfect centre for walking or touring the Cotswolds, Malverns, or Royal Forest of Dean.

Bed & Breakfast per night: single occupancy £30.00; double room £45.00

Bedrooms: 1 double, 1 twin
Bathrooms: 2 en-suite
Parking for 10

159 Edgewood House

HIGHLY COMMENDED

Churcham, Gloucester, Gloucestershire GL2 8AA Tel (01452) 750232

Edgewood House, built in the 1930s, is set in two acres of gardens, with lawns and mature trees. A restful and friendly atmosphere is combined with spacious bedrooms, which are tastefully furnished with comfortable beds, all with views overlooking the garden. Guests' own television lounge. Generous cooked breakfast. Ideal for visiting the Forest of Dean, Malverns, Wye Valley and the Cotswolds. Opposite RSPB reserve, near viewpoint for the Severn Bore tidal wave. Dinner available at good local pubs. Totally non-smoking. Brochure available.

Bed & Breakfast per night: single occupancy from £25.00–£29.00; double room from £36.00–£45.00

Bedrooms: 1 double, 1 twin, 1 family room
Bathrooms: 2 en-suite, 1 private
Parking for 6

At-a-glance symbols are explained on the flap inside the back cover

160 TUDOR FARMHOUSE HOTEL AND RESTAURANT

HIGHLY COMMENDED

Clearwell, Coleford, Gloucestershire GL16 8JS Tel (01594) 833046 Fax (01594) 837093

This charming 13th-century Grade II Listed farmhouse, with 14 acres of grounds, is set in the picturesque village of Clearwell, which nestles between the Wye Valley and the Forest of Dean. Accommodation comprises fully equipped en-suite bedrooms, including four-posters and two family suites. The award-winning restaurant serves delicious home-made food, with a vegetarian selection, and comprehensive wine list.

Bed & Breakfast per night: single room £47.50; double room from £57.00–£90.00
Half board per person: £42.50–£57.50 daily; £255.00–£365.00 weekly
Evening meal 1900 (last orders 2100)

Bedrooms: 2 single, 6 double, 1 twin, 4 triple
Bathrooms: 13 en-suite
Parking for 20
Cards accepted: Mastercard, Visa, Amex, Switch/Delta

Westonbirt Arboretum

WHEN CAPTAIN ROBERT HOLFORD planted his first tree on his father's land in 1829 he did so, in part, for posterity, knowing he could never live to see the mature fulfilment of his botanical vision. The eldest son of the owner of the wealthy Weston Birt estate on the edge of the Cotswolds, Holford was just 21 when he began the outstanding collection of tree specimens which now forms Westonbirt Arboretum. Today, almost 170 years later, visitors may view the spectacular culmination of his life's work.

Holford was primarily a plantsman. His aim was to collect as many species as possible, nurturing them in a climate and ecosystem which was, in many cases, very different from that of their country of origin. Today some 4,000 species flourish here, with exotic specimens at every turn: the Chilean fire-bush, the tulip tree, the corkscrew hazel, the handkerchief tree...

Holford aimed not only to grow a wide range of species, but also to create a landscape of great beauty, designed to provide colour and interest throughout the year. In what is now the main arboretum, he began planting a series of rides and glades laid out to create ever-changing vistas. Here, sheltered by especially planted belts of evergreens, azaleas, camellias and rhododendrons flourish, a mass of vivid colour in spring. Summer is the best time to appreciate the 'colour circle' designed by Holford as a congenial picnic spot, while autumn sets the trees on fire, especially acers and maples.

Later, with the help of his son, George, who inherited his father's passion, Holford cut further drives and avenues through nearby Silk Wood. Here he devoted space to collections of oak, beech, ash and lime, creating an opportunity to see familiar native species side by side with more exotic foreign cousins. The giant evergreen conifers – pines, spruces, sequoias, cedars and cypresses – are particularly impressive in winter, especially when covered in snow.

In total the arboretum covers 600 acres (242.5 hectares) of woodland with 17 miles (27.2km) of paths and 18,000 listed specimens of plants. To view it in its entirety is an impossible challenge, but by its nature it rewards many visits throughout the year (tel: 01666 880220).

Entries are cross referenced by number to the maps on pages 66–67

161 THE OLD RECTORY

HIGHLY COMMENDED

Didmarton, Gloucestershire GL9 1DS Tel (01454) 238233

This small former rectory is set in the south Cotswolds on the A433. It has a very friendly informal atmosphere and is an ideal base for touring or, since we are close to Bath and the M4/5, is a convenient and comfortable overnight stop. Westonbirt Arboretum is five minutes away and the antiques centre of Tetbury is less than ten. There is ample parking and food is available within walking distance.

Bed & Breakfast per night: single occupancy from £25.00; double room from £38.00–£40.00

Bedrooms: 2 double, 1 twin
Bathrooms: 2 en-suite, 1 private
Parking for 4

---

162 TAVERN HOUSE

DE LUXE

Willesley, Tetbury, Gloucestershire GL8 8QU Tel (01666) 880444 Fax (01666) 880254

A delightfully situated 17th-century Grade II Listed former staging-post, this elegant Cotswold-stone country house is only one mile from Westonbirt Arboretum which has one of Europe's largest collections of trees and shrubs. The four en-suite bedrooms have direct-dial telephone, television, hairdryer and much more. A charming secluded garden offers peace and tranquillity, far from the madding crowd. Convenient for Bath, Gloucester, Cheltenham and Stow. A country house atmosphere with attention to detail being our keynote. ETB 'England for Excellence' Silver Award, 1993.

Bed & Breakfast per night: single occupancy from £45.00–£55.00; double room from £57.00–£65.00

Bedrooms: 3 double, 1 twin
Bathrooms: 4 en-suite
Parking for 4
Cards accepted: Mastercard, Visa

---

163 THE GREY COTTAGE

DE LUXE

Bath Road, Leonard Stanley, Stonehouse, Gloucestershire GL10 3LU Tel (01453) 822515 Fax (01453) 822515

Situated in the undiscovered south Cotswolds, nevertheless with good communications. Andrew and Rosemary Reeves welcome you to their rugged stone-built cottage which permeates warmth and ambience. Fresh flowers abound as we endeavour to maintain our half-acre garden to a high standard throughout the year. Prior reservation is essential as we try to cater for individual preferences and tastes using authentic ingredients.

Bed & Breakfast per night: single room from £29.00–£32.00; double room from £46.00–£54.00
Half board per person: £45.00–£50.00 daily
Evening meal 1915

Bedrooms: 1 single, 1 double, 1 twin
Bathrooms: 2 en-suite, 1 private
Parking for 7

164 PRETORIA VILLA

Listed HIGHLY COMMENDED

Wells Road, Eastcombe, Stroud, Gloucestershire GL6 7EE Tel (01452) 770435

Eastcombe, a south Cotswold village set above the beautiful Toadsmoor Valley, is ideally placed for touring the Cotswolds. Within easy reach of the spa towns of Bath and Cheltenham and the market towns of Cirencester and Gloucester. Discover the towns along the ancient Fosse Way – Northleach, Bourton-on-the-Water, Stow-on-the-Wold – and nearby Broadway. Close to hand are excellent golf courses, riding stables and leisure centres. For walking enthusiasts, there is the famous Cotswold Way.

Bed & Breakfast per night: single room £20.00; double room £40.00
Half board per person: £32.00 daily; £210.00 weekly
Evening meal 1830 (last orders 2030)

Bedrooms: 1 single, 1 double, 1 twin
Bathrooms: 1 en-suite, 2 private, 1 public
Parking for 3

165 GILBERT'S

HIGHLY COMMENDED

Gilbert's Lane, Brookthorpe, Gloucester GL4 0UH Tel (01452) 812364 Fax (01452) 812364 E-mail jenny@gilbertsbb.demon.co.uk

This beautiful listed 16th-century house has been tastefully brought up to date with modern comforts and conveniences whilst retaining the dignity and atmosphere of the past. This is also reflected in the surrounding organic grounds. Here goodies are grown for the table amongst a rich tapestry of flora and fauna. Centrally placed beneath the dramatic Cotswold edge, ten minutes from Gloucester and Stroud, this makes an excellent base for exploring Bath, Oxford, Stratford and much more.

Bed & Breakfast per night: single room from £25.00–£37.00; double room from £48.00–£57.00

Bedrooms: 1 single, 2 double, 1 twin
Bathrooms: 3 en-suite, 1 private
Parking for 6

166 CHARLTON KINGS HOTEL

HIGHLY COMMENDED

London Road, Charlton Kings, Cheltenham, Gloucestershire GL52 6UU Tel (01242) 231061 Fax (01242) 241900

Situated in an area of outstanding natural beauty on the edge of Cheltenham Spa. An ideal touring centre for the walker (the famous Cotswold Way is only a half mile away) or motorist (ask for your free 'Romantic Road' when booking). The sporting/activity enthusiast is also well catered for. Whatever you choose, come back and enjoy the creative skills of our talented chef. Although we have high standards, the hotel is informally run by the proprietor and his team of enthusiastic staff.

Bed & Breakfast per night: single room from £55.50–£75.50; double room from £84.00–£94.00
Half board per person: £58.95–£63.95 daily; £301.00–£322.00 weekly
Lunch available: 1200–1400

Evening meal 1900 (last orders 2045)
Bedrooms: 2 single, 8 double, 2 twin, 1 triple, 1 family room
Bathrooms: 14 en-suite
Parking for 26
Cards accepted: Mastercard, Visa, Amex, Switch/Delta

Entries are cross referenced by number to the maps on pages 66–67

167 THE SWAN HOTEL

DE LUXE

Bibury, Cirencester, Gloucestershire GL7 5NW Tel (01285) 740695 Fax (01285) 740473

A luxurious hotel with cosy parlours, elegant dining room, sumptuous bedrooms (a few with four-poster beds) and lavish bathrooms (some with large jacuzzi baths). Our head chef, Paul Mingo-West, presents a regularly changing menu in a modern English style which is occasionally influenced by classical cuisine. An ideal base for touring the Cotswolds, visiting Shakespeare's Stratford, Roman Bath, antiques in Burford and the Oxford colleges. Take pleasure in our private garden on the banks of the River Coln – enjoy the ambience or fish for your own trout. Licensed for weddings. Ideal venue for special occasions.

Bed & Breakfast per night: single occupancy from £99.00–£119.00; double room from £150.00–£220.00
Half board per person: £90.00–£125.00 daily; £630.00–£875.00 weekly
Lunch available: 1200–1430

Evening meal 1930 (last orders 2130)
Bedrooms: 13 double, 4 twin, 1 family room
Bathrooms: 18 en-suite
Parking for 20
Cards accepted: Mastercard, Visa, Amex, Switch/Delta

168 THE NEW INN AT COLN

HIGHLY COMMENDED

Coln St-Aldwyns, near Cirencester, Gloucestershire GL7 5AN Tel (01285) 750651 Fax (01285) 750657

Set in a tranquil Cotswold village close to Bibury, The New Inn at Coln is a 16th-century coaching inn with log fires, oak beams and smiling, efficient service. Discerning visitors travel miles to experience its restaurant, which has an enviable reputation. Self-styled as "a private castle of comfort", The New Inn at Coln has over the last five years become generally regarded as one of England's finest and best-run inns.

Bed & Breakfast per night: single room £59.00–£78.00; double room from £87.00–£120.00
Half board per person: £60.00–£82.50 daily; £400.00–£525.00 weekly
Lunch available: 1200–1400

Evening meal 1900 (last orders 2100)
Bedrooms: 1 single, 11 double, 2 twin
Bathrooms: 14 en-suite
Parking for 25
Cards accepted: Mastercard, Visa, Amex, Switch/Delta

169 COOMBE HOUSE

HIGHLY COMMENDED

Rissington Road, Bourton-on-the-Water, Gloucestershire GL54 2DT Tel (01451) 821966 Fax (01451) 810477

Quietly located just a river-side walk from the centre of this beautiful Cotswold Village, Coombe House offers a haven of cleanliness, comfort and personal attention from your hosts. Gentle elegance, charming bedrooms and reception rooms, and a delightful garden with unusual plants. Perfect central base for discovering the superb Cotswolds, gardens and castles. London 75 miles. Oxford/Stratford 26 miles. Anticipated assistance with routes, ideas and restaurants. No smoking.

Bed & Breakfast per night: single occupancy from £46.00–£48.00; double room from £59.00–£68.00

Bedrooms: 3 double, 2 twin, 2 triple
Bathrooms: 6 en-suite, 2 private
Parking for 10
Cards accepted: Mastercard, Visa, Amex

170 DIAL HOUSE

HIGHLY COMMENDED

The Chestnuts, Bourton-on-the-Water, Gloucestershire GL54 2AN Tel (01451) 822244 Fax (01451) 810126

Built in 1698 of Cotswold stone, the Dial House is set in secluded gardens and reflects the ambience, charm and good manners of times gone by. Tastefully furnished rooms provide bathrooms, satellite television and beverage trays, some have antique four-posters. Dine in style in an intimate restaurant with inglenook fireplace and oak beams. Chef Calum Williamson has achieved awards for his excellent cuisine. There is ample parking within the grounds.

Bed & Breakfast per night: single room from £35.00–£55.00; double room from £90.00–£110.00
Half board per person: £58.50–£68.00 daily; £346.00–£409.00 weekly
Lunch available: 1200–1400

Evening meal 1900 (last orders 2100)
Bedrooms: 1 single, 6 double, 3 twin
Bathrooms: 9 en-suite, 1 private
Parking for 18
Cards accepted: Mastercard, Visa, Amex, Switch/Delta

171 STOW LODGE HOTEL

HIGHLY COMMENDED

The Square, Stow-on-the-Wold, Gloucestershire GL54 1AB Tel (01451) 830485 Fax (01451) 831671

Privately owned and family-run Cotswold Manor House Hotel set back in its own gardens in a secluded corner of the market square. Bedrooms are comfortably furnished with a private bathroom, and the no smoking restaurant offers excellent home cooking and an interesting extensive wine list. There are warm open fires for those cooler days in both the bar and residents' lounge. The hotel is ideal for those touring the Cotswolds and Shakespeare country and requiring a relaxing holiday.

Bed & Breakfast per night: single room from £45.00–£95.00; double room from £65.00–£105.00
Half board per person: £230.00–£360.00 weekly
Lunch available: 1200 –1400
Evening meal 1900 (last orders 2100)

Bedrooms: 1 single, 9 double, 9 twin, 2 triple
Bathrooms: 21 en-suite
Parking for 30
Open: February–December
Cards accepted: Mastercard, Visa, Diners, Switch/Delta

172 COLLEGE HOUSE

DE LUXE

Chapel Street, Broadwell, Moreton-in-Marsh, Gloucestershire GL56 0TW Tel (01451) 832351

College House is a 17th-century residence of great character located in a quiet and enchanting Cotswold village. It has superb bedrooms and luxurious bathrooms, of which two are en-suite, and a sitting-room with a large inglenook fireplace for exclusive guest use. Breakfast and, if desired, three-course dinners are served in the beamed dining-room. Broadwell is just two miles from Stow-on-the-Wold. Oxford, Cheltenham and Stratford-upon-Avon are all easily accessible.

Bed & Breakfast per night: double room from £46.00–£62.00
Half board per person: £40.50–£48.50 daily; £283.00–£339.00 weekly
Evening meal 1800 (last bookings 1200)

Bedrooms: 3 double
Bathrooms: 2 en-suite, 1 private
Parking for 6

Entries are cross referenced by number to the maps on pages 66–67

173 GRAPEVINE HOTEL

HIGHLY COMMENDED

Sheep Street, Stow-on-the-Wold, Gloucestershire GL54 1AU Tel (01451) 830344 Fax (01451) 832278 E-mail enquiries@vines.co.uk

An award-winning 17th-century market town hotel in the antiques centre of the Cotswolds. Romantic conservatory restaurant crowned by a magnificent historic vine and finely furnished garden and vine rooms. The outstanding personal service provided by a loyal team of staff is perhaps the secret of the hotel's success. This, along with the exceptionally high standard of overall comfort, hospitality and fine food, has earned the Grapevine its many accolades.

Half board per person: £59.00–£120.00 daily; £354.00–£634.00 weekly
Lunch available: 1200–1400
Evening meal 1900 (last orders 2130)

Bedrooms: 3 single, 7 double, 10 twin, 2 triple
Bathrooms: 22 en-suite
Parking for 23
Cards accepted: Mastercard, Visa, Diners, Amex, Switch/Delta

174 GUITING GUESTHOUSE

HIGHLY COMMENDED

Post Office Lane, Guiting Power, Cheltenham, Gloucestershire GL54 5TZ Tel (01451) 850470 Fax (01451) 850034

The house is a delightful and carefully-restored 16th-century Cotswold stone farmhouse. Everywhere there are exposed beams, inglenook fireplaces, open fires and polished solid pine floors from the Wychwood forest. Three rooms have four-poster beds and are en-suite, whilst the other room has totally private facilities. Television and generously-filled hospitality tray in each room. Access to the guesthouse is available at all times. Delicious evening meals, served by candle light, are prepared and presented by the hosts (with the exception of Sunday and Monday).

Bed & Breakfast per night: single occupancy £30.00; double room from £48.00–£50.00
Half board per person: £39.00–£45.00 daily
Evening meal 1845 (last orders 1845)

Bedrooms: 3 double, 1 family room
Bathrooms: 3 en-suite, 1 private
Parking for 4
Cards accepted: Mastercard, Visa, Switch/Delta

175 CLEEVE HILL HOTEL

DE LUXE

Cleeve Hill, Cheltenham, Gloucestershire GL52 3PR Tel (01242) 672052 Fax (01242) 679969

This award-winning hotel, perched on the slopes of Cleeve Hill, the highest point in the Cotswolds, is a mere ten minute drive from the centre of Cheltenham. The immaculate Edwardian house is elegantly decorated with quality furnishings and fabrics and all of the bedrooms are equipped to a very high standard with all the little extras that make this a very special place to stay. The hotel upholds a strict 'No Smoking' policy.

Bed & Breakfast per night: single room from £45.00–£65.00; double room from £60.00–£75.00

Bedrooms: 1 single, 5 double, 2 twin, 1 family room
Bathrooms: 9 en-suite
Parking for 12
Cards accepted: Mastercard, Visa, Amex

At-a-glance symbols are explained on the flap inside the back cover

176 COTSWOLD SPA HOTEL

HIGHLY COMMENDED

Cleeve Hill, Cheltenham, Gloucestershire GL52 3QE Tel (01242) 582727 Fax (01242) 257327

Cotswold Spa Hotel is a Cotswold stone-built country house hotel of character. Set in four acres of mature secluded landscaped gardens and grounds, occupying a semi-rural hillside setting in an area of outstanding natural beauty. Views to Leckhampton, the Malvern Hills and Cheltenham Race Course. Our Spa packages give you real luxurious value for your money. Just a few days away from it all will leave you feeling relaxed, revived and energised.

Bed & Breakfast per night: single room from £35.00–£55.00; double room from £65.00–£80.00
Lunch available: 1230–1400
Evening meal 1900 (last orders 2030)

Bedrooms: 3 single, 2 double, 2 twin, 3 triple
Bathrooms: 8 en-suite, 2 private, 1 public
Parking for 20
Cards accepted: Mastercard, Switch/Delta

S TV SC SP T

---

177 ALMSBURY FARM

HIGHLY COMMENDED

Vineyard Street, Winchcombe, Cheltenham, Gloucestershire GL54 5LP Tel (01242) 602403 Fax (01242) 603957

Almsbury Farm is a 17th-century Cotswold farmhouse on the edge of the Sudeley Castle estate, only a few minutes' walk from the town centre. Set in peaceful countryside, the house provides an elegant countryside retreat in which to relax, and is perfectly located for touring and walking. Winchcombe offers several good restaurants, pubs and shops. A warm welcome and comfort are assured.

Bed & Breakfast per night: single occupancy from £28.00–£32.00; double room from £44.00–£55.00

Bedrooms: 1 double, 1 triple
Bathrooms: 2 en-suite
Parking for 6

10 UL TV SP T

---

178 ISBOURNE MANOR HOUSE

HIGHLY COMMENDED

Castle Street, Winchcombe, Cheltenham, Gloucestershire GL54 5JA Tel (01242) 602281 Fax (01242) 602281

This beautiful listed house is quietly situated within attractive gardens which are bordered by the River Isbourne. We are adjacent to the lovely grounds of Sudeley Castle and only two minutes' walk away from both stunning Cotswold countryside and the centre of historic Winchcombe. All rooms are decorated and furnished to the highest standard, combining modern comfort with family antiques and beautiful fabrics. Guests have the sole use of two elegant reception rooms, private parking and garden.

Bed & Breakfast per night: double room from £50.00–£65.00

Bedrooms: 2 double, 1 twin
Bathrooms: 2 en-suite, 1 private
Parking for 4

10 UL SP T

Entries are cross referenced by number to the maps on pages 66–67

179 SUDELEY HILL FARM

HIGHLY COMMENDED

Winchcombe, Cheltenham, Gloucestershire GL54 5JB Tel (01242) 602344 Fax (01242) 602344

A friendly welcome awaits you on our eight hundred acre sheep and arable farm. The 15th-century listed farmhouse is situated above Sudeley Castle, with a large garden and panoramic views across the valley. A comfortable lounge, log fires, separate dining room, no smoking en-suite bedrooms with television and facilities for hot drinks. Central for exploring the Cotswolds. Good pub food in Winchcombe, half a mile away.

Bed & Breakfast per night: single occupancy from £28.00; double room from £44.00

Bedrooms: 1 double, 2 triple
Bathrooms: 3 en-suite
Parking for 10

180 DORMY HOUSE

HIGHLY COMMENDED

Willersey Hill, Broadway, Worcestershire WR12 7LF Tel (01386) 852711 Fax (01386) 858636

The 17th-century Dormy House is ideally located for visiting the picturesque villages of the Cotswolds as well as Shakespeare's Stratford-upon-Avon. Enjoy the beautifully appointed rooms, superb restaurant and high standard of cuisine and service. Our croquet lawn, putting green, sauna/steam room, gym, games room and nature trail offer the chance to combine leisure with pleasure. Pamper yourself with a Champagne Weekend or a carefree midweek break in the Heart of England.

Bed & Breakfast per night: single room from £69.00–£91.00; double room from £138.00–£182.00
Half board per person: £98.50–£120.50 daily
Lunch available: 1230–1400 (except Saturday)
Evening meal 1900 (last orders 2130)

Bedrooms: 6 single, 16 double, 26 twin, 1 family room
Bathrooms: 49 en-suite
Parking for 90
Cards accepted: Mastercard, Visa, Diners, Amex, Switch/Delta

181 TUDOR COTTAGE

HIGHLY COMMENDED

High Street, Broadway, Worcestershire WR12 7DT Tel (01386) 852674

Situated on Broadway's famous High Street, this traditional 17th-century stone Cotswold cottage is full of character and charm. All bedrooms are en-suite and have been tastefully decorated, furnished with style and equipped with modern comforts, including the four-poster bedroom which is ideal for a romantic weekend. Walks across open countryside lie within a few yards of the cottage. Or simply stroll the High Street with its interesting shops, pubs and restaurants.

Bed & Breakfast per night: single occupancy from £30.00–£40.00; double room from £45.00–£60.00

Bedrooms: 2 double, 1 twin
Bathrooms: 3 en-suite

182 ORCHARD HILL HOUSE

HIGHLY COMMENDED

Broad Campden, Chipping Campden, Gloucestershire GL55 6UU Tel (01386) 841473 Fax (01386) 841030

Situated in one of the most picturesque villages in the Cotswolds, Orchard Hill House dates back to 1646 and has been beautifully restored to provide comfort and style with old original charm. The rooms are beautifully furnished. Two are in the main house and, for something more private, a converted hayloft offers total individuality. Breakfast at our ten-foot elm refectory table in our flagstone-floored dining hall. The friendliest atmosphere you could wish to find. Orchard Hill House is a totally non-smoking establishment.

Bed & Breakfast per night: single occupancy from £40.00–£50.00; double room from £45.00–£57.00

Bedrooms: 2 double, 1 twin, 1 triple
Bathrooms: 3 en-suite, 1 private
Parking for 6

183 THE OLD RECTORY

DE LUXE

Church Street, Willersey, Broadway, Worcestershire WR12 7PN Tel (01386) 853729 Fax (01386) 858061 E-mail beauvoisin@btinternet.com

Built of Cotswold stone, the 17th-century Rectory is quietly tucked away opposite the church. Enclosed by its dry-stone wall, the garden with its ancient mulberry tree is truly idyllic. Superb breakfasts served in the elegant dining room (beside a log fire in winter). The Bell Inn, one minute walk away, offers excellent meals. The immaculate bedrooms, including four-posters, are furnished and decorated to a high standard and include all facilities. All rooms have their own bathroom with Crabtree & Evelyn toiletries. E-mail: if no reply, owners are away – please use fax.

Bed & Breakfast per night: single occupancy from £35.00–£85.00; double room from £60.00–£95.00

Bedrooms: 5 double, 1 twin, 2 triple
Bathrooms: 6 en-suite, 2 private
Parking for 10
Cards accepted: Mastercard, Visa, Switch/Delta

184 ROOSTERS

HIGHLY COMMENDED

Todenham, Moreton-in-Marsh, Gloucestershire GL56 9PA Tel (01608) 650645

Beautifully situated for exploring the Cotswolds and Shakespeare country. This lovely 17th-century Cotswold stone house has spacious beamed rooms and a delightful dining room with inglenook fireplace. Freshly cooked meals for those who would like them, and the comforts of home for all. Two twin en-suite rooms plus a double with private sunken bath. All rooms have TVs, hairdryers and tea/coffee-making facilities. Guests can sit and appreciate the superb view from the large landscaped gardens.

Bed & Breakfast per night: single occupancy from £22.00–£25.00; double room from £42.00–£45.00
Half board per person: £32.00–£36.00 daily
Evening meal 1900 (last orders 2100)

Bedrooms: 1 double, 2 twin
Bathrooms: 2 en-suite, 1 private
Parking for 3

Entries are cross referenced by number to the maps on pages 66–67

185 FOLLY FARM COTTAGE

HIGHLY COMMENDED

Ilmington, Shipston-on-Stour, Warwickshire CV36 4LJ Tel (01608) 682425 Fax (01608) 682425 E-mail slowe@mcmail.com

A large country cottage in a delightful, undiscovered and quiet Cotswold village, with country pubs and pretty cottages. Within easy reach of Stratford-upon-Avon and Warwick. Offering outstanding accommodation for that special occasion. Romantic en-suite double or four-poster rooms, with TVs and hospitality trays. As an added luxury, breakfast may be served in your room overlooking the pretty cottage gardens. Luxury honeymoon apartment suite with whirlpool bath. Brochure available. Internet: http://www.stratford-upon-avon.co.uk/follyfrm.htm

Bed & Breakfast per night: double room from £46.00–£60.00

Bedrooms: 3 double
Bathrooms: 3 en-suite
Parking for 8

186 ETTINGTON PARK HOTEL

HIGHLY COMMENDED

Alderminster, Stratford-upon-Avon, Warwickshire CV37 8BU Tel (01789) 450123 Fax (01789) 450472

Situated in 40 acres of landscaped parkland, this Grade I Listed 19th-century, neo-gothic mansion offers you the opportunity of experiencing the elegance of bygone days. The Oak Room restaurant serves the best of English dishes, whilst the chandeliered Great Drawing Room offers a place to relax. The park offers a myriad of leisure activities including tennis, croquet, riding and fishing. Our indoor leisure centre has a heated pool and solarium.

Bed & Breakfast per night: single occupancy £125.00; double room from £175.00–£350.00
Half board per person: from £155.50 daily
Lunch available: 1200–1400
Evening meal 1900 (last orders 2130)

Bedrooms: 41 double, 7 twin
Bathrooms: 48 en-suite
Parking for 90
Cards accepted: Mastercard, Visa, Diners, Amex, Switch/Delta

187 CRANDON HOUSE

HIGHLY COMMENDED

Avon Dassett, Leamington Spa, Warwickshire CV33 0AA Tel (01295) 770652 Fax (01295) 770652

This lovely country house, set in twenty acres with beautiful views over unspoilt countryside, offers affordable luxury and an especially warm welcome. Attractive bedrooms with colour television, tea tray, hairdryer and many extras to make your stay enjoyable. Guests' dining room and sitting rooms with full central heating and log fires in chilly weather. Delicious breakfasts from extensive menu. Peaceful and quiet, yet within easy reach of Stratford, Warwick, Oxford and the Cotswolds. Located between Junctions 11 and 12/M40. Special winter breaks.

Bed & Breakfast per night: single occupancy from £26.00–£32.00; double room from £39.00–£46.00

Bedrooms: 2 double, 3 twin
Bathrooms: 4 en-suite, 1 private
Parking for 22
Cards accepted: Mastercard, Visa

12 UL S TV SP

At-a-glance symbols are explained on the flap inside the back cover

188 LOXLEY FARM

HIGHLY COMMENDED

Loxley, Warwick, Warwickshire CV35 9JN Tel (01789) 840265 Fax (01789) 840265

Picturesque thatched, half-timbered farmhouse and barn, surrounded by one and a half acres of garden and orchard, in a quiet village on the edge of the Cotswolds. Three and a half miles from Stratford-upon-Avon, seven miles from Warwick. Accommodation is in the recently restored single-storey barn, which has two private suites of rooms, one of which includes a small kitchen. Traditional English breakfasts are served in the farmhouse dining room. Mrs Horton is happy to book theatre tickets at no extra charge.

Bed & Breakfast per night: single occupancy from £33.00–£36.00; double room from £50.00–£55.00

Bedrooms: 2 double
Bathrooms: 2 en-suite
Parking for 10

---

189 GRAVELSIDE BARN

HIGHLY COMMENDED

Binton, Stratford-upon-Avon, Warwickshire CV37 9TU Tel (01789) 750502 or (01789) 297000 Fax (01789) 298056

Serenely situated on a hilltop in the middle of rolling Warwickshire farmland, with magnificent views of the surrounding countryside and Cotswold Hills, Gravelside Barn offers the discerning traveller all of today's modern conveniences and comforts in a stunning and tranquil setting. A great base for exploring Shakespeare country and the Heart of England, or simply a place to relax. Three and a half miles from Stratford and ten minutes from Junction 15/M40. Please ring for a brochure. Totally non-smoking.

Bed & Breakfast per night: single occupancy £35.00; double room from £50.00–£60.00

Bedrooms: 2 double, 1 twin
Bathrooms: 3 en-suite
Parking for 6
Cards accepted: Mastercard, Visa

---

190 THE MILL AT HARVINGTON

HIGHLY COMMENDED

Anchor Lane, Harvington, Evesham, Worcestershire WR11 5NR Tel (01386) 870688 Fax (01386) 870688

Friendly, owner-run hotel, sensitively converted from a beautiful Georgian house and former baking mill. Situated on the banks of the River Avon in acres of private parkland, our hotel offers peace, tranquillity and a view over the garden and river towards the morning sun from every bedroom. Find gentle elegance without formality, good food without fussiness, and friendly staff who will help you relax immediately.

Bed & Breakfast per night: single occupancy £58.00; double room from £79.00–£107.00
Half board per person: £62.50–£81.00 daily; £297.50–£525.00 weekly
Lunch available: 1145–1345

Evening meal 1900 (last orders 2045)
Bedrooms: , 12 double, 3 twin
Bathrooms: 15 en-suite
Parking for 45
Cards accepted: Mastercard, Visa, Diners, Amex, Switch/Delta

10

Entries are cross referenced by number to the maps on pages 66–67

191 Arbour House Bed and Breakfast — HIGHLY COMMENDED

Main Road, Wyre Piddle, Pershore, Worcestershire WR10 2HU Tel (01386) 555833

Arbour House Bed and Breakfast is a charming old home with oak beams, real fires and flagstone floors, containing a fascinating collection of china and objets d'art. We offer beautifully prepared bedrooms with hospitality trays, a good selection of quality teas, fresh flowers, and many other personal touches that will make your stay thoroughly enjoyable. Situated in the vale of Evesham, there are several good hostelries here, and the Cotswolds, Stratford and Worcester are all nearby.

Bed & Breakfast per night: single occupancy from £25.00–£26.00; double room from £40.00–£42.00
Half board per person: £32.50–£34.00 daily; £220.00–£238.00 weekly
Evening meal 1800 (last orders 1900)

Bedrooms: 1 double, 2 twin
Bathrooms: 3 en-suite
Parking for 5

10 UL S TV SP T

192 Stratford Court Hotel — HIGHLY COMMENDED

Avenue Road, Stratford-upon-Avon, Warwickshire CV37 6UX Tel (01789) 297799 Fax (01789) 262449

This beautiful Edwardian residence is situated in one of Stratford's finest locations and is surrounded by an acre of walled gardens, providing a peaceful setting where our guests can relax and be looked after with care and courtesy. All our bedrooms are en-suite, having been refurbished to the highest standard in keeping with the style of the hotel. On the ground floor, antiques, oak and comfy sofas in both the garden bar and lounge ensure a warm and welcoming atmosphere.

Bed & Breakfast per night: single room from £50.00–£60.00; double room from £90.00–£140.00
Half board per person: £65.00–£75.00 daily; £390.00–£450.00 weekly
Evening meal 1800 (last orders 2030)

Bedrooms: 4 single, 5 double, 2 twin, 2 triple
Bathrooms: 13 en-suite
Parking for 32
Cards accepted: Mastercard, Visa

G S TV SP T

193 Brook Lodge — HIGHLY COMMENDED

192 Alcester Road, Stratford-upon-Avon, Warwickshire CV37 9DR Tel (01789) 295988 Fax (01789) 295988

This immaculately maintained guesthouse is run to the highest standards and has a most warm and friendly atmosphere. The property is only a five-minute walk from Anne Hathaway's cottage and is well situated for all local attractions. The prettily decorated en-suite bedrooms are equipped to ensure that your stay is both happy and comfortable. The knowledgeable local hosts are delighted to assist their guests with information and advice. Ample car parking.

Bed & Breakfast per night: single occupancy from £30.00–£40.00; double room from £40.00–£50.00

Bedrooms: 4 double, 1 twin, 2 triple
Bathrooms: 6 en-suite, 1 private
Parking for 10
Cards accepted: Mastercard, Visa, Amex, Switch/Delta

5 UL S TV SP T

194 Peartree Cottage

HIGHLY COMMENDED

7 Church Road, Wilmcote, Stratford-upon-Avon, Warwickshire CV37 9UX Tel (01789) 205889 Fax (01789) 262862

Situated in the Shakespearean village of Wilmcote, this Elizabethan Grade II Listed building is set in nearly an acre of shady garden, overlooking Mary Arden's House. The cottage, and its later extension, is furnished throughout with country antiques. Breakfast is served in the stone-flagged and beamed dining room. Dinners are available at two good pub/restaurants within walking distance. The cottage provides a convenient centre for Shakespeare country, the Cotswolds and the NEC.

Bed & Breakfast per night: single occupancy £30.00; double room £45.00

Bedrooms: 4 double, 2 twin, 1 triple
Bathrooms: 7 en-suite
Parking for 8

195 Victoria Spa Lodge

HIGHLY COMMENDED

Bishopton Lane, Stratford-upon-Avon, Warwickshire CV37 9QY Tel (01789) 267985 Fax (01789) 204728

An elegant Grade II Listed spa lodge in a country setting close to the town centre, with seven beautifully-appointed en-suite bedrooms. Built in 1837 and the former home of cartoonist Bruce Bairnsfather (Old Bill) and Sir Barry Jackson (Founder, Birmingham Repertory Theatre), this is the first hotel Queen Victoria gave her name to – the Royal Coat of Arms is built into the gables. Full fire certificate. Paul & Dreen Tozer are your hosts and look forward to welcoming you. Totally non-smoking.

Bed & Breakfast per night: single occupancy from £38.00–£45.00; double room from £48.00–£55.00

Bedrooms: 3 double, 1 twin, 3 family rooms
Bathrooms: 7 en-suite, 1 public
Parking for 12
Cards accepted: Mastercard, Visa

196 Abberley

HIGHLY COMMENDED

12 Albany Road, Stratford-upon-Avon, Warwickshire CV37 6PG Tel (01789) 295934

Abberley is centrally situated within easy walking distance of the town centre, the Royal Shakespeare Company theatres and the riverside gardens. We provide the perfect base from which to visit the Shakespearean properties and nearby Warwick Castle. To ensure an enjoyable stay we offer you a comfortable room, a delicious full English breakfast freshly prepared and all the advice you may require. A non-smoking house with private parking on site.

Bed & Breakfast per night: single occupancy from £30.00–£35.00; double room from £44.00–£46.00

Bedrooms: 1 twin
Bathrooms: 1 en-suite
Parking for 2

Entries are cross referenced by number to the maps on pages 66–67

197 8 Clarendon Crescent

HIGHLY COMMENDED

Leamington Spa, Warwickshire CV32 5NR Tel (01926) 429840

A Grade II Listed Regency house in a crescent with its own private dell. Elegantly furnished with antiques, with individually designed en-suite bedrooms with tea and coffee-making facilities. Situated in a quiet backwater of Leamington Spa, yet only a five-minute walk from the town centre. Warwick, Stratford and the Royal Agricultural Centre are all within an easy drive.

Bed & Breakfast per night: single room from £30.00–£40.00; double room £50.00

Bedrooms: 2 single, 1 double, 1 twin
Bathrooms: 3 en-suite, 1 private
Parking for 1

Packwood Yew Garden

THERE IS SOMETHING RATHER SURREAL about the famous Yew Garden at Packwood House. On the manicured green lawn, smooth and flat as a billiard table, immaculately clipped yew bushes stand to attention. Seen from a distance they are strangely people-like, resembling a gathering of hooded figures, poised waiting, listening, ready to hurry off about their business. It is no wonder that a human symbolism has been attributed to them; the arrangement of trees with its single large yew 'the Master' standing atop a mound, surrounded by a 'multitude' of others, is said to represent the 'Sermon on the Mount'. Further refinements to the scheme include four large trees near the 'Master' known as 'the Apostles', and a row of twelve on a raised terrace called 'the Evangelists'.

Whether the original designer of the garden intended such a scheme is unknown, for references to the 'Sermon on the Mount' idea do not appear in documents until the late 19th century, some 200 years after the first trees were planted. All that is known about the origins of the Yew Garden is that John Fetherston, who inherited Packwood in 1634, laid out at least part of it between 1650 and 1670, but it is possible that many of the trees were planted some time later.

It was probably John Fetherston's father, another John, who began the fine timber-framed mansion which still forms the core of the present house. Though less famous than the garden, this too is of considerable interest. During the course of the Fetherston family's ownership the original Tudor building underwent considerable alterations, in particular the addition of fine stables and outbuildings in the 1670s. Packwood left the Fetherston family in 1869 and was eventually bought by Alfred Ash, a wealthy industrialist, in 1905. Ash's son, Graham Baron Ash, lavished meticulous care on it, restoring it to match his vision of the perfect Tudor mansion. He was a punctiliously correct and obsessively tidy man who kept everything, including the gardens, in perfect order. The restoration of his house became his passion – until he tired of it and bought a moated castle in Sussex. Donating Packwood to the National Trust, he hoped it would be kept forever as he created it, and so it has been. It remains the kind of museum piece it always was in his lifetime, a perfect monument to the Tudor age.

198 LANSDOWNE HOTEL

HIGHLY COMMENDED

87 Clarendon Street, Leamington Spa, Warwickshire CV32 4PF Tel (01926) 450505 Fax (01926) 421313

An elegant Regency hotel, the Lansdowne offers a tranquil atmosphere. The comprehensive menus change daily, providing guests with a choice of freshly prepared dishes. David and Gillian Allen's personal selection of good quality wines underlines their policy of excellent value and complements the high standard of cuisine which is recognised by most discerning guides. Licensed bar, ample parking. Discount tickets to Warwick Castle. The Lansdowne is in the town centre, so easy for browsing round the shops.

Bed & Breakfast per night: single room from £49.95–£54.95; double room from £63.90–£69.90
Half board per person: from £46.50 daily; from £297.50 weekly
Evening meal 1830 (last orders 2130)

Bedrooms: 5 single, 5 double, 5 twin
Bathrooms: 12 en-suite, 1 public
Parking for 12
Cards accepted: Mastercard, Visa, Amex

199 NORTHLEIGH HOUSE

HIGHLY COMMENDED

Five Ways Road, Hatton, Warwick, Warwickshire CV35 7HZ Tel (01926) 484203 or 0374 101894 Fax (01926) 484006

A personal welcome, the individually-designed rooms with colour co-ordinated furnishings, en-suite bathrooms, television, fridge, kettle and many thoughtful extras make this the perfect hide-away in rural Warwickshire. A full English breakfast is freshly cooked to suit guests' individual tastes. Evening meals can be arranged, although there are excellent country pubs nearby, as well as the historic towns of Stratford-upon-Avon and Warwick, and the exhibition centres. Please call Sylvia Fenwick for brochures. No smoking.

Bed & Breakfast per night: single room from £33.00–£40.00; double room from £46.00–£58.00

Bedrooms: 1 single, 5 double, 1 twin
Bathrooms: 7 en-suite
Parking for 8
Open: February–November
Cards accepted: Mastercard, Visa

200 ALCOTT FARM

HIGHLY COMMENDED

Weatheroak, Alvechurch, Worcestershire B48 7EH Tel (01564) 824051 or 0374 163253 Fax (01564) 824051

Alcott Farm is situated in the middle of beautiful grounds and rolling countryside, yet is only a twenty-minute drive from Birmingham Airport, the Conference Centre, the National Exhibition Centre, Solihull, Stratford and Redditch. It is only five minutes from Junction 3/M42. This beautiful country home has luxurious en-suite bedrooms with all the facilities, and unlimited safe parking and stabling available. Good pubs and restaurants are nearby. John and Jane Poole offer a warm welcome.

Bed & Breakfast per night: single occupancy £30.00; double room £50.00

Bedrooms: 1 double, 2 twin
Bathrooms: 3 en-suite
Parking for 20

Entries are cross referenced by number to the maps on pages 66–67

201 BROCKENCOTE HALL

DE LUXE

Chaddesley Corbett, Kidderminster, Worcestershire DY10 4PY Tel (01562) 777876 Fax (01562) 777872

Nestling in the heart of the Worcestershire countryside, Brockencote Hall is set in seventy acres of private parkland with its own lake. It is the perfect place for relaxation. Proprietors Alison and Joseph Petitjean have created a charming Gallic oasis in the heart of England, combining traditional French comfort and friendliness with superb French cuisine. The hotel offers a choice of seventeen magnificent en-suite bedrooms, including one that has been especially designed to make stays comfortable for disabled guests.

Bed & Breakfast per night: single occupancy from £90.00–£102.00; double room from £120.00–£145.00
Half board per person: £84.50–£126.50 daily
Lunch available: 1200–1330
Evening meal 1900 (last orders 2130)

Bedrooms: 13 double, 3 twin, 1 triple
Bathrooms: 17 en-suite
Parking for 50
Cards accepted: Mastercard, Visa, Diners, Amex, Switch/Delta

202 NUTHURST GRANGE COUNTRY HOUSE HOTEL & RESTAURANT

HIGHLY COMMENDED

Nuthurst Grange Lane, Hockley Heath, Warwickshire B94 5NL Tel (0156478) 3972 Fax (0156478) 3919

Nuthurst Grange nestles in seven and a half acres of landscaped gardens and woodlands. The hotel has fifteen luxurious bedrooms, all with private bathrooms and air-spa baths, with rural views. It has an award-winning restaurant using only the freshest of produce. The hotel is perfectly placed at the heart of England's motorway network and close to the international railway and airport. Also an ideal venue for parties, wedding receptions, meetings and conferences.

Bed & Breakfast per night: single occupancy £120.00; double room from £140.00–£165.00
Lunch available: 1200–1400
Evening meal 1900 (last orders 2130)

Bedrooms: 10 double, 5 twin
Bathrooms: 15 en-suite
Parking for 86
Cards accepted: Mastercard, Visa, Diners, Amex, Switch/Delta

203 THE EDWARDIAN GUEST HOUSE

HIGHLY COMMENDED

7 St Bernards Road, Olton, Solihull, West Midlands B92 7AU Tel (0121) 706 2138

The charm of this Edwardian residence, with its large, beautiful gardens, stained glass windows, large rooms, comfort, style and elegance, makes your stay a memorable one. A warm welcome to all. Television, tea/coffee-making facilities and hairdryers in all rooms. En-suite showers. Ideally situated for easy access, One and a quarter miles to Solihull town centre, 10 minutes to National Exhibition Centre, airport and railway station, 5 minutes to junction 5/M42, 15 minutes to Birmingham and Convention Centre. A no-smoking establishment.

Bed & Breakfast per night: single occupancy from £30.00–£35.00; double room from £50.00–£60.00

Bedrooms: 2 twin
Bathrooms: 2 en-suite
Parking for 7

At-a-glance symbols are explained on the flap inside the back cover

204 Arden Hotel and Leisure Club

HIGHLY COMMENDED

Coventry Road, Bickenhill, Solihull, West Midlands B92 0EH Tel (01675) 443221 Fax (01675) 443221

Ideally located next to the National Exhibition Centre, railway, airport and motorway network, this privately-owned hotel has 146 bedrooms, all with bath and shower. Conference facilities for up to 200. Free car parking. Leisure complex includes swimming pool, sauna and jacuzzi. Two restaurants: one offering high quality cuisine; the other bistro-style and health foods. Conservatory overlooks landscaped rock gardens.

Bed & Breakfast per night: single room from £60.00–£81.00; double room from £66.00–£98.50
Half board per person: £74.00–£95.00 daily
Lunch available: 1200–1430
Evening meal 1800 (last orders 2200)

Bedrooms: 28 single, 14 double, 98 twin, 6 triple
Bathrooms: 146 en-suite
Parking for 300
Cards accepted: Mastercard, Visa, Diners, Amex, Switch/Delta

Birmingham's Pre-Raphaelite Collection

Artists of the Pre-Raphaelite movement, in general, lived and worked in London and the South, but their paintings found an appreciative audience further north. Birmingham's City Museum and Art Gallery (tel: 0121 303 2834) houses the largest (and arguably finest) collection of Pre-Raphaelite art in the world. Manchester's City Art Gallery (tel: 0161 236 5244) and Port Sunlight's Lady Lever Gallery (tel: 0151 644 6466) also have extensive, high-quality collections.

Of the seven founding members of the so-called Pre-Raphaelite brotherhood the most talented and influential were Dante Gabriel Rossetti, William Holman Hunt and John Everett Millais. Later, William Morris and Edward Burne-Jones were attracted to the movement, and Morris applied its principles to develop his medieval-revival Arts and Craft movement.

All these artists are represented in Birmingham's City Museum and Art Gallery, where visitors may gaze at some of the most famous of English paintings. Holman Hunt's *The Last of England, The Blind Girl* by Millais and Rossetti's *Beata Beatrix,* for example, are always on display, together with a vast number of other paintings, drawings and crafts. When the Pre-Raphaelites began exhibiting in 1848, these beautiful works were greeted by howls of protest, for they were a radical departure from the staid, formulaic art of the day, governed by strict rules of composition and an artificial scale of colour. The Pre-Raphaelites instead emulated the more 'truthful' art of the early renaissance (i.e. before Raphael), favouring subjects from literature, the Bible or contemporary life (usually moral scenes), which they rendered with meticulous detail and the true, vivid colours of out-of-doors.

At this time Birmingham was enjoying great prosperity. A new class of rich entrepreneurs, untrammelled by the opinions of the art establishment, responded readily to the Pre-Raphaelites' naturalistic approach, becoming important patrons of their work. One such magnate was Samuel Theodore Mander whose house, Wightwick Manor, just outside Wolverhampton, is open to the public (tel: 01902 761108). His Elizabethan-style home, completed in 1893, was entirely furnished and decorated by the most prominent Pre-Raphaelite artists, and it remains one of the finest monuments to their movement.

From October 1998 until the following March, Birmingham City Art Gallery will be marking the centenary of the death of Burne-Jones, a native of the city, with a major international exhibition of his work (Burne-Jones' *Phillys & Demophoon* is shown above). Visitors to Birmingham may also see some superb stained glass windows designed by the artist in St Philip's Cathedral.

205 NAILCOTE HALL HOTEL AND RESTAURANT

HIGHLY COMMENDED

Nailcote Lane, Berkswell, West Midlands CV7 7DE Tel (01203) 466174 Fax (01203) 470720

Nailcote Hall is a charming Elizabethan country house hotel set in 15 acres of gardens and surrounded by Warwickshire countryside. Built in 1640, the house was used by Cromwell during the Civil War. Guests can enjoy the relaxing atmosphere of the Piano Bar Lounge and the intimate Tudor Oak Room restaurant or the lively mediterranean style of Rick's Garden Café and Bar. Leisure facilities include a championship 9-hole par 3s golf course, a superb indoor leisure complex with Roman-style swimming pool, gymnasium, steam room, solarium, and health and beauty salon.

Bed & Breakfast per night: single occupancy from £125.00–£195.00; double room from £135.00–£195.00
Half board per person: from £85.00 daily; £521.50 weekly
Lunch available: 1200–1400
Evening meal 1900 (last orders 2130)

Bedrooms: 25 double, 13 twin
Bathrooms: 38 en-suite
Parking for 130
Cards accepted: Mastercard, Visa, Diners, Amex, Switch/Delta

206 LEA MARSTON HOTEL AND LEISURE COMPLEX

HIGHLY COMMENDED

Haunch Lane, Lea Marston, Warwickshire B76 0BY Tel (01675) 470468 Fax (01675) 470871

Set in its own extensive grounds in rural Warwickshire, this hotel is truly a first class venue for a relaxing break. Choose from a host of superb indoor and outdoor activities including golf, tennis and swimming. Or relax in the tranquil surroundings of the beauty salon. With an excellent restaurant and bars, luxury accommodation including suites (some with four-poster beds), this is 'Somewhere Special'. For a colour brochure, telephone 01675 470468. CATEGORY 3

Bed & Breakfast per night: single room from £69.00–£90.00; double room from £69.00–£160.00
Lunch available: 1200–1400
Evening meal 1900 (last orders 2200)

Bedrooms: 2 single, 68 double, 13 twin
Bathrooms: 83 en-suite
Parking for 190
Cards accepted: Mastercard, Visa, Amex, Switch/Delta

207 OAK TREE FARM

HIGHLY COMMENDED

Hints Road, Hopwas, Tamworth, Staffordshire B78 3AA Tel (01827) 56807 or 0836 387887 Fax (01827) 56807

A country farmhouse with river frontage. Recently renovated to luxurious standards. Large, warm and welcoming bedrooms, all en-suite, with all comforts provided – sofas, courtesy tray, trouser press, hairdryer, iron, mineral water, etc. Set in the pretty village of Hopwas, between the River Tame and the Fazely Canal, Oak Tree Farm offers tranquil surroundings, but is very convenient for Tamworth, Lichfield, NEC and the airport.

Bed & Breakfast per night: single occupancy from £32.00–£35.00; double room from £42.00–£45.00

Bedrooms: 4 double, 1 twin, 2 triple
Bathrooms: 7 en-suite
Parking for 10

208 LAKE ISLE HOTEL

HIGHLY COMMENDED

16 High Street East, Uppingham, Oakham, Leicestershire LE15 9PZ Tel (01572) 822951 Fax (01572) 822951

The personal touch we provide will make your stay extra special, starting with a decanter of sherry, home-made biscuits and fresh fruit in your room. Our menus, changed weekly, offer fresh produce and a list of over 300 wines, with special 'Wine Dinners' held throughout the year. Whirlpool baths and cottage suites are available. The shops of this sleepy market town surround us, yet we are within a short drive of Rutland Water, Burghley House and many pretty villages.

Bed & Breakfast per night: single room from £45.00–£52.00; double room from £60.00–£80.00
Lunch available: 1215–1345
Evening meal 1930 (last orders 2130)

Bedrooms: 1 single, 9 double, 2 twin
Bathrooms: 12 en-suite
Parking for 7
Cards accepted: Mastercard, Visa, Diners, Amex

209 THE MANOR HOUSE

HIGHLY COMMENDED

Louth Road, West Barkwith, Lincoln, Lincolnshire LN3 5LF Tel (01673) 858253 or (0402) 460537 Fax (01673) 858253

Delightful manor house standing in extensive landscaped grounds overlooking lawns, ornamental pond, rock garden and lake. Situated between Lincoln and Louth on the western edge of the Wolds, ideal for exploring the best of Lincolnshire.

Bed & Breakfast per night: double room £45.00
Half board per person: £38.00 daily; £231.00 weekly

Bedrooms: 1 double, 1 twin
Bathrooms: 2 en-suite
Parking for 10
Open: February–December

12

210 BARNSDALE LODGE HOTEL

HIGHLY COMMENDED

The Avenue, Exton, Oakham, Leicestershire LE15 8AH Tel (01572) 724678 Fax (01572) 724961

Set in the heart of Rutland's beautiful countryside overlooking Rutland Water, this 17th-century farmhouse welcomes you with luxury and warmth. Traditional English fayre, using fresh, locally-grown produce, is served in an Edwardian dining room. International wines complement the menus. Afternoon tea, elevenses and buttery lunches are available in the conservatory. Our 29 en-suite bedrooms are filled with antique furniture (with 16 additional bedrooms, a 6-metre spa pool and stress therapy centre available from April 1998). The ideal retreat from everyday life. Come and discover the tranquillity of Rutland.

Bed & Breakfast per night: single room from £58.00–£65.00; double room from £75.00–£90.00
Lunch available: 1200–1400
Evening meal 1900 (last orders 2145)

Bedrooms: 8 single, 12 double, 7 twin, 2 triple
Bathrooms: 29 en-suite
Parking for 107
Cards accepted: Mastercard, Visa, Switch/Delta

Entries are cross referenced by number to the maps on pages 66–67

211 THE PRIORY

HIGHLY COMMENDED

Church Road, Ketton, Stamford, Lincolnshire PE9 3RD Tel (01780) 720215 Fax (01780) 721881 E-mail Priory.a0504924@infotrade.co.uk

Historic listed country house in quiet village near Stamford. Award-winning bed and breakfast with spacious en-suite bedrooms offering every comfort and many thoughtful extras. Bedrooms are individually designed with oversize hand-made beds, high ceilings, luxurious fabrics, original panelling and splendid views over the gardens. Each has a resident Teddy. Luxury bathrooms have shower and bath. Resident chef prepares a choice of dishes every day from fresh local produce. Private parking. Close to Rutland Water. Send for our colour brochure.

Bed & Breakfast per night: single occupancy from £40.00–£60.00; double room from £69.00–£75.00
Half board per person: £54.50–£57.50 daily; £357.00–£375.00 weekly
Evening meal 1900 (last orders 2000)

Bedrooms: 2 double, 1 twin
Bathrooms: 3 en-suite
Parking for 10
Cards accepted: Mastercard, Visa

Stamford

SOME WILL HAVE YOU BELIEVE that Stamford is the most perfect town in England. If such an accolade existed, this small town on Lincolnshire's southern edge would certainly be a prime candidate. Chosen in 1967 as England's first conservation area, its fame recently received a boost when it was chosen as the location for the BBC adaptation of George Eliot's *Middlemarch*.

Stamford, of course, owes its rich architectural heritage – its 600 or so listed buildings form almost half of all those to be found in Lincolnshire – to its location. The proximity of several different quarries yielding building stone of subtly different hues is just one benefit of its setting. Others that brought prosperity to the town in the Middle Ages included the River Welland giving access to the sea, and the fertile grazing lands of surrounding South Lincolnshire and nearby Leicestershire. Merchants grew wealthy on the export of Stamford cloth (famed throughout Europe as being of the highest quality) and during the 13th, 14th and 15th centuries the churches of All Saints, St George's, St John's, St Martin's and St Mary's were all built. Few towns can boast such a concentration of medieval churches: St George's and St John's have fine stained glass while St Mary's and St Martin's contain notable statuary. In this last church is the enormous tomb of gargantuan Daniel Lambert, reputedly over 52 stone (330kg) at his death in 1809.

Medieval Stamford was also a place of learning, and for a few years a group of disaffected Oxford students set up a breakaway university in Brasenose Hall. On their return to Oxford in 1336 they gave the name of their former Stamford home to their college; the door knocker in the shape of a 'brazen-nosed' bull can be seen at Brasenose College, Oxford, while a replica adorns Brasenose Gate – all that now remains of the Hall. Much more complete is the magnificent Browne's Hospital, dating from 1494, one of the finest medieval almshouses in the country. Also of great age, but much altered up until the 18th century is the George Inn. It enjoyed its heyday in the 17th and 18th centuries as a coaching stop on the busy route of the Great North Road between London and York.

Another stop for the modern visitor is Burghley House on Stamford's southern edge, scene of the famous Burghley Horse Trials held each September. The town's main attraction, however, is no single building, it is simply wandering through narrow twisting streets encountering at almost every turn houses and churches which have barely changed in 500 years.

212 PIPWELL MANOR

HIGHLY COMMENDED

Washway Road, Saracens Head, Holbeach, Spalding, Lincolnshire PE12 8AL Tel (01406) 423119

This handsome listed Georgian manor house, circa 1730, has many original features and is situated in a small village in the Lincolnshire Fens, in the midst of the flower-growing area. Guests are welcomed with afternoon tea in the comfortable sitting room, which has a log fire in winter. Traditional English breakfast is served in the elegant dining room and includes home-made preserves and home-produced fruit and eggs. Pipwell Manor is a lovely place to stay.

Bed & Breakfast per night: single room maximum £30.00; double room maximum £40.00

Bedrooms: 1 single, 2 double, 1 twin
Bathrooms: 2 en-suite, 2 private
Parking for 6

213 CORFIELD HOUSE

HIGHLY COMMENDED

Sporle, Swaffham, Norfolk PE32 2EA Tel (01760) 723636

Corfield House is an attractive brick-built house standing in half an acre of lawned gardens in the peaceful village of Sporle near Swaffham, an ideal base for touring Norfolk. Some of the comfortable en-suite bedrooms (one ground floor) have fine views across open fields and all have television, clock radio and a fact-file on places to visit. Good home-cooked food using excellent local produce. No smoking throughout.

Bed & Breakfast per night: double room from £37.00–£43.00
Half board per person: £31.00–£34.00 daily; £205.00–£220.00 weekly
Evening meal 1900 (last bookings 1730)

Bedrooms: 2 double, 2 twin
Bathrooms: 4 en-suite
Parking for 5
Open: April–December
Cards accepted: Mastercard, Visa

214 THE HOSTE ARMS

HIGHLY COMMENDED

The Green, Burnham Market, King's Lynn, Norfolk PE31 8HD Tel (01328) 738777 Fax (01328) 730103 E-mail 106504.2472@compuserve.com

Situated in the idyllic village of Burnham Market, close to some of the most beautiful country walks and birdwatching sites in Norfolk. The Hoste Arms has twenty bedrooms, all elegantly furnished, with some having a private entrance into the tranquil setting of our gardens. An excellent menu with British, French and Oriental influences, and a superb wine list. Local ales served from the cask. Jazz on Friday evenings.

Bed & Breakfast per night: single room from £60.00; double room from £86.00–£98.00
Lunch available: 1200–1400
Evening meal 1900 (last orders 2130)

Bedrooms: 3 single, 12 double, 4 twin, 1 family room
Bathrooms: 20 en-suite
Parking for 60
Cards accepted: Mastercard, Visa, Switch/Delta

Entries are cross referenced by number to the maps on pages 66–67

215 WINGATE

HIGHLY COMMENDED

Two Furlong Hill, Wells-next-the-Sea, Norfolk NR23 1HQ Tel (01328) 711814 or (01328)710122 Fax (01328) 710122

Located in the charming small fishing port of Wells-next-the-Sea, Wingate is an ideal base for walking, exploring the local beaches and historic houses, or simply relaxing with a game of croquet on the front lawn. Overlooking fields to the west, yet only a few minutes' walk from the harbour and town centre, the house offers good quality accommodation, excellent breakfasts and a soothing atmosphere.

Bed & Breakfast per night: double room from £40.00–£43.00

Bedrooms: 2 double, 1 twin
Bathrooms: 2 en-suite, 1 private
Parking for 3

216 MORDEN HOUSE

HIGHLY COMMENDED

20 Cliff Avenue, Cromer, Norfolk NR27 0AN Tel (01263) 513396

Morden House is a charming detached, late Victorian residence, peacefully situated in a quiet avenue in Cromer, just minutes away from the beach and town centre. Decorated and furnished tastefully throughout, the house still retains the character of that period. Morden House offers warm, friendly accommodation with welcoming log fires, genuine hospitality and lots of delicious home-cooked food.

Bed & Breakfast per night: single room from £21.00–£22.50; double room from £42.00–£45.00
Half board per person: £32.00–£34.00 daily; £196.00–£203.00 weekly
Evening meal 1830 (last orders 1900)

Bedrooms: 1 single, 4 double, 1 twin
Bathrooms: 4 en-suite, 1 public
Parking for 3

217 THE OLD HALL

Listed HIGHLY COMMENDED

Edingthorpe, North Walsham, Norfolk NR28 9TJ Tel (01692) 650189 Fax (01692) 650189

A handsome and historic Elizabethan Grade II family home. A beamed ceiling and log fires await you in our guests' sitting room. Candle-lit dinners, by prior arrangement, are our speciality. Luxurious rooms with draped beds. Standing in beautiful mature gardens. Ample parking and seating area. A relaxing, calming retreat in our hectic world. Two miles from the coast, surrounded by farmland and woods. Near to the Norfolk Broads and an abundance of sporting facilities. National Trust estates close by.

Bed & Breakfast per night: single occupancy from £19.50–£27.50; double room from £39.00–£55.00
Half board per person: £37.00–£45.00 daily; £239.50–£287.50 weekly
Evening meal 1800 (last orders 2000)

Bedrooms: 1 double, 1 twin, 1 triple
Bathrooms: 1 en-suite, 2 private, 1 public
Parking for 6

At-a-glance symbols are explained on the flap inside the back cover

218 BEECHWOOD HOTEL

HIGHLY COMMENDED

20 Cromer Road, North Walsham, Norfolk NR28 0HD Tel (01692) 403231 Fax (01692) 407284

As soon as you arrive at the Beechwood Hotel you know you are somewhere very special. Chosen by Agatha Christie as her Norfolk hideaway, the hotel is an ivy-clad Georgian house with a warm and friendly atmosphere. Set in an acre of mature gardens, there are nine well-appointed bedrooms. In the attractive dining room the menu features fresh Norfolk produce and always includes classic English dishes, as well as the chef's personal suggestions.

Bed & Breakfast per night: single occupancy from £42.00–£53.00; double room from £60.00–£76.00
Half board per person: £45.00–£53.00 daily; £224.00–£345.00 weekly
Lunch available: 1200–1400

Evening meal 1900 (last orders 2100)
Bedrooms: 6 double, 3 twin
Bathrooms: 9 en-suite
Parking for 15
Cards accepted: Mastercard, Visa, Amex, Switch/Delta

219 HOTEL NELSON

HIGHLY COMMENDED

Prince of Wales Road, Norwich, Norfolk NR1 1DX Tel (01603) 760260 Fax (01603) 620008

The Hotel Nelson has a prime city-centre location on the banks of the River Wensum. All bedrooms have an en-suite bathroom, refrigerator with fresh milk, tea/coffee-making facilities and remote control Teletext TV. The hotel also has its own leisure club with 40ft indoor pool, spa-pool, sauna, steam room, air-conditioned exercise studio and a gymnasium which is free for residents' use. Other facilities include two riverside restaurants, two bars, a large free car park at the rear of the hotel, its own river quay and riverside gardens.

Bed & Breakfast per night: single room from £85.00–£89.00; double room from £100.00–£104.00
Lunch available: 1230–1400
Evening meal 1845 (last orders 2145)

Bedrooms: 27 single, 67 double, 38 twin
Bathrooms: 132 en-suite
Parking for 214
Cards accepted: Mastercard, Visa, Diners, Amex

220 BEECHES HOTEL & VICTORIAN GARDENS

HIGHLY COMMENDED

4-6 Earlham Road, Norwich, Norfolk NR2 3DB Tel (01603) 621167 Fax (01603) 620151 E-mail beeches.hotel@paston.co.uk

'An oasis in the heart of Norwich' with three acres of English Heritage Victorian garden to enjoy, this hotel provides a peaceful retreat from the bustle of the city, which is just ten minutes' walk away. Two listed Victorian houses and a modern annexe have been tastefully refurbished and extended to offer high standards of comfort in a relaxed, informal setting. Non-smoking bedrooms are individually designed, enhancing their own character and charm. Our licensed restaurant offers mouth-watering contemporary cuisine. The photograph shows Plantation House, which is part of the Beeches. CATEGORY 2

Bed & Breakfast per night: single room from £54.00–£59.00; double room from £65.00–£80.00
Half board per person: £45.00–£55.00 daily; £311.00–£400.00 weekly (based on 2 sharing)
Evening meal 1830 (last orders 2100)

Bedrooms: 8 single, 14 double, 3 twin
Bathrooms: 25 en-suite
Parking for 24
Cards accepted: Mastercard, Visa, Diners, Amex, Switch/Delta

Entries are cross referenced by number to the maps on pages 66–67

221 THE LODGE

DE LUXE

Cargate Lane, Saxlingham Thorpe, Norwich, Norfolk NR15 1TU Tel (01508) 471422 Fax (01508) 471682

A listed Regency house, the home of Sally and Roger Dixon, set in three acres of secluded grounds, conveniently located close to the A140 south of Norwich. All the rooms are elegantly furnished in the best country house tradition to provide luxury accommodation in lovely surroundings. Imaginative candle-lit dinners are a speciality, using top quality produce and seasonal contributions from the herb garden. Licensed. East of England Tourist Board "England for Excellence" regional award winner 1997.

Bed & Breakfast per night: single room from £34.00; double room from £56.00–£60.00
Half board per person: £46.50–£52.50 daily; £306.00–£343.50 weekly
Evening meal 1930 (last orders 2000)

Bedrooms: 1 single, 2 double/twin
Bathrooms: 2 en-suite, 1 private
Parking for 12

222 IVY HOUSE FARM

HIGHLY COMMENDED

Ivy Lane, Oulton Broad, Lowestoft, Suffolk NR33 8HY Tel (01502) 501353 or (01502)588144 Fax (01502) 501539

Relax amid intertwining herbaceous beds or tarry awhile beside the ponds. Take a gentle stroll down a garden path to view Oulton Broad, with its sailing boats, or wander a little further to enjoy a boat trip. Ivy House Farm enjoys a peaceful setting amidst forty acres in the Broads National Park. The accommodation is individually designed with en-suite bathrooms. Lunch and dinner is served in The Crooked Barn – an eighteenth-century thatched barn. ♿ CATEGORY 1

Bed & Breakfast per night: single occupancy from £59.00–£65.00; double room from £79.00–£89.00
Lunch available: 1200–1400
Evening meal 1900 (last orders 2130)

Bedrooms: 7 double, 2 twin, 1 triple, 1 family room
Bathrooms: 11 en-suite
Parking for 50
Cards accepted: Mastercard, Visa, Diners, Amex, Switch/Delta

223 ABBE HOUSE HOTEL

HIGHLY COMMENDED

322 London Road South, Lowestoft, Suffolk NR33 0BG Tel (01502) 581083 Fax (01502) 581083

Britain's most easterly 2 Crown Highly Commended hotel. Abbe, situated on the Sunrise Coast with Lowestoft's award-winning beach only two minutes' walk away, is a tiny Victorian townhouse hotel where emphasis is big on comfort and quality. We offer an excellent choice of fine home cooking, using mainly local produce, from our breakfast and candle-lit dinner menus. The hotel is an excellent base from which to explore East Anglia.

Bed & Breakfast per night: single occupancy from £25.00–£30.00; double room from £38.00–£48.00
Half board per person: £38.00–£43.00 daily
Evening meal 1900 (last bookings 1200)

Bedrooms: 3 double
Bathrooms: 2 en-suite, 1 private
Parking for 1

224 STARSTON HALL

HIGHLY COMMENDED

Starston, Harleston, Norfolk IP20 Tel (01379) 854252 Fax (01379) 852966

Starston Hall is a Grade II Listed house of Elizabethan origin, standing in four acres of gardens, which include the original moat, and is surrounded by a large estate. It has recently been extensively renovated, and many of the original features have been sympathetically restored. It is now comprehensively furnished with antiques. Your hostess, who is fluent in French, German and Italian, offers varied dinner menus, including vegetarian, by prior arrangement. Children over 12 years are welcome.

Bed & Breakfast per night: single occupancy from £30.00–£35.00; double room from £60.00–£70.00
Half board per person: £55.00–£60.00 daily
Evening meal 2000

Bedrooms: 2 double, 1 twin
Bathrooms: 2 en-suite, 1 private
Parking for 12

12

Thetford Forest

AT 50,000 ACRES THETFORD FOREST is the largest lowland forest in the country, but vast and established as it now seems, it is in fact a relatively recent feature of the landscape. The Forestry Commission planted its first trees here in 1922. For the previous 4,000 years, ever since Neolithic man began felling the primeval forest to cultivate the land, the region was known as a sandy heath, barren and almost treeless. Evidence may still be seen of the ways in which man scraped a living in inhospitable surroundings, a fascinating record of ingenuity and survival.

To the north-west of Thetford, Grimes Graves, a bare, pock-marked stretch of heath, is the site of a prehistoric flint mine, one of the oldest industrial workings in Europe. Here, over the course of several millennia, Neolithic man tunnelled some 700–800 shafts each about 40ft (12m) deep and extracted nodules of flint for the production of tools and implements (shown right). One shaft has been excavated and is open to visitors.

Neolithic farmers cultivated the light soil of the region, but the ground was easily exhausted and by medieval times was mostly used for grazing, not just sheep, but rabbits, which were farmed for meat and fur. Many place-names within the Forest, once sites of rabbit farms, still incorporate the word 'warren', and Thetford Warren Lodge (open to the public) was built around 1400 to house the Prior of Thetford's warrener.

By the 17th century over-grazing by both sheep and rabbits had resulted in erosion on a massive scale, and for 200 years the Forest became a barren desert of shifting sand. Shelter belts of trees, usually Scots pines, were planted to check erosion, the gnarled and twisted remains of which are still a characteristic feature of the landscape.

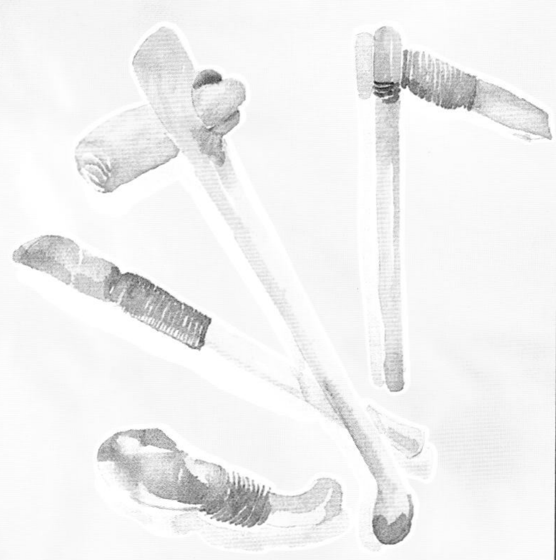

Today, forestry is a productive and sustainable use of the land. Primarily functioning as a commercial resource with around 2,500 trees felled every working day, the forest is also an important wildlife habitat, where interspersed heathland and woodland encourage many rare bird species. In 1990 Thetford Forest became a designated Forest Park, attracting over a million visitors a year to walk, camp, cycle or simply drink in the peace of this great, uninhabited tract of English countryside. The High Lodge Forest Centre (where there is also a maze) is located just off the Thetford–Brandon road (tel: 01842 815434).

Entries are cross referenced by number to the maps on pages 66–67

225 CHIPPENHALL HALL

HIGHLY COMMENDED

Fressingfield, Eye, Suffolk IP21 5TD Tel (01379) 588180 or (01379) 586733 Fax (01379) 586272

A listed Tudor manor of Saxon origin, recorded in the Domesday Book, enjoying total rural seclusion in seven acres of gardens with ponds, and a heated outdoor pool set in a rose-covered courtyard. The manor is heavily beamed with inglenook log fireplaces. For that special anniversary with friends, arrange for pre-dinner drinks served in the bar and fine food and wines served by candle light. Located one mile south of Fressingfield, B1116.

Bed & Breakfast per night: single occupancy from £53.00–£59.00; double room from £59.00–£65.00
Half board per person: £52.50–£56.50 daily; £354.00–£373.00 weekly
Lunch available: 1200–1400

Evening meal 1930 (last bookings 1600)
Bedrooms: 3 double
Bathrooms: 3 en-suite
Parking for 12
Cards accepted: Mastercard, Visa

15

226 FORNHAM HALL

HIGHLY COMMENDED

Fornham All Saints, Bury St Edmunds, Suffolk IP28 6JJ Tel (01284) 725266 Fax (01284) 703424

Georgian country home, with Tudor origins, set in quiet peaceful gardens, two miles from Bury St Edmunds and major roads. A traditionally furnished home with superior accommodation, crisp white linens, bone china tea services, fresh flowers and many extras. Enjoy afternoon tea on the lawn, a game of croquet, or relax by the pond and feed the resident ducks. Informal, warm and friendly – do come!

Bed & Breakfast per night: single occupancy from £35.00–£45.00; double room from £50.00–£70.00

Bedrooms: 1 double, 1 twin, 1 triple
Bathrooms: 3 en-suite, 1 public
Parking for 10
Open: February–November
Cards accepted: Mastercard, Visa

227 THE ANGEL HOTEL

HIGHLY COMMENDED

Angel Hill, Bury St Edmunds, Suffolk IP33 1LT Tel (01284) 753926 Fax (01284) 750092

During the past 400 years, royal guests, artists and renowned writers have stayed at The Angel. Charles Dickens wrote part of the Pickwick Papers while in residence. This beautiful, historic coaching inn dates back to 1452 and has 42 bedrooms, including four four-posters and a suite, all individually decorated and with a private bathroom, colour TV, direct dial telephone and trouser press.

Bed & Breakfast per night: single room from £43.00–£72.50; double room from £76.00–£120.00
Half board per person: £58.00 daily
Lunch available: 1230–1400
Evening meal 1900 (last orders 2200)

Bedrooms: 11 single, 19 double, 12 twin
Bathrooms: 42 en-suite
Parking for 58
Cards accepted: Mastercard, Visa, Diners, Amex, Switch/Delta

228 Cherry Tree Farm

HIGHLY COMMENDED

Mendlesham Green, Stowmarket, Suffolk IP14 5RQ Tel (01449) 766376

Martin and Diana Ridsdale invite guests to enjoy their hospitality in this timber-framed farmhouse. Situated in the very heart of rural Suffolk, it makes an ideal base for exploring this and neighbouring counties. Great care is taken in the preparation and cooking of all meals which are served around a refectory table. Bread is home-baked and vegetables garden-fresh. The wine list includes an extensive range of East Anglian-produced wines.

Bed & Breakfast per night: double room from £44.00–£48.00
Half board per person: £37.00–£39.00 daily
Evening meal 1900 (last bookings 1400)

Bedrooms: 3 double
Bathrooms: 3 en-suite
Parking for 3
Open: February–December

229 The Great House Restaurant and Hotel

HIGHLY COMMENDED

Market Place, Lavenham, Sudbury, Suffolk CO10 9QZ Tel (01787) 247431 Fax (01787) 248007

Ideally located on the Market Square of the beautiful medieval village of Lavenham, we are the perfect place for a relaxing get-away. Our four spacious bedrooms offer the best comfort, with luxury bathrooms and sitting rooms or sitting areas. The creative French cuisine of our award-winning restaurant is complemented by excellent and friendly service from our professional staff. Choose from the daily menu or from the à la carte for that something 'special'. Special leisure breaks from Monday to Thursday.

Bed & Breakfast per night: single occupancy from £50.00–£88.00; double room from £68.00–£98.00
Half board per person: from £51.95 daily
Lunch available: 1200–1430
Evening meal 1900 (last orders 2130)

Bedrooms: 4 double, 1 twin
Bathrooms: 5 en-suite
Parking for 10
Cards accepted: Mastercard, Visa

230 College Farm

HIGHLY COMMENDED

Hintlesham, Ipswich, Suffolk IP8 3NT Tel (01473) 652253 Fax (01473) 652253

Relax and unwind at our peaceful 15th-century farmhouse (Grade II Listed) where comfortable accommodation, hearty breakfasts and a warm welcome are assured. The three spacious bedrooms are tastefully furnished to high standards with every facility. Guests' TV lounge has an inglenook fireplace with log fires. Six miles west of Ipswich with easy access to the A12 and A14 roads. Explore 'Constable Country', Lavenham and Heritage Coast. Country walks with golf, riding and sailing nearby. Good restaurants locally.

Bed & Breakfast per night: single room from £17.50–£23.00; double room from £35.00–£40.00

Bedrooms: 1 single, 1 double, 1 triple
Bathrooms: 1 en-suite, 1 public
Parking for 6

10

Entries are cross referenced by number to the maps on pages 66–67

231 MILE HILL BARN

HIGHLY COMMENDED

Main Road, Kelsale, Saxmundham, Suffolk IP17 2RG Tel (01728) 668519

Welcome to our home – a superb 15th-century Suffolk oak barn, converted to the highest standards, situated in the heart of the heritage coast. Ideal for Snape, RSPB Minsmere, Aldeburgh and Southwold. Three delightful en-suite double rooms, individually furnished, with own access and private parking. Relax in our pretty walled garden or in front of the log fire in our magnificent beamed and vaulted lounge. Farmhouse Aga cooking using fresh local ingredients for candle-lit dinners in our cosy dining room.

Bed & Breakfast per night: double room from £45.00–£65.00
Half board per person: £36.50–£46.50 daily
Evening meal 1900 (by prior arrangement only)

Bedrooms: 3 double
Bathrooms: 3 en-suite
Parking for 12

232 THE OLD HOUSE

HIGHLY COMMENDED

Eyke, Woodbridge, Suffolk IP12 2QW Tel (01394) 460213

Jan and Tony Warnock invite you to their lovely listed home, which dates from the 16th century. We have open fires, beams, a beautiful garden, and we overlook the Deken Valley on the edge of the heritage coast. Attractive forest and river walks are within easy reach. All rooms have central heating, en-suite facilities, sofas and easy chairs. We cater for all diets and offer a wide choice for breakfast. Evening meals by special arrangement.

Bed & Breakfast per night: single occupancy from £26.00–£30.00; double room from £42.00–£45.00
Half board per person: £34.00–£40.00 daily
Evening meal 1800 (last bookings 1000)

Bedrooms: 1 double, 2 twin
Bathrooms: 3 en-suite
Parking for 8

233 SECKFORD HALL HOTEL

HIGHLY COMMENDED

Woodbridge, Suffolk IP13 6NU Tel (01394) 385678 Fax (01394) 380610

A romantic Elizabethan mansion set in 32 acres of landscaped gardens and woodlands. Personally supervised by the owners, Seckford Hall is a haven of seclusion and tranquillity. Oak panelling, beamed ceilings, antique furniture, four-poster bedrooms, suites, leisure club with indoor pool, gym and spa bath and adjacent 18-hole golf course. Two restaurants featuring fresh lobster and game from local farms, extensive wine cellar. Picturesque Woodbridge with its tide mill, antique shops and yacht harbour is a short walk away. 'Constable Country' and Suffolk coast nearby.

Bed & Breakfast per night: single room from £79.00–£115.00; double room from £110.00–£150.00
Lunch available: 1200–1400
Evening meal 1915 (last orders 2130)

Bedrooms: 3 single, 14 double, 10 twin, 1 triple, 4 family rooms
Bathrooms: 32 en-suite
Parking for 102
Cards accepted: Mastercard, Visa, Diners, Amex

234 HIGHFIELD

 HIGHLY COMMENDED

Harkstead Road, Holbrook, Ipswich, Suffolk IP9 2RA Tel (01473) 328250

Relax in the quiet charm of the Suffolk countryside with your hosts Bryan and Sally Morris in their home on the outskirts of Holbrook and 'Constable Country'. All bedrooms and the garden have views over the Stour valley and river. There are many walks in the area, including the River Orwell and Stour estuaries which are havens for bird-watching and sailing. Many excellent pubs serving food can also be found nearby. Sorry, no smoking, children or pets.

Bed & Breakfast per night: single occupancy from £27.00–£33.00; double room from £35.00–£42.00

Bedrooms: 3 double/twin
Bathrooms: 2 en-suite, 1 private
Parking for 6

235 THE BAUBLE

 HIGHLY COMMENDED

Higham, Colchester, Essex CO7 6LA Tel (01206) 337254 Fax (01206) 337263

The Bauble is an old property, carefully restored and ideally placed in the picturesque hamlet of Higham for touring East Anglia. With one and a half acres of mature gardens overlooking water meadows in the heart of 'Constable Country', Dedham, Flatford, Lavenham and Beth Chatto's garden are close by and Cambridge, Norwich, Aldeburgh and the coast are all within an hour's drive. Find us on the B1068 from the A12, through the village, immediately over River Brett, on the left towards Stoke-by-Nayland.

Bed & Breakfast per night: single room from £25.00–£30.00; double room from £40.00–£45.00

Bedrooms: 1 single, 2 twin
Bathrooms: 1 en-suite, 2 private
Parking for 5

236 HOCKLEY PLACE

HIGHLY COMMENDED

Hockley Place, Frating, Colchester, Essex CO7 7HG Tel (01206) 251703 Fax (01206) 251578

Peace and tranquillity greet you at this country house built in the 'Lutyens' style. The individually designed bedrooms are en-suite, the standard of cuisine is high and guests eat in the beamed dining room. The outdoor swimming pool and gymnasium are open to guests throughout the day. The coastline of Frinton, Clacton and Brightlingsea, Beth Chatto's garden, Colchester's Roman castle and the picturesque countryside of Dedham and 'Constable Country' are all within easy reach.

Bed & Breakfast per night: single occupancy from £28.00–£40.00; double room from £56.00–£60.00
Half board per person: £44.00–£50.00 daily; £251.00–£298.00 weekly

Bedrooms: 1 double, 2 twin
Bathrooms: 3 en-suite
Parking for 20
Cards accepted: Mastercard, Visa, Switch/Delta

12

Entries are cross referenced by number to the maps on pages 66–67

237 TOWNSFORD MILL

Listed HIGHLY COMMENDED

Mill House, The Causeway, Halstead, Essex CO9 1ET Tel (01787) 474451

Halstead is a market town which boasts plenty of pubs and restaurants, including traditional, Indian, Italian and excellent Chinese. Mill House is an 18th-century listed town house with a delightful garden which slopes down to the River Colne. Adjoining the house and straddling the river is Townsford Mill Antiques Centre, with three floors of antiques and collectables, which was used recently for filming in the Lovejoy television series. All rooms are decorated in period style with tea-making facilities and TV. Major credit cards accepted.

Bed & Breakfast per night: single occupancy £30.00; double room £48.00

Bedrooms: 2 double, 1 twin
Bathrooms: 3 en-suite
Parking for 20
Open: February–December
Cards accepted: Mastercard, Visa

Greensted's log church

ST ANDREW'S CHURCH, Greensted, near Chipping Ongar in Essex, has long been famed as the oldest wooden building in Europe, and the oldest wooden church in the world. In 1995, however, its nave timbers were submitted to dendrochronological examination, a method of dating wood by examining the spacing of its tree rings. Embarrassingly, given that the church's fame lay in part in its antiquity, the tests revealed that the oldest sections of the building were 220 years younger than had previously been thought. Instead of dating from Saxon times (around 845AD) the church could not have been built earlier than 1066, the date of the Norman conquest.

The new date also threw into doubt one of the most significant events in the church's history: its rôle as a resting place for the body of the martyred King Edmund on its way from London to Bury St Edmunds. The church makes much of this claim, with a stained glass window dedicated to the saint, a picture of his martyrdom, and a finely carved beam depicting one of the legends surrounding his death. But Edmund's body was transported in 1013, some half century before the present church was built. Though it is likely that there were earlier buildings on the site, this particular structure clearly never housed the saint.

The claims of being the oldest wooden building, however, still stand. The primitive wooden church now forms the nave of the present building and is constructed from huge logs, split in half and joined with wooden wedges; the rounded sides of the logs form the exterior wall, while the smooth sides face the interior. The original church had no windows and was lit by oil lamps, and it is thought that dark patches in the wood may be scorch marks.

The early church has undergone a gradual transformation, with substantial additions in Tudor and Victorian times, and now has every appearance of a pretty English parish church, lovingly cared for in neatly manicured surroundings. Only its heavy wooden walls hark back to a darker age, when religion and civilisation maintained a tenuous footing in wild, forested lands. Greensted church is now one of the most visited in the country, attracting some 100,000 visitors every year.

238 CANFIELD MOAT

HIGHLY COMMENDED

High Cross Lane West, Little Canfield, Dunmow, Essex CM6 1TD Tel (01371) 872565 or (01385) 384648 Fax (01371) 876264

A peaceful Georgian rectory set among eight acres in the heart of the Essex countryside yet only ten minutes from the M11 and Stansted Airport and within easy reach of London, Cambridge, St Albans and 'Constable Country'. The large, elegant en-suite bedrooms are supplied with almost every conceivable luxury. Breakfasts include our own eggs and produce from our vegetable garden, and guests are welcome to use the tennis court, croquet lawn and, in season, heated outdoor swimming pool.

Bed & Breakfast per night: single occupancy £33.00; double room £55.00
Evening meal 1930 (by arrangement only)

Bedrooms: 1 double, 1 twin
Bathrooms: 2 en-suite
Parking for 10

8

---

239 THE HALL

Listed HIGHLY COMMENDED

Steeple Bumpstead Road, Helions Bumpstead, Haverhill, Suffolk CB9 7BT Tel (01440) 730285

Situated in beautiful rolling farmland where Suffolk, Essex and Cambridgeshire meet. Iain and Joy Gemmill's attractive old Tudor farmhouse provides an ideal centre to explore Cambridge, Newmarket, Bury St Edmunds and many other towns and villages of rural East Anglia. The accommodation includes a large, beamed double bedroom with en-suite shower and toilet. Guests' lounge and breakfast room overlooking mature gardens and open farmland.

Bed & Breakfast per night: double room £44.00

Bedrooms: 1 double
Bathrooms: 1 en-suite
Parking for 2
Open: January and March–December

---

240 SOPWELL HOUSE HOTEL AND COUNTRY CLUB

HIGHLY COMMENDED

Cottonmill Lane, Sopwell, St Albans, Hertfordshire AL1 2HQ Tel (01727) 864477 Fax (01727) 844741

Just minutes from four major motorways, half an hour from central London, Sopwell House stands in eleven acres of landscaped gardens and grounds amongst pleasant Hertfordshire countryside. An extensive refurbishment has further enhanced its country-style ambience. The Country Club and Spa, a haven for relaxation and pampering, features an ozone-treated indoor pool, jacuzzi, steam room and sauna, together with beauty and hairdressing salons, full-size snooker table and superbly-equipped fitness studio. Golf available nearby.

Bed & Breakfast per night: single room from £79.50–£125.00; double room from £115.00–£156.00
Lunch available: 1230–1430 (except Saturday)
Evening meal 1930 (last orders 2200)

Bedrooms: 12 single, 60 double, 14 twin, 6 family rooms
Bathrooms: 92 en-suite
Parking for 200
Cards accepted: Mastercard, Visa, Diners, Amex, Switch/Delta

Entries are cross referenced by number to the maps on pages 66–67

241 WALLIS FARM

HIGHLY COMMENDED

98 Main Street, Hardwick, Cambridge, Cambridgeshire CB3 7QU Tel (01954) 210347 Fax (01954) 210988

A warm welcome awaits you at our traditional Victorian farmhouse on our working farm in the picturesque village of Hardwick. We are seven miles from the university town of Cambridge and ideally situated for touring Cambridgeshire, Norfolk and Suffolk. All rooms are ground floor, en-suite, twin/double, furnished to a high standard and look out onto large gardens and farmland which guests are welcome to use. All have colour TVs and tea/coffee-making facilities.

Bed & Breakfast per night: single occupancy from £30.00–£35.00; double room from £40.00–£45.00

Bedrooms: 3 double, 1 twin
Bathrooms: 4 en-suite
Parking for 8

Brasses of East Anglia

EAST ANGLIA HAS A PLETHORA of superb churches that house a wealth of medieval art. One branch of this is that of the monumental brass. Created to mark a grave and to glorify the dead person, brasses are now a lesson in medieval life. The inscriptions provide information on local families, the coats of arms give genealogical material, the depictions of the men, women and children are a source book for costume.

The earliest brasses date from the late 13th and early 14th centuries. In Isleham church in Cambridgeshire, for instance, Sir Geoffrey Bernard is dated to 1275 by the type of tailed surcoat he wears over his armour. Many soldiers are shown lying with a dog as a foot-rest – as at Trumpington, another Cambridgeshire church. This brass is in memory of Sir Roger Trumpington, who died in 1289, and here his dog bites the scabbard of his sword. Sir Roger was a Crusader – a fact indicated by his crossed legs. The most famous military brass in England, however, is that of Sir Robert de Bures in Acton, Suffolk, dated to 1302. He, too, was a Crusader and wears a splendid set of chainmail, with decorative knee-pieces of *cuir-bouilli* (boiled leather), pryck spurs and a surcoat whose folds are gathered with a waist-girdle.

Other brasses show husband and wife side by side, sometimes with rows of children too. John Daye, the printer, is commemorated in Little Bradley, Suffolk, with a wife, six sons and five daughters, plus two babies under the table. Weston Colville, Cambridgeshire, has two good brasses: one to Sir Robert Leverer (1427), depicted in armour and surrounded by flowers, beside his wife in flowing head dress. In the same church, a brass in a much later style (1636) to Abraham Gates shows him with his wife at a prie-dieu and surrounded by cherubs, skulls and an angel with trumpet flying off to tell St Peter of his arrival. The earliest known brass of a priest in a cope is found in East Anglia, at Fulbourn, Cambridgeshire.

Since they are floor monuments, brasses have always been subjected to heavy wear and their conservation is now of great concern. The best places to take rubbings are brass-rubbing centres such as that in St Mary's Church, Bury St Edmunds (tel: 01284 706668), the Round Church, Cambridge (tel: 01223 871621), or Ely Cathedral (tel: 01353 667735), where replicas from all over Britain include the elegant Lady Margaret Peyton II of Isleham.

242 HOLIDAY INN (CAMBRIDGE)

HIGHLY COMMENDED

Downing Street, Cambridge, Cambridgeshire CB2 3DT Tel (01223) 464466 Fax (01223) 464440 E-mail hicam@hicam.demon.co.uk

Situated in the city centre, our fully air-conditioned hotel is close to the historic University Colleges, Kings College Chapel, Ely Cathedral and 'Constable Country'. Bloomsburys Bar Restaurant, which is open all day, offers a wide choice of dishes, including Hibachi cooking - based on an ancient Japanese style of cooking – prepared by our chefs in the theatre-style kitchen. As an alternative, Quinns is a traditional Irish pub, ideal for relaxing and winding down from the stresses of the day. CATEGORY 2

Bed & Breakfast per night: single occupancy maximum £130.00; double room maximum £167.00
Lunch available: all day
Evening meal (last orders 2230)

Bedrooms: 84 double, 112 twin
Bathrooms: 196 en-suite
Valet parking available
Cards accepted: Mastercard, Visa, Diners, Amex, Switch/Delta

S SP

243 THE OLD BRIDGE HOTEL

HIGHLY COMMENDED

1 High Street, Huntingdon, Cambridgeshire PE18 6TQ Tel (01480) 458410 Fax (01480) 411017

A handsome 18th-century building overlooking the River Ouse, and yet only 500 yards from the town centre. The atmosphere of a beautiful luxurious hotel, yet also a busy meeting place for the local community. All rooms are individually decorated, with satellite TVs and power showers – many with air conditioning and CD-stereos. An eclectic, modern menu, award-winning wine list, and real ales.

Bed & Breakfast per night: single room from £79.50–£99.50; double room from £89.50–£139.50
Lunch available: 1200–1430
Evening meal 1830 (last orders 2230)

Bedrooms: 5 single, 16 double, 4 twin
Bathrooms: 25 en-suite, 4 public
Parking for 70
Cards accepted: Mastercard, Visa, Diners, Amex, Switch/Delta

S SP T

Key to Symbols

For ease of use, the key to symbols appears on the back of the cover flap and can be folded out while consulting individual entries. The symbols which appear at the end of each entry are designed to enable you to see at a glance what's on offer, and whether any particular requirements you have can be met. Most of the symbols are clear, simple icons and few require any further explanation, but the following points may be useful:

Alcoholic drinks: Alcoholic drinks are available at all types of accommodation listed in the guide unless the symbol (unlicensed) appears. However, even in licensed premises there may be some restrictions on the serving of drinks, such as being available to diners only.

Smoking: Many establishments offer facilities for non-smokers, indicated by the symbol. These may include no smoking bedrooms and parts of communal rooms set aside for non-smokers. Some establishments prefer not to accommodate smokers at all, and if this is the case it will be made clear in the establishment description in the guide entry.

Pets: The symbol is used to show that dogs are not accepted in any circumstances. Some establishments will accept pets, but we advise you to check this at the time of booking and to enquire as to whether any additional charge will be made to accommodate them.

Entries are cross referenced by number to the maps on pages 66–67

England's West Country

SPRING COMES early to the Isles of Scilly, 28 miles (45km) west of Land's End – and the islanders wisely take full advantage of it. The two chief industries, flower-growing and tourism, both benefit from the benign climate, said by some to consist of just two seasons, spring and summer. Tresco, with its famous sub-tropical gardens at Tresco Abbey, perhaps forms the highlight of an island trip. It's also one of England's few havens from the car: local transport needs are satisfied by tractors. For those keener to use two legs than four wheels, gentle walks around the coast afford close views of the Scillies' plentiful marine life, often including grey seals, dolphins and porpoises.

Coastal paths of a more rugged and challenging nature combine to form the Cornish leg of the South-West Coast Path, one of the most dramatic long-distance paths on offer. Reaching Cornwall from the north you enter a landscape forever associated with an eccentric 19th-century Cornish clergyman and poet, Robert Hawker. From a lonely driftwood hut (open to the public) on the cliffs near Morwenstow, he would seek inspiration from the waves and from opium. He also rescued more than one seaman from the wrecks that litter much of the north Cornish coast. On calmer days the breakers are welcomed by the surfers who flock to resorts such as Bude in search of England's biggest waves. With America the next landfall some 3,000 miles (4,800km) away, they can reach impressive proportions. The Tate Gallery's south-western outpost at St Ives even offers visitors a cupboard for stowing surfboards. Past the spectacular scenery around Land's End – further south and particularly memorable – al fresco culture is available in the precariously positioned Minack Theatre, Porthcurno. Along the more sheltered southern coast two typically Cornish fishing villages to visit are Fowey and Polperro; Portscatho is perhaps lesser-known, but all are popular in season.

Devon, too, has both north and south coasts, but these are far apart. Foreland Point (near Lynmouth) is roughly 75 miles (120km) north of Prawle Point (near Salcombe), considerably further, for example, than the distance between Carlisle and Newcastle-upon-Tyne. Devon has countless miles of majestic coastline; some stretches, such as the Devon Riviera around Torquay, are well-trodden, while others, such as the rocky margins of Lundy Island, are known to but a handful of visitors. The island's granite stacks bear a striking similarity to the tors of Dartmoor, southern England's last tract of wilderness and a place of almost bleak beauty. Exploring Dartmoor's softer, wooded fringes by meandering along their quiet, sunken lanes, discovering unspoilt pubs or indulging in sumptuous cream teas is surely the perfect way to idle away a lazy afternoon. There's also Lutyens' remarkable Castle Drogo, designed early this century and often billed as the last castle built in Britain. If northern Devon receives less attention it's not through want of attractions; the headlong rush of high moorland into crashing waves along the Exmoor coast provides scenery of an improbable splendour little touched by mankind. This is the area RD Blackmore chose as the backdrop for his celebrated novel, *Lorna Doone*.

Though renowned for its natural beauty, the West Country also boasts exquisite architecture. Exeter Cathedral contains the longest span of Gothic vaulting in the world. By way of contrast, visitors can also dive beneath the streets of the city to explore an extensive network of underground passages. Every bit as memorable is Wells, nestling in the Mendip Hills and home to what some believe to be the finest cathedral in the country, an achievement crowned by the West Front, a 13th-century tour de force which manages to find room for over 350 statues of saints and martyrs. Joseph of Arimathea, the man who gave his tomb to Jesus, may not be amongst their number but legend records that he left his mark at nearby Glastonbury. The thorn tree that grows in the grounds of the ruined abbey is purportedly a cutting of the tree that sprang from his staff around two thousand years ago.

Beyond the Mendips is a city which can justly claim to be composed of countless works of art. Bath manages to combine architectural masterpiece with shopper's paradise – and is understandably popular. An intriguing alternative, given its 150-year-old suspension bridge, caves and *camera obscura*, is the well-to-do Bristol suburb of Clifton. One of its Georgian crescents, Royal York, is reputed to be the longest in Europe. Both Bath and Clifton

► Thomas Hardy's Dorset

It's a measure of the success of his novels that the names Hardy gave the towns, villages and heaths of his native Dorset are almost as familiar as their real counterparts. Dorchester is perhaps as well known as Casterbridge (*The Mayor of Casterbridge*), the Frome Valley as the Valley of the Great Dairies (*Tess of the d'Urbervilles*). Hardy devotees can visit his birthplace at Higher Bockhampton (the house appears in *Under the Greenwood Tree*) while Dorchester contains both a museum preserving the novelist's study, and Max Gate, the home he built for himself (both open to the public).

► Lundy Island

Lundy is as remote an island as England has to offer and makes a magnificent day out from Ilfracombe and Bideford, both some 24 miles (38.5km) distant on the north Devon coast. The island, 3 miles (5km) long and never much more than half a mile (1km) wide, boasts some superb scenery, and there can be no better way of passing time here than strolling its gentle paths. The west coast is the highlight of the island: here Soay sheep and feral goats pick their way over stacks of granite tumbling hundreds of feet to the Atlantic while ravens wheel above.

played host to Jane Austen on several occasions. One of the former's lesser-known connections is with American history and culture: the American Museum in Britain is housed in Claverton Manor, to the east of the city. Two other excursions to consider south of Bath are Mells, a most attractive village largely undiscovered by tourism, and Norton St Philip, whose 15th-century George Inn has many a story to tell – often involving violent death.

Wiltshire, the only inland county of the region, has an open feel. Here the views from the extensive chalk downlands are vast and golden in the shimmering heat haze of high summer. In this huge farmland, man's influence is paradoxically everywhere, yet hard to discern. Thousands of years ago the rolling downs were clad in trees, but our ancestors, who needed wood for warmth and shelter, and pasture for their growing flocks, long ago transformed their surroundings. The past two centuries have witnessed a change almost as profound, with huge tracts of pasture falling to the plough. The landscape has altered but retains a majesty and grandeur all its own. Peopling this land is a concentration of prehistoric remains unmatched in the country. Barbury Castle and Wayland's Smithy, both close to the Ridgeway Path in the east of the county, see few visitors. In the opposite, south-western corner, from the Nadder valley south to Cranborne Chase are many nooks and crannies asking to be explored. Nearby are Shaftesbury and the intriguingly named Sixpenny Handley, and to the south the strange Chesil Beach where the sea grades all the stones according to size: largest in the east, smallest in the west.

Left: Fisherman's Bay, Cornwall; inset: Brixham, Devon

► The Tate at St Ives

At the end of the Second World War St Ives became home to an influential clan of artists. Following the death of the sculptress Barbara Hepworth in 1975, her studio was given to the Tate Gallery in London and is now open as a museum. The Tate slowly acquired other works by St Ives artists, but was unable to display them until the opening of the magnificent and airy former gasworks as a gallery in 1993. Overlooking Porthmeor beach, few arts venues can boast a closet specially designed for visitors to leave their surfboards...

► Dartmoor longhouses

A defining feature of the longhouse is that humans and livestock lived under a single roof. This arrangement, common on the continent, is very rare in England, and only occurs where it was vital to keep livestock warm and near at hand in harsh winter conditions. Around a hundred longhouses remain on Dartmoor: low, rectangular buildings, built between 1150 and 1700 from huge blocks of granite, often partly recessed into the hillside to maximise shelter.

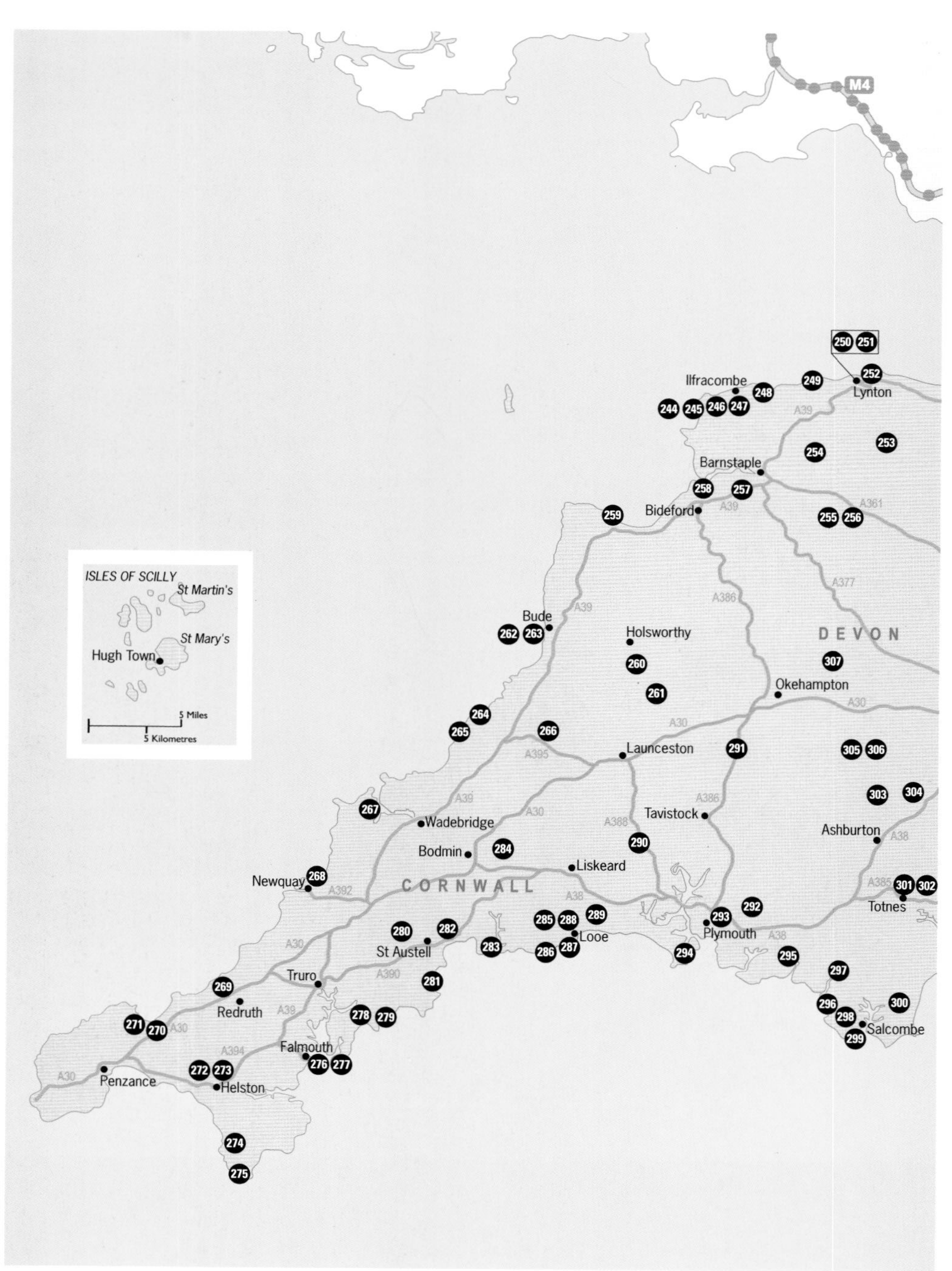

M4
ISLES OF SCILLY
St Martin's
St Mary's
Hugh Town
5 Miles
5 Kilometres
250 251
252
Lynton
Ilfracombe
244 245 246 247
248
249
A39
253
254
Barnstaple
258
257
259
Bideford
A39
A361
255 256
A377
A386
A39
Bude
262 263
Holsworthy
DEVON
307
260
261
Okehampton
A30
A30
264
265
266
Launceston
291
305 306
A395
303
304
267
A39
Wadebridge
A30
A386
A388
Tavistock
Ashburton
A38
Bodmin
284
290
Liskeard
Newquay
268
A392
CORNWALL
A38
A385
301 302
Totnes
292
285 288
289
Looe
293
Plymouth
A38
280
282
St Austell
283
286 287
294
295
A30
297
Truro
A390
281
269
Redruth
A39
296
300
278 279
298
Salcombe
299
271 270
A30
A394
Falmouth
A30
Penzance
272 273
276 277
Helston
274
275

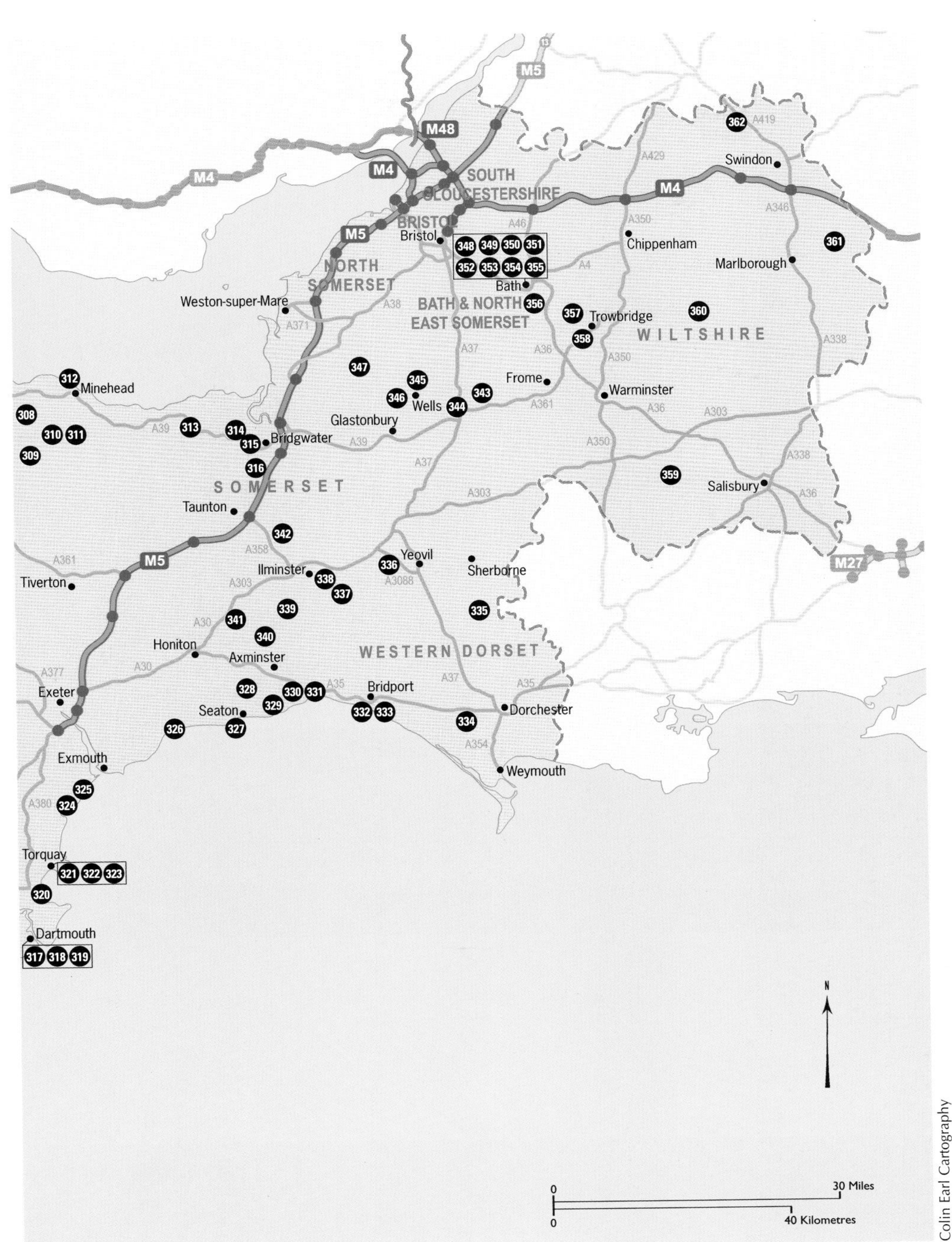
M5
M48
M4
SOUTH GLOUCESTERSHIRE
BRISTOL
Bristol
NORTH SOMERSET
Weston-super-Mare
BATH & NORTH EAST SOMERSET
Bath
Chippenham
Swindon
Marlborough
Trowbridge
WILTSHIRE
Frome
Warminster
Wells
Glastonbury
Minehead
Bridgwater
SOMERSET
Taunton
Salisbury
Yeovil
Sherborne
Ilminster
Tiverton
Honiton
Axminster
WESTERN DORSET
Exeter
Seaton
Bridport
Dorchester
Weymouth
Exmouth
Torquay
Dartmouth
M27
30 Miles
40 Kilometres
Colin Earl Cartography

244 LITTLE BEACH HOTEL

HIGHLY COMMENDED

The Esplanade, Woolacombe, Devon EX34 7DJ Tel (01271) 870398 Fax (01271) 870051

A small, friendly and family-run hotel with superb seafront location. The three miles of Woolacombe's golden sands, the cliffs of Baggy Point, the Isle of Lundy, the rock pools of Barricane Beach and the heathland of Morte Point all form the view from the hotel. Ideal for the walker or just to relax and enjoy our comfort and cuisine. We have awards for food, hospitality and service.

Bed & Breakfast per night: single room from £28.00–£35.00; double room from £52.00–£76.00
Half board per person: £36.00–£53.00 daily; £224.00–£324.00 weekly
Evening meal 1915 (last orders 2000)

Bedrooms: 1 single, 7 double, 1 twin
Bathrooms: 8 en-suite, 1 public
Parking for 5
Open: March–October
Cards accepted: Mastercard, Visa

245 WOOLACOMBE BAY HOTEL

HIGHLY COMMENDED

Woolacombe, Devon EX34 7BN Tel (01271) 870388 Fax (01271) 870613

Set in six acres of quiet gardens gently leading to three miles of EC Blue Flag golden sands. Built in the halcyon days of the mid-1800s, the hotel has a relaxed style of comfort and good living. Guests can enjoy unlimited use of superb sporting facilities, or just relax with a good book in spacious lounges overlooking the Atlantic. The 'Hothouse' offers fitness, massage and beauty treatments. Superb cooking of traditional and French dishes. Shooting, fishing, horse-riding and boating available.

Bed & Breakfast per night: single occupancy from £55.00–£75.00; double room from £110.00–£150.00
Half board per person: £75.00–£95.00 daily; £365.00–£515.00 weekly
Lunch available: 1230–1330 (Sunday only)

Evening meal 1930 (last orders 2130)
Bedrooms: 27 double, 11 twin, 5 triple, 22 family rooms
Bathrooms: 65 en-suite
Parking for 150 Open: February–December
Cards accepted: Mastercard, Visa, Diners, Amex, Switch/Delta

246 WATERSMEET HOTEL

HIGHLY COMMENDED

Mortehoe, Woolacombe, Devon EX34 7EB Tel (01271) 870333 Fax (01271) 870890

Set on the National Trust Atlantic coastline with panoramic views of Hartland Point and Lundy Island, the three acres of garden enclose a lawn tennis court, an open air swimming pool and steps to the beach below. A superb new indoor pool and spa is popular with everybody. The resident owners ensure the Watersmeet offers the comfort and peace of a country house, and all the main bedrooms, lounges and the octagonal restaurant overlook the sea. The Watersmeet offers a wine list to complement its national award-winning cuisine and service.

Bed & Breakfast per night: single room from £57.00–£79.00; double room from £90.00–£170.00
Half board per person: £60.00–£101.00 daily; £385.00–£655.00 weekly
Lunch available: 1200–1345

Evening meal 1900 (last orders 2030)
Bedrooms: 3 single, 10 double, 9 twin, 2 triple
Bathrooms: 22 en-suite
Parking for 50 Open: February–November
Cards accepted: Mastercard, Visa, Diners, Amex, Switch/Delta

Entries are cross referenced by number to the maps on pages 120–121

247 THE CLEEVE HOUSE

HIGHLY COMMENDED

Mortehoe, Woolacombe, Devon EX34 7ED Tel (01271) 870719 Fax (01271) 870719

The Cleeve offers a holiday to remember and our friendly hotel is renowned for its top-quality cuisine, using fresh local produce, with lobster a speciality. Excellent accommodation with en-suite rooms individually designed for your every comfort. We also have ample private parking. There are plenty of activities for everyone: golf, fishing, surfing, riding, walks and boat trips as well as National Trust properties, gardens and smugglers coves to explore. Brochure with pleasure from David and Anne Strobel.

Bed & Breakfast per night: single occupancy from £24.00–£28.00; double room from £48.00–£56.00
Half board per person: £40.00–£42.00 daily; £238.00–£266.00 weekly
Evening meal 1930 (last bookings 1800)

Bedrooms: 5 double, 1 twin
Bathrooms: 6 en-suite
Parking for 9
Open: March–October
Cards accepted: Mastercard, Visa, Switch/Delta

12 S SP T

248 BESSEMER THATCH HOTEL AND RESTAURANT

HIGHLY COMMENDED

Berrynarbor, Devon EX34 9SE Tel (01271) 882296

Situated in one of Devon's prettiest villages and only two miles from the Exmoor border, Bessemer Thatch is the perfect retreat from life's stresses and strains. Four-poster bedrooms with charming decor and furnishings complement this lovely old 13th-century building that offers peace and quiet, with more than a little comfort. In the dining room with its cosy inglenook fireplace enjoy the very best of traditional English menus which are always carefully prepared and presented. Truly somewhere special.

Bed & Breakfast per night: double room from £50.00–£66.00
Half board per person: £40.00–£48.00 daily; £250.00–£275.00 weekly
Evening meal 1930 (last orders 2130)

Bedrooms: 5 double
Bathrooms: 5 en-suite
Open: January–November
Cards accepted: Mastercard, Visa, Switch/Delta

S SP

249 HEDDONS GATE HOTEL

HIGHLY COMMENDED

Heddons Mouth, Parracombe, Barnstaple, Devon EX31 4PZ Tel (01598) 763313 Fax (01598) 763363

Six miles west of Lynton and beneath the winding lanes of Martinhoe is a private drive leading to Heddons Gate Hotel. This Victorian house overlooks the spectacular wooded hills of coastal Exmoor and terraced gardens lead down to the famous South West peninsular footpath with the river and sea beyond. Finest English cooking by chef/proprietor Robert Deville. Log fires, all en-suite rooms, elegant public rooms and ample private parking complete this haven of peace.

Bed & Breakfast per night: single room from £28.00–£37.00; double room from £49.00–£92.00
Half board per person: £54.00–£63.00 daily; £356.00–£430.00 weekly
Evening meal 2000

Bedrooms: 1 single, 8 double, 5 twin
Bathrooms: 14 en-suite
Parking for 14
Open: April–October
Cards accepted: Mastercard, Visa, Amex

10 S SP T

At-a-glance symbols are explained on the flap inside the back cover

250 HIGHCLIFFE HOUSE

 DE LUXE

Sinai Hill, Lynton, Devon EX35 6AR Tel (01598) 752235 Fax (01598) 752235

Small luxury Victorian gentleman's summer residence, 800ft above picturesque bay, commanding panoramic views of Exmoor and its fine coastline. Antiques, fine furnishings, beautifully decorated spacious en-suite rooms with all the modern comforts one could wish for. Roaring log fires throughout the cooler months. Our cuisine embodies the best of Victorian values, assembled with love and presented with panache. Come and share our lovely house – we'd like to pamper you. Totally non-smoking.

Bed & Breakfast per night: single occupancy maximum £53.00; double room from £76.00–£84.00
Half board per person: £63.00–£67.00 daily; £413.00–£441.00 weekly
Evening meal 1900

Bedrooms: 4 double, 2 twin
Bathrooms: 6 en-suite
Parking for 12
Cards accepted: Mastercard, Visa, Switch/Delta

251 SEAWOOD HOTEL

HIGHLY COMMENDED

North Walk Drive, Lynton, Devon EX35 6HJ Tel (01598) 752272

Seawood is situated at one of the loveliest spots on the North Devon coast, right in the heart of Lorna Doone country. Nestling on wooded cliffs 400ft above the sea, the hotel has some magnificent views. It looks right out across Lynmouth Bay and the Grand Headland of Countisbury where Exmoor meets the sea. On a clear night you can easily see the twinkling lights of Wales.

Bed & Breakfast per night: single room from £27.00–£29.00; double room from £54.00–£58.00
Half board per person: £39.00–£41.00 daily; from £269.00 weekly
Evening meal 1900 (last orders 1930)

Bedrooms: 1 single, 9 double, 2 twin
Bathrooms: 12 en-suite, 2 public
Parking for 10
Open: April–October

12

252 RISING SUN HOTEL

HIGHLY COMMENDED

Harbourside, Lynmouth, Devon EX35 6EQ Tel (01598) 753223 Fax (01598) 753480 E-mail risingsunlynmouth@easynet.co.uk

An award-winning 14th-century thatched smugglers' inn overlooking a tiny picturesque harbour and Lynmouth Bay with its stunning backdrop of the highest hogback cliffs in England. The Rising Sun Hotel is steeped in history, with oak panelling, crooked ceilings and creaky, uneven floorboards. Lynmouth Bay lobster, local game and salmon served in the romantic candle-lit, oak-panelled dining room, all add to the atmosphere of quintessential British innkeeping at its best.

Bed & Breakfast per night: single room £55.00; double room from £79.00–£130.00
Half board per person: £57.00–£87.00 daily; £365.00–£505.00 weekly
Lunch available: 1200–1400

Evening meal 1900 (last orders 2100)
Bedrooms: 1 single, 12 double, 2 twin, 1 triple
Bathrooms: 16 en-suite
Cards accepted: Mastercard, Visa, Diners, Amex, Switch/Delta

7

Entries are cross referenced by number to the maps on pages 120–121

253 SIMONSBATH HOUSE HOTEL

HIGHLY COMMENDED

Simonsbath, Minehead, Somerset TA24 7SH Tel (01643) 831259 Fax (01643) 831557

The first house to be built within the Royal Forest of Exmoor in 1654, Simonsbath House is now a small and friendly family-run country house hotel situated in an ideal position for exploring the Exmoor National Park and the north Devon coastline, on foot or by car. Receive peace and quiet, unstinting comfort, generous and deliciously interesting home-cooked food, rooms with log fires and panelling and some four-poster beds.

Bed & Breakfast per night: single occupancy from £50.00–£65.00; double room from £85.00–£95.00
Half board per person: £65.00–£85.00 daily; £420.00–£490.00 weekly
Evening meal 1900 (last orders 2030)

Bedrooms: 4 double, 3 twin
Bathrooms: 7 en-suite
Parking for 30 Open: February–November
Cards accepted: Mastercard, Visa, Diners, Amex, Switch/Delta

10 S SP T

Lorna Doone's Exmoor

RICHARD BLACKMORE (1825–1900) was a prolific, but largely unsuccessful writer. Of fourteen novels only one achieved lasting fame, but its impact was so pervasive that a small region of north Exmoor will always be associated with it. *Lorna Doone*, published in 1869, initially seemed destined for the same obscurity as its fellows, but, by a fortuitous coincidence, in 1870 a daughter of Queen Victoria became engaged to the Marquis of Lorne. Many mistakenly believed that Lorna Doone, descendant of the Lords of Lorne, was an ancestor of this fashionable aristocrat and, almost overnight, the book became a runaway success. It was to put Doone Country, quite literally, on the map.

The Doones of Blackmore's story were a band of 17th-century outlaws who lived by pillage and highway robbery. Although there are no contemporary records of their existence, by Blackmore's time their exploits had become legendary. They were supposed to have inhabited a remote stronghold on the upper reaches of Badgworthy Water, near Lynmouth. Following *Lorna Doone*'s publication this lonely region became so famously associated with them that it now appears on Ordnance Survey maps as the Doone Valley.

Where Hoccombe Combe joins Badgworthy Water there are, in fact, remains of an ancient settlement which may have inspired Blackmore in his depiction of the brigands' lair. Admirers of the book have tried to pin down other nearby landmarks, identifying a rocky waterfall at the bottom of Lank Combe as the famous waterslide through which the hero, John Ridd, enters the Doone stronghold, and pointing to a window in Oare church as the opening through which Carver Doone shoots Lorna. More tenuously, a shepherd's cottage built in 1860 from stones of the old settlement is known as Lorna's Cott, while a farm at Malmsmead is now Lorna Doone Farm; neither are described as such in the book.

The problem for the Doone sleuth is that Blackmore, though sticking to existing placenames, allows himself considerable poetic licence in his descriptions. Blackmore himself admitted, 'If I had dreamed that it would have been more than a book of the moment, the descriptions of the scenery – which I know as well as I know my garden – would have been kept nearer to their fact'. An appreciation of Exmoor's wild and unspoilt beauty will undoubtedly enhance a reading of the text, but the novel's topographical landmarks will always remain tantalisingly elusive.

254 BRACKEN HOUSE COUNTRY HOTEL

HIGHLY COMMENDED

Bratton Fleming, Barnstaple, Devon EX31 4TG Tel (01598) 710320

On the western edge of Exmoor. An attractive former Victorian rectory set in eight peaceful acres of garden, pasture, pond and woodland. Extensive views. A haven of rural tranquillity. Eight en-suite bedrooms, including two on the ground floor. Interesting Devon food cooked with care in the Aga. Friendly and efficient service. Dogs welcome to bring well-trained owners. Convenient for Arlington, Rosemoor, Marwood and the spectacular Exmoor coastline. CATEGORY 3

Bed & Breakfast per night: double room from £58.00–£72.00
Half board per person: £44.00–£51.00 daily; £266.00–£315.00 weekly
Evening meal 1900 (last orders 1930)

Bedrooms: 4 double, 4 twin
Bathrooms: 8 en-suite
Parking for 12
Open: March–November
Cards accepted: Mastercard, Visa

8 S SP

255 WHITECHAPEL MANOR

HIGHLY COMMENDED

South Molton, Devon EX36 3EG Tel (01769) 573377 Fax (01769) 573797

Whitechapel Manor is a Grade I Listed Elizabethan manor house set within fifteen acres of terraced gardens, woodlands and pastures. It is the ideal base for exploring Exmoor with its ancient woodlands, dramatic coastline, hidden valleys, high moors and thatched villages. The National Trust has many attractions nearby and The Royal Horticultural Society's gardens at Rosemoor are also close by. The restaurant is recognised as one of the West Country's best and has won many accolades over the years.

Bed & Breakfast per night: single room from £70.00–£85.00; double room from £110.00–£170.00
Half board per person: £75.00–£110.00 daily; £500.00–£750.00 weekly
Lunch available: 1200–1345

Evening meal 1900 (last orders 2045)
Bedrooms: 1 single, 4 double, 5 twin, 1 family room
Bathrooms: 11 en-suite
Parking for 40
Cards accepted: Mastercard, Visa, Diners, Switch/Delta

S SP T

256 MARSH HALL COUNTRY HOUSE HOTEL

HIGHLY COMMENDED

Marsh Hall, South Molton, Devon EX36 3HQ Tel (01769) 572666 Fax (01769) 574230

Marsh Hall is a lovely Victorian country house with stained-glass windows, chandeliers and log fires in winter, set in three acres of gardens and woodland. With its spacious lounges, gallery and bedrooms, it is the ideal place in which to relax and enjoy the comforts of life. The delightful award-winning restaurant serves a four-course dinner with mouth-watering dishes devised from local fare and fresh produce grown in the hotel's herb, vegetable and fruit gardens.

Bed & Breakfast per night: single room from £45.00–£50.00; double room from £75.00–£94.00
Half board per person: £64.00–£69.00 daily; £340.00–£400.00 weekly
Evening meal 1900 (last orders 2030)

Bedrooms: 1 single, 4 double, 2 twin
Bathrooms: 7 en-suite
Parking for 20
Cards accepted: Mastercard, Visa, Switch/Delta

12 S SP

Entries are cross referenced by number to the maps on pages 120–121

257 THE RED HOUSE

HIGHLY COMMENDED

Brynsworthy, Roundswell, Barnstaple, Devon EX31 3NP Tel (01271) 45966

A period country house situated in an elevated position with panoramic views. Although being within two miles of the historic market town of Barnstaple, the house is set in the countryside with its own half acre garden. All rooms have colour TV, showers, hairdryers, tea/coffee-making facilities and central heating. Visitors will find that they are well situated for visiting the historic towns, sandy beaches and natural beauty of the moors, and can enjoy a good and varied selection of pub food, all within a short driving distance.

Bed & Breakfast per night: single occupancy from £16.00–£20.00; double room from £32.00–£40.00

Bedrooms: 1 double, 1 twin
Bathrooms: 1 public, 2 private showers
Parking for 6
Open: February–November

12

258 YEOLDON COUNTRY HOUSE HOTEL AND RESTAURANT

HIGHLY COMMENDED

Durrant Lane, Northam, Bideford, Devon EX39 2RL Tel (01237) 474400 Fax (01237) 476618

Set in two acres of gardens overlooking the River Torridge, Yeoldon House offers real hospitality and a refreshingly casual atmosphere in this uniquely unspoilt part of Devon. Individually decorated rooms with an air of elegance and charm – all en-suite with tea/coffee-making facilities. Imaginative à la carte cuisine using fresh local produce and an extensive wine list.

Bed & Breakfast per night: single occupancy from £45.00–£55.00; double room from £70.00–£95.00
Evening meal 1900 (last orders 2100)

Bedrooms: 7 double, 3 twin
Bathrooms: 10 en-suite
Parking for 22
Cards accepted: Mastercard, Visa, Diners, Amex, Switch/Delta

5 S SP T

259 THE NEW INN

HIGHLY COMMENDED

High Street, Clovelly, Bideford, Devon EX39 5TQ Tel (01237) 431303 Fax (01237) 431636

A fascinating 17th-century inn nestling amongst the cobbled streets and flower-strewn cottages of this historic and picturesque sea-faring village. Luxurious bedrooms with lovely views of the village or the sea. Cosy lounges serving Devon cream teas. A restaurant serving traditional regional dishes and a bar with real ale and, from time to time, interesting local personalities. In this traffic-free village, luggage is portered in by sledge and carried up to your car by donkeys. A short break paradise.

Bed & Breakfast per night: single room from £28.50–£51.25; double room from £57.00–£72.50
Half board per person: £49.00–£54.25 daily; £234.50–£313.25 weekly
Lunch available: 1200–1430 (bar snacks)

Evening meal 1900 (last orders 2100)
Bedrooms: 1 single, 7 double
Bathrooms: 8 en-suite
Cards accepted: Mastercard, Visa, Switch/Delta

S SP T

260 COURT BARN COUNTRY HOUSE HOTEL

HIGHLY COMMENDED

Clawton, Holsworthy, Devon EX22 6PS Tel (01409) 271219 Fax (01409) 271309

Pure Devon air, magical skies and countryside, combined with crackling log fires, antiques and fresh flowers, create a warm and relaxing atmosphere for a romantic break. Set in park-like grounds, Court Barn is one of the South West's great small touring hotels. Close to the Atlantic heritage coast, Blue Flag beaches, nature walks, cycle trails, National Trust houses and gardens, and midway between the moors. Our award-winning restaurant, which features an extensive wine list, teas and hospitality make Court Barn a place to remember.

Bed & Breakfast per night: single room from £39.00–£49.00; double room from £70.00–£86.00
Half board per person: £56.00–£63.00 daily; £350.00–£390.00 weekly
Lunch available: 1200–1400

Evening meal 1900 (last orders 2130)
Bedrooms: 1 single, 3 double, 2 twin, 2 triple
Bathrooms: 8 en-suite, 1 public
Parking for 17
Cards accepted: Mastercard, Visa, Diners, Amex, Switch/Delta

S TV SC SP T

261 BLAGDON MANOR COUNTRY HOTEL

DE LUXE

Ashwater, Beaworthy, Devon EX21 5DF Tel (01409) 211224 Fax (01409) 211634

Welcome to Blagdon Manor. A truly wonderful 17th-century manor nestling in twenty acres with superb views of the rolling countryside. Beautifully appointed en-suite guest rooms. Log fires during the cooler months, and a profusion of fresh flowers throughout the spring and summer, provide a relaxing and welcoming atmosphere. Guests dine together in a country houseparty atmosphere and enjoy the best of English cuisine, the ingredients of which will be the finest available. Smoking restricted.

Bed & Breakfast per night: single occupancy from £60.00–£70.00; double room from £95.00–£110.00
Evening meal 2000 (last orders 2000)

Bedrooms: 5 double, 2 twin
Bathrooms: 7 en-suite
Parking for 8
Cards accepted: Mastercard, Visa, Amex, Switch/Delta

SP

262 THE FALCON HOTEL

HIGHLY COMMENDED

Breakwater Road, Bude, Cornwall EX23 8SD Tel (01288) 352005 Fax (01288) 356359

Overlooking the famous Bude Canal, with beautiful walled gardens and yet only a short stroll from the beaches and shops, the Falcon has one of the finest settings in North Cornwall. Established in 1798, it still retains an old-world charm and atmosphere. The bedrooms are furnished to a very high standard, and have televisions with Teletext and Sky. Excellent local reputation for the quality of the food, both in the bar and candle-lit restaurant.

Bed & Breakfast per night: single room from £34.00–£36.00; double room from £68.00–£72.00
Half board per person: £47.50–£49.50 daily; £285.00–£297.00 weekly
Lunch available: 1200–1400

Evening meal 1900 (last orders 2100)
Bedrooms: 4 single, 14 double, 5 twin
Bathrooms: 23 en-suite
Parking for 40
Cards accepted: Mastercard, Visa, Diners, Amex, Switch/Delta

S SP T

Entries are cross referenced by number to the maps on pages 120–121

263 THE CLIFF HOTEL

HIGHLY COMMENDED

Crooklets Beach, Bude, Cornwall EX23 8NG Tel (01288) 353110 Fax (01288) 353110

The Cliff has a wonderful location, being 200 yards from Crooklets Beach and next to the National Trust cliff walk – "an area of outstanding natural beauty". Our facilities are first class, with indoor swimming pool, gym, all-weather bowling green and tennis court – all set within five acres of lawns and wild-flower meadow. We feel our greatest attribute, though, is the home-cooked fresh food and informal ambience.

Bed & Breakfast per night: single room from £23.50–£30.00; double room from £46.00–£60.00
Half board per person: £32.00–£40.00 daily; £215.00–£265.00 weekly
Lunch available: 1230–1400

Evening meal 1830 (last orders 2030)
Bedrooms: 2 single, 3 double, 1 twin, 9 triple
Bathrooms: 15 en-suite
Parking for 15 Open: April–September
Cards accepted: Mastercard, Visa, Switch/Delta

S TV SP T

The South-West Coast Path

'POOLE 500 MILES' reads the signpost pointing west along the Somerset coast at Minehead. In this daunting manner begins the South-West Coast Path, a walk around England's 'toe' taking in some of the most magnificent coastal scenery in the land. The walk starts dramatically as it enters the Exmoor National Park, hugging steep, wooded slopes that drop precipitously down to the sea, with stupendous views of the Welsh coast. Further on, the section of Devon coastline from Westward Ho! (the only British placename to include an exclamation mark) to the Cornish border is equally lovely as it passes the huddled village of Clovelly and the heights of Hartland Point with fine views of Lundy Island.

The Cornish Coast, both north and south, displays a stunning array of rocky promontories and soaring cliffs, interspersed with superb sandy beaches and fishing villages nestling in tiny coves. In general, the south coast, here and further on, is harder to negotiate than the north because of the many estuaries cutting into the lower-lying terrain, often requiring long detours inland.

The path re-enters Devon and, almost immediately, Plymouth, the largest city on its route. After rounding the wild promontories of Bolt Head and Prawle Point, it meanders through the gentler landscape of the 'Devon Riviera' and the seaside resorts of Paignton, Torquay, Teignmouth, and Dawlish. In Dorset, chalk cliffs run from Lyme Regis to Lulworth, interrupted by the long finger of shingle, Chesil Bank, pointing out to sea. The walk ends on a scenic high point as it negotiates the limestone heights of the Isle of Purbeck, an island in name only, for it remains firmly attached to the mainland.

As well as offering stunning scenery, the walk is rich in historical interest, from prehistoric hillforts in Dorset to Palmerston forts in Plymouth, or the abandoned village of Tyneham (Dorset) taken over by the army in 1943. In Cornwall, defunct engine houses and empty pilchard 'palaces' are relics of a rich industrial past.

The naturalist, as well as the historian, will find much of interest. The protruding coastline provides a landfall for migrating birds, while sub-tropical species of plants flourish in the mild climes of the South-West. The Lizard, in particular, supports a unique flora, while army ranges at Lulworth, untouched by modern farming practices, have preserved a rare botanical habitat.

There are several guides to the South-West Coast Path available, some suggesting shorter, circular walks and offering advice on accommodation, local attractions and other practical information.

At-a-glance symbols are explained on the flap inside the back cover

264 TOLCARNE HOUSE HOTEL AND RESTAURANT

HIGHLY COMMENDED

Tintagel Road, Boscastle, Cornwall PL35 0AS Tel (01840) 250654 Fax (01840) 250654

Tolcarne is a charming Victorian residence providing modern comforts in an old-world atmosphere and occupying a favoured location in this unspoilt coastal village, with spectacular views of the Jordan Valley and to the coastline and sea. There are lovely gardens with a croquet lawn. Relax in our comfortable guestrooms and enjoy peaceful rural and coastal views. Our dining room offers a choice of menus and good English cuisine with a well chosen wine list.

Bed & Breakfast per night: single room from £27.00–£30.00; double room from £44.00–£60.00
Half board per person: £35.00–£43.00 daily; £230.00–£280.00 weekly
Evening meal 1900 (last orders 2100)

Bedrooms: 1 single, 5 double, 2 twin
Bathrooms: 8 en-suite, 1 public
Parking for 15
Open: March–October
Cards accepted: Mastercard, Visa

2 SP T

265 POLKERR GUEST HOUSE

HIGHLY COMMENDED

Molesworth Street, Tintagel, Cornwall PL34 0BY Tel (01840) 770382 or (01840) 770132

Somewhere special was what we envisaged when we planned the decor of our bedrooms, dining room and the recently constructed large and restful sun lounge that overlooks the garden: guests visiting Polkerr Guest House enjoy accommodation of the highest standard. Situated within a few minutes' walk of Tintagel village, the historic castle and cliffs that offer superb views of the coast, we are also ideally located for exploring the beauty of the countryside.

Bed & Breakfast per night: single room from £18.00–£22.00; double room from £36.00–£46.00
Half board per person: £27.00–£31.00 daily; £189.00–£217.00 weekly
Evening meal 1830 (last bookings 1200)

Bedrooms: 1 single, 3 double, 1 twin, 1 triple, 1 family room
Bathrooms: 6 en-suite, 1 private
Parking for 9

UL S

266 THE OLD VICARAGE

HIGHLY COMMENDED

Treneglos, Launceston, Cornwall PL15 8UQ Tel (01566) 781351

An elegant Grade II Listed Georgian vicarage in an idyllic, peaceful rural setting near the spectacular north Cornwall coast. Ideally located as a touring base. Renowned for our hospitality and excellent food, which together with personal service and the highest standards throughout, assure your absolute comfort. A restful conservatory overlooks the garden. The en-suite bedrooms are individually furnished, together with fresh flowers and personal touches. Superb food, imaginative cuisine using produce from our own organic kitchen gardens. Non-smoking.

Bed & Breakfast per night: double room from £46.00–£48.00
Half board per person: £38.00–£39.00 daily
Evening meal 1900–2000

Bedrooms: 2 double
Bathrooms: 2 en-suite
Parking for 10
Open: March–November

2 UL S TV

Entries are cross referenced by number to the maps on pages 120–121

267 THE DOWER HOUSE

HIGHLY COMMENDED

Fentonluna Lane, Padstow, Cornwall PL28 8BA Tel (01841) 532317 Fax (01841) 532667

As you step on to our terrace and smile at this beautiful old house, you'll glance to your right over the rooftops of old Padstow, and marvel at the magnificent view of the Camel Estuary and distant hills of Bodmin Moor. Paul and Patricia will greet you and introduce you to their house. You will be delighted with the individually-decorated rooms and the care with which your breakfast is freshly prepared and presented in their elegant dining room.

Bed & Breakfast per night: single room from £37.50–£50.50; double room from £50.00–£82.00
Lunch available: 1200–1400

Bedrooms: 1 single, 2 double, 3 twin
Bathrooms: 6 en-suite
Parking for 8
Open: March–November
Cards accepted: Mastercard, Visa, Switch/Delta

268 WINDWARD HOTEL

HIGHLY COMMENDED

Alexandra Road, Porth Bay, Newquay, Cornwall TR7 3NB Tel (01637) 873185 or (01637) 852436 Fax (01637) 852436

A modern hotel of fine quality, set in its own grounds overlooking Porth Bay, and having a large car park and garden. All 14 rooms have colour TV, hairdryer, clock radio, en-suite bathrooms and beverage-making facilities. The licensed bar/lounge and elegant dining room enjoy spectacular views. Freshly prepared in the hotel is an excellent varied menu featuring old English favourites and a few modern additions, all served by caring, friendly staff to make your holiday memorable.

Bed & Breakfast per night: single occupancy from £28.00–£33.00; double room from £44.00–£54.00
Half board per person: £38.00–£43.00 daily; £140.00–£209.00 weekly
Evening meal 1830 (last orders 1900)

Bedrooms: 10 double, 1 twin, 1 triple, 2 family rooms
Bathrooms: 14 en-suite
Parking for 14
Open: March–October
Cards accepted: Mastercard, Visa, Amex, Switch/Delta

269 AVIARY COURT HOTEL

HIGHLY COMMENDED

Marys Well, Illogan, Redruth, Cornwall TR16 4QZ Tel (01209) 842256 Fax (01209) 843744

A charming three-hundred-year-old Cornish country house set in its own grounds on the edge of Illogan Woods, ideal for touring the South West peninsular and its many local attractions. Six well-equipped individual bedrooms with tea/coffee-making facilities, biscuits, mineral water, fresh fruit, direct dial telephone, remote control television and a view of the gardens. The resident family proprietors ensure personal service, offering well-cooked varied food that uses as much Cornish produce as possible.

Bed & Breakfast per night: single occupancy from £40.00–£44.00; double room from £56.00–£60.00
Half board per person: £53.00–£57.00 daily; £246.00–£258.00 weekly
Lunch available: 1230–1330 (Sunday only)

Evening meal 1900 (last orders 2030)
Bedrooms: 4 double, 1 twin, 1 triple
Bathrooms: 6 en-suite
Parking for 25
Cards accepted: Mastercard, Visa, Diners, Amex

270 TREGLISSON

HIGHLY COMMENDED

11 Wheal Alfred Road, Hayle, Cornwall TR27 5JT Tel (01736) 753141 Fax (01736) 753141

Situated in the quiet Cornish countryside, Treglisson is a listed 18th-century farmhouse which offers pretty bedrooms with comfortable beds, antique furniture and fresh flowers. Start the day with a swim in the heated indoor pool before tucking into a hearty breakfast served in the elegant dining room or conservatory. St Michael's Mount, St Ives and Land's End are all within easy reach of Treglisson.

Bed & Breakfast per night: single occupancy £25.00; double room £40.00

Bedrooms: 2 double, 1 twin, 2 family rooms
Bathrooms: 5 en-suite
Parking for 20
Cards accepted: Mastercard, Visa, Switch/Delta

271 CARBIS BAY HOTEL

HIGHLY COMMENDED

Carbis Bay, St Ives, Cornwall TR26 2NP Tel (01736) 795311 Fax (01736) 797677

Built in 1894 by the famous Cornish architect Sylvanus Trevail, this award-winning hotel has one of the most enchanting and romantic locations in the country – situated on the perfect golden sands of Carbis Bay beach itself. The idyllic surroundings offer peace and tranquillity, making it a natural haven for visitors wishing to escape the stresses and strains of everyday life. Set in its own grounds, the hotel commands breathtaking views across the beautiful landlocked bay of St Ives to Godrevy lighthouse and beyond.

Bed & Breakfast per night: single room from £40.00–£100.00; double room from £70.00–£120.00
Half board per person: £40.00–£140.00 daily; £295.00–£395.00 weekly
Evening meal 1800 (last orders 2030)

Bedrooms: 3 single, 13 double, 6 twin, 4 triple, 7 family rooms
Bathrooms: 33 en-suite, 1 public
Parking for 66 Open: March–December
Cards accepted: Mastercard, Visa, Diners, Amex, Switch/Delta

272 NANSLOE MANOR

HIGHLY COMMENDED

Meneage Road, Helston, Cornwall TR13 0SB Tel (01326) 574691 Fax (01326) 564680

This Grade II Listed building is located at the head of the magnificent Loe Valley, in some four acres of grounds. Character, style and elegance are complemented by the warm, friendly and relaxed atmosphere. The Manor's enchanting, award-winning restaurant creates the perfect ambience to experience the most imaginatively prepared food. Each luxurious bedroom reflects its own individual charm, and all double and twin rooms offer en-suite facilities, direct dial telephone, television, hairdryer and beverage maker.

Bed & Breakfast per night: single room from £44.00–£60.00; double room from £90.00–£120.00
Half board per person: £60.00–£75.00 daily
Lunch available: 1200–1330
Evening meal 1900 (last orders 2030)

Bedrooms: 1 single, 2 double, 4 twin
Bathrooms: 6 en-suite, 1 private
Parking for 30
Cards accepted: Mastercard, Visa, Switch/Delta

Entries are cross referenced by number to the maps on pages 120–121

273 TREGILDRY HOTEL

HIGHLY COMMENDED

Gillan, Manaccan, Helston, Cornwall TR12 6HG Tel (01326) 231378 Fax (01326) 231561

An elegant small hotel with stunning sea views. Tucked away in an undiscovered corner of the Lizard Peninsula, this is for those seeking relaxed and stylish comfort in "away from it all" surroundings. Large, light lounges with panoramic sea views have comfy sofas, fresh flowers and the latest books and magazines. The stylish restaurant has won awards for cuisine and the pretty sea-view bedrooms are attractively decorated with colourful fabrics. Near coastal path walks and an ideal peaceful base for exploring Cornwall.

Half board per person: £55.00–£60.00 daily;
£345.00–£365.00 weekly
Evening meal 1900 (last orders 2030)

Bedrooms: 7 double, 3 twin
Bathrooms: 10 en-suite
Parking for 15
Open: March–November
Cards accepted: Mastercard, Visa, Switch/Delta

SP T

The Lizard

IF IT'S BRITAIN'S MOST southerly point you're after, then come to the Lizard (Land's End is the westernmost point). This small Cornish peninsula has much to interest the visitor besides its location, being especially rich both geologically and botanically. Like almost every part of the county, the Lizard also has many historical connections and a glorious coastline.

Opinions vary as to how it got its name: some claim it means high palace, others that it derives from a Celtic word for outcast. Both explanations are plausible, for the Lizard is a level moorland plateau about 200ft (61m) above sea level, almost cut off from the rest of the county. Much of the peninsula is formed of serpentine stone, a soft, easily-worked material used in local churches (and on sale in the shops of Lizard village). A farmer reputedly chanced upon its ornamental qualities when he erected some large rocks in his field as rubbing posts for his cows. He soon noticed that the 'polished' areas showed patterns resembling snakeskin, and colours ranging from grey-green to pink. Once Queen Victoria had chosen it for Osborne House its popularity was assured. In the church of St Winwalloe at Landewednack it can be seen alternated with granite. This, the most southerly church in Britain, is where the last sermon was preached in Cornish (1678).

Kynance Cove, owned by the National Trust, is typical of the majestic coastline of the Lizard. Its rocky outcrops enjoy some unlikely names, including Man-o'-War Rock, the Devil's Postbox, the Devil's Bellows and Asparagus Island (where the plant grows wild). There are some intriguing caves (the Parlour and the Drawing Room), but take care not to be stranded by the incoming tide.

The flora of the Lizard is a botanist's delight. Here can be found plants too tender to grow outdoors elsewhere in the country (such as tamarisks and the Hottentot fig) and others which are unique to this corner of England, such as Cornish Heath. These plants have to be able to withstand the frequent onslaught of sea gales, something which countless local vessels have not managed. More shipwrecks have occurred here than almost anywhere else in the country. Off the eastern coast of the peninsula are the Manacles, a group of ferocious rocks extending over a couple of square miles. In 1770 parishioners of the nearby church of St Arkerveranus (in the village of St Deverne) redesigned the steeple as a landmark to warn passing ships. They may have been successful, but there are still over 400 victims of shipwrecks buried in the churchyard.

274 POLURRIAN HOTEL, APARTMENTS AND LEISURE CLUB HIGHLY COMMENDED

Polurrian Cove, Mullion, Helston, Cornwall TR12 7EN Tel (01326) 240421 Fax (01326) 240083

Polurrian is a family-run hotel in a magnificent cliff-top setting with 12 acres of gardens leading down to a secluded sandy cove. The National Trust coastline surrounding the hotel offers unrivalled scenic walks and there are many interesting and historic places to visit, all within easy distance. At Polurrian, our aim is to offer good value, quality and service in an atmosphere of comfort and friendliness.

Half board per person: £45.00–£90.00 daily;
£280.00–£475.00 weekly
Evening meal 1900 (last orders 2100)

Bedrooms: 18 double, 17 twin, 4 triple
Bathrooms: 39 en-suite, 1 public
Parking for 60
Open: February–December
Cards accepted: Mastercard, Visa, Diners, Amex

275 HOUSEL BAY HOTEL HIGHLY COMMENDED

Housel Cove, The Lizard, Helston, Cornwall TR12 7PG Tel (01326) 290417 or (01326) 290917 Fax (01326) 290359

An elegant Victorian hotel at Britain's most southerly coast. The views across the ocean are spectacular and a secluded and sandy beach nestles below the hotel. The Cornish coastal path, which runs through the hotel gardens, leads east towards Cadgwith and Coverack and west towards Kynance Cove. Fully licensed with a stylish restaurant and a bar with panoramic views. All bedrooms are en-suite with satellite television and there is a passenger lift.

Bed & Breakfast per night: single room from
£32.00–£57.00; double room from £64.00–£98.00
Half board per person: £50.00–£75.00 daily;
£288.00–£393.00 weekly
Lunch available: 1200–1400/1430 (in Ocean View bar)

Evening meal 1900 (last orders 2100/2130)
Bedrooms: 4 single, 10 double, 6 twin, 1 family room
Bathrooms: 21 en-suite
Parking for 30
Cards accepted: Mastercard, Visa, Amex, Switch/Delta

276 GREEN LAWNS HOTEL HIGHLY COMMENDED

Western Terrace, Falmouth, Cornwall TR11 4QJ Tel (01326) 312734 Fax (01326) 211427 E-mail green.lawns@dial.pipex.com

Where can you relax in an elegant, centrally positioned, chateau-style hotel with views across a beautiful bay? The Green Lawns Hotel and the famous Garras restaurant! If you are looking for a holiday where high standards and personal attention are paramount, you will enjoy an excellent choice of imaginative cuisine from a table d' hôte or à la carte menu. All our guests enjoy free membership to the Garras Leisure Club with its magnificent indoor swimming pool. 'Britain in Bloom' winners 1995, 1996 and 1997.

Bed & Breakfast per night: single room from
£55.00–£88.00; double room from £88.00–£126.00
Half board per person: £62.00–£106.00 daily;
£385.00–£480.00 weekly
Lunch available: 1200–1345

Evening meal 1845 (last orders 2145)
Bedrooms: 6 single, 16 double, 9 twin, 2 triple, 6 family rooms
Bathrooms: 39 en-suite
Parking for 60
Cards accepted: Mastercard, Visa, Diners, Amex, Switch/Delta

Entries are cross referenced by number to the maps on pages 120–121

277 CRILL MANOR HOTEL

HIGHLY COMMENDED

Roscarrack Road, Budock Water, Falmouth, Cornwall TR11 5BL Tel (01326) 211880 Fax (01326) 211229

Peace, quiet, comfort and delicious cuisine combined with Crill Manor's informal, friendly atmosphere promise you a relaxing break at any time of year. This small country house in lovely countryside between Falmouth and the Helford river is an ideal centre for exploring the west of Cornwall. The coastal path, golf and gardens galore plus boat trips are all nearby. Brochure on request gives details of special breaks, including free entry to the Lost Gardens of Heligan.

Bed & Breakfast per night: single room from £35.00–£39.00; double room from £70.00–£78.00
Evening meal 1900 (last orders 2030)

Bedrooms: 2 single, 9 double, 3 twin
Bathrooms: 14 en-suite
Parking for 16
Cards accepted: Mastercard, Visa, Amex, Switch/Delta

10 S SP

278 THE HUNDRED HOUSE HOTEL

HIGHLY COMMENDED

Ruan Highlanes, near Truro, Cornwall TR2 5JR Tel (01872) 501336 Fax (01872) 501151

Delightful 19th-century Cornish country house set in three acres. Near St Mawes on the Fal estuary and surrounded by superb countryside and unspoilt sandy coves. It is now a charming small hotel, beautifully decorated and furnished like an elegant English home. Delicious candle-lit dinners, Cornish cream teas, log fires and croquet on the lawn make a relaxing short break or a longer stay a memorable delight. Ideal for exploring Cornwall, its sub-tropical gardens or walking the coastal path.

Bed & Breakfast per night: single room from £36.00–£39.50; double room from £72.00–£79.00
Half board per person: £54.00–£59.00 daily; £336.00–£373.00 weekly
Evening meal 1930 (last bookings 1900)

Bedrooms: 2 single, 4 double, 4 twin
Bathrooms: 10 en-suite
Parking for 15
Open: March–October
Cards accepted: Mastercard, Visa, Amex

S SP T

279 LUGGER HOTEL AND RESTAURANT

HIGHLY COMMENDED

Portloe, Truro, Cornwall TR2 5RD Tel (01872) 501322 Fax (01872) 501691

Dating from the 17th century and originally an inn frequented by smugglers, the Lugger is situated at the very water's edge of a picturesque cove on the beautiful and unspoilt Cornish Roseland Peninsula. Internationally renowned for its first-class accommodation, superb food and wide selection of wines, the hotel has been in the ownership of the welcoming Powell family for three generations. It is the perfect place for lovers of nature and those in search of peace and seclusion.

Bed & Breakfast per night: single room £55.00; double room £110.00
Half board per person: £60.00–£75.00 daily; £420.00–£490.00 weekly
Lunch available: 1200–1400

Evening meal 1900 (last orders 2130)
Bedrooms: 3 single, 9 double, 7 twin
Bathrooms: 19 en-suite
Parking for 25 Open: March–October
Cards accepted: Mastercard, Visa, Diners, Amex, Switch/Delta

12 S SP T

280 HEMBAL MANOR

HIGHLY COMMENDED

Hembal Lane, Trewoon, St Austell, Cornwall PL25 5TD Tel (01726) 72144 Fax (01726) 72144

Hembal Manor is a Grade II Listed 16th-century dwelling, set in six acres of tranquil gardens. In 1569 Hembal was mentioned in the 'Feet of Fines'. Within the walled garden is a rare twin-seater loo – well worth a visit! All rooms are tastefully decorated and furnished with period furniture to a high standard. Ideally situated for exploring the Lost Gardens of Heligan and other places of historic interest. A warm welcome always assured.

Bed & Breakfast per night: single occupancy from £25.00–£28.00; double room from £45.00–£50.00

Bedrooms: 2 double, 1 twin
Bathrooms: 3 en-suite, 1 public
Parking for 6

12 TV SP

281 KERRY ANNA COUNTRY HOUSE

HIGHLY COMMENDED

Treleaven Farm, Mevagissey, St Austell, Cornwall PL26 6RZ Tel (01726) 843558 Fax (01726) 843558

Kerry Anna Country House is set amidst beautiful gardens with an outdoor heated summer pool. Overlooking the village, which is just a few minutes' walk away, with outstanding views of the countryside and with sea glimpses. Romantic en-suite bedrooms, all with their own personal touches. Three lounges, two of which are non-smoking. The dining room serves the best of farmhouse cooking using fresh local produce. Car parking close to the house. Sorry, no pets. Children over five most welcome during school holidays.

Bed & Breakfast per night: double room from £42.00–£50.00
Half board per person: £32.00–£36.00 daily
Evening meal 1900 (last bookings 1200)

Bedrooms: 4 double, 1 twin, 1 family room
Bathrooms: 6 en-suite
Parking for 6
Open: April–October

5 S TV SP

282 BOSCUNDLE MANOR

HIGHLY COMMENDED

Tregrehan, St Austell, Cornwall PL25 3RL Tel (01726) 813557 Fax (01726) 814997

A lovely house in over twelve acres of secluded grounds with a practice golf area. The rooms are very attractively furnished with antiques, pictures and family possessions. The bedrooms are extremely comfortable and most have spa baths and power showers. There is an outstanding wine list and beautifully prepared fresh food is served. Andrew and Mary Flint have been here for over nineteen years and their personal involvement and enthusiasm create a relaxed and happy atmosphere.

Bed & Breakfast per night: single room from £65.00–£85.00; double room from £120.00–£130.00
Half board per person: £80.00–£110.00 daily; £490.00–£595.00 weekly
Evening meal 1930 (last orders 2030)

Bedrooms: 2 single, 3 double, 5 twin
Bathrooms: 10 en-suite
Parking for 15
Open: April–October
Cards accepted: Mastercard, Visa, Amex, Switch/Delta

S SP T

Entries are cross referenced by number to the maps on pages 120–121

283 MARINA HOTEL

HIGHLY COMMENDED

Esplanade, Fowey, Cornwall PL23 1HY Tel (01726) 833315 Fax (01726) 832779

This Georgian hotel, originally built as the summer residence of the Bishop of Truro, is situated on the waterside with its own moorings. The hotel faces south and most rooms (four have balconies) overlook the estuary. The walled garden provides an ideal spot for observing the waterside traffic. The restaurant overlooking the water provides a feast of local fish, shellfish and meat. Early and late season offers of two nights for the price of one.

Bed & Breakfast per night: double room from £54.00–£90.00
Half board per person: £42.00–£62.00 daily; £266.00–£406.00 weekly
Lunch available: 1200–1700

Evening meal 1900 (last orders 2030)
Bedrooms: 5 double, 5 twin
Bathrooms: 10 en-suite
Open: March–December
Cards accepted: Mastercard, Visa, Amex, Switch/Delta

12 S SP

Daphne Du Maurier's Cornwall

IN 1926, AFTER MANY holidays in Cornwall, Daphne Du Maurier's parents found the second home they had been looking for – Ferryside, Bodinnick (now her son's private home), on the Fowey Estuary (shown below). When her family returned to London, Daphne stayed on, alone for the first time. 'Here', she wrote, 'was the freedom I desired, long sought-for, not yet known. Freedom to write, to walk, to wander, freedom to climb hills, to pull a boat, to be alone.' So began her lifelong love affair with Cornwall.

By the time she died in 1989, Du Maurier had written several best-selling novels, as well as biographies, short stories, plays, and *Vanishing Cornwall*, recommended reading for anyone interested in the history and spirit of the county. All reveal a profound love and knowledge of Cornwall's landscape and history. *The Loving Spirit*, written at Ferryside and inspired by the boat-building Slade family of Polruan, was the first novel set in the Fowey area (published in 1931). Menabilly, the house Daphne and her husband, Major Tommy Browning (they married in Lanteglos Church, where Slade graves can still be seen), rented from 1943 to 1969, was the Manderley of *Rebecca* and featured in the *The King's General* (about the Civil War in Cornwall) and *My Cousin Rachel*. Several scenes in *Rebecca* are set on the beach at nearby Polridmouth. Kilmarth, the house in *The House on the Strand*, was Du Maurier's home from 1969 until her death. (Neither Kilmarth nor Menabilly is open to the public.) The Fowey district also features in *Frenchman's Creek*, *Rule Britannia* and *Castle Dor*, the novel written in collaboration with Arthur Quiller Couch based on the Cornish legend of Tristan and Iseult. It climaxes on the hillfort Castle an Dinas, near St Columb Major.

Further afield, the 'silent, desolate country' of Bodmin Moor is the setting for Du Maurier's tale of smuggling, *Jamaica Inn*. The inn, and accompanying museum, are at Bolventor, between Launceston and Bodmin. The old rectory at Altarnun was home to the same novel's villain, Reverend Francis Davy, while Launceston Castle and Lanhydrock House both feature in *The King's General*. More action in *Jamaica Inn* takes place in the Helford Estuary, also the main setting for *Frenchman's Creek*.

Circular walks taking in several Du Maurier sites can be made from Fowey, either on the coast path around Gribben Head or, using ferries, around Bodinnick and Polruan. The Daphne Du Maurier Visitor Centre, 5 South Street, Fowey (tel: 01726 833619, closed winter), has displays, as well as details of the Daphne Du Maurier Festival, 8–17 May 1998.

284 MOUNT PLEASANT MOORLAND HOTEL — HIGHLY COMMENDED

Mount, Bodmin, Cornwall PL30 4EX Tel (01208) 821342 Fax (01208) 821417

A warm welcome and a relaxing atmosphere await you at our delightful countryside hotel hidden away in the heart of Cornwall. Our comfortable en-suite bedrooms have tea-making facilities and many enjoy splendid country views. Sample a delicious home-cooked dinner, perhaps followed by ice cream made on the premises, then enjoy a pleasant evening in our cosy bar or relax in the "indoor garden" (sun lounge). Safe parking, attractive gardens, beautiful secluded swimming pool, peace and tranquillity guaranteed!

Bed & Breakfast per night: single room from £23.00–£26.00; double room from £46.00–£52.00
Half board per person: £35.00–£38.00 daily; £210.00–£240.00 weekly
Evening meal 1900 (last bookings 1700)

Bedrooms: 1 single, 3 double, 1 twin, 1 triple, 1 family room
Bathrooms: 6 en-suite, 1 private
Parking for 10
Open: April–September
Cards accepted: Mastercard, Visa, Switch/Delta

285 TRELASKE HOTEL AND RESTAURANT — HIGHLY COMMENDED

Polperro Road, Looe, Cornwall PL13 2JS Tel (01503) 262159 Fax (01503) 265360

Trelaske is situated just off, but not visible from, the main Looe to Polperro Road, making it a perfect place for peace and tranquillity. The hotel is privately owned by Sylvia and Roger Rawlings, who are both Cornish and local to the area. Trelaske has an enviable reputation for fine food and luxurious accommodation. Each of the seven bedrooms has been individually furnished to the highest possible standard. Executive rooms with jacuzzi. Set in four acres of beautiful mature gardens, making a perfect retreat to return to after visiting Poldark country.

Bed & Breakfast per night: single occupancy from £42.50; double room from £65.00
Half board per person: from £50.00 daily; from £300.00 weekly
Evening meal 1900 (last orders 2130)

Bedrooms: 3 double, 2 twin, 1 triple, 1 family room
Bathrooms: 7 en-suite
Parking for 50
Cards accepted: Mastercard, Visa, Amex, Switch/Delta

286 TALLAND BAY HOTEL — HIGHLY COMMENDED

Talland Bay, Looe, Cornwall PL13 2JB Tel (01503) 272667 Fax (01503) 272940

A delightful old Cornish manor house set in two acres of gardens overlooking the sea. All bedrooms are furnished to a high standard and many have sea views. Dinners feature fresh regional produce – local seafood, Cornish lamb, West Country cheeses. Talland Bay is a magically peaceful spot from which to explore this part of Cornwall. Breathtaking cliff paths lead to Looe and Polperro, and there are fascinating sub-tropical gardens and National Trust properties within easy reach.

Half board per person: £59.00–£94.00 daily; £371.70–£592.20 weekly
Lunch available: 1230–1400
Evening meal 1900 (last orders 2100)

Bedrooms: 3 single, 5 double, 9 twin, 2 family rooms
Bathrooms: 19 en-suite
Parking for 20
Open: February–December
Cards accepted: Mastercard, Visa, Diners, Amex, Switch/Delta

Entries are cross referenced by number to the maps on pages 120–121

287 FIELDHEAD HOTEL

HIGHLY COMMENDED

Portuan Road, Hannafore, West Looe, Looe, Cornwall PL13 2DR Tel (01503) 262689 Fax (01503) 264114

Built around the turn of the century, our hotel occupies a premier site in Looe, offering panoramic views over Looe Bay, St George's Island, the surrounding coastline, and as far out as the Eddystone Lighthouse. We have 14 pretty, coordinated en-suite bedrooms, mostly with sea views, and some with balconies. An intimate candle-lit restaurant with an extensive menu and the pick of local produce and fresh fish. Our garden has a heated swimming pool in season. Car parking within the grounds. Internet: http://www.chycor.co.uk/fieldhead/

Bed & Breakfast per night: single room £38.50; double room from £66.00–£78.00
Half board per person: £49.50–£53.50 daily; £285.00–£342.00 weekly
Evening meal 1830 (last orders 2030)

Bedrooms: 1 single, 9 double, 3 twin, 1 triple
Bathrooms: 14 en-suite
Parking for 14
Open: February–December
Cards accepted: Mastercard, Visa, Amex, Switch/Delta

5 S TV SP T

288 COMMONWOOD MANOR HOTEL

HIGHLY COMMENDED

St Martins Road, Looe, Cornwall PL13 1LP Tel (01503) 262929 Fax (01503) 262632 E-mail commonwood@compuserve.com

Formerly a spacious and elegant Victorian family villa, Commonwood is set in six acres of landscaped gardens and woodland, enjoying spectacular views over the Looe river valley and countryside. Here you can relax in one of the lounges, around the swimming pool – which is a real suntrap – or in the garden. Our friendly unhurried service, with the best of local food and fresh fish, makes the Commonwood an ideal base. Only a few minutes' walk to Looe town, harbour and beaches.

Bed & Breakfast per night: single room from £31.00–£38.00; double room from £62.00–£76.00
Half board per person: £44.50–£54.00 daily; £311.50–£336.00 weekly
Evening meal 1900 (last orders 2000)

Bedrooms: 1 single, 6 double, 3 twin, 1 family room
Bathrooms: 11 en-suite
Parking for 20
Cards accepted: Mastercard, Visa, Amex, Switch/Delta

8 S TV SP T

289 COOMBE FARM

HIGHLY COMMENDED

Widegates, near Looe, Cornwall PL13 1QN Tel (01503) 240223 Fax (01503) 240895

Relax in a wonderful tranquil setting of lawns, meadows, woods and streams, with superb views down a wooded valley to the sea. Enjoy warm friendly hospitality in a house lovingly furnished with antiques and interesting objects. There are open log fires, a beautiful outdoor pool, a stone barn for snooker, table tennis and a candle-lit dining room in which we serve a delicious four-course dinner every evening. Nearby National Trust houses, glorious walks and beaches.

Bed & Breakfast per night: single occupancy from £26.00–£36.00; double room from £52.00–£72.00
Half board per person: £41.00–£51.00 daily; £273.00–£340.00 weekly
Evening meal 1900 (last orders 1900)

Bedrooms: 3 double, 3 twin, 2 triple, 2 family rooms
Bathrooms: 10 en-suite
Parking for 12
Open: March–October
Cards accepted: Mastercard, Visa, Diners, Amex, Switch/Delta

5 S TV SP

290 East Cornwall Farmhouse

 HIGHLY COMMENDED

Fullaford Road, Callington, Cornwall PL17 8AN Tel (01579) 350018

Beautifully situated, former silver-mine Captain's home. Sympathetically restored in the style of a farmhouse. Close to National Trust's Cotehele House, the Rivers Tamar and Lynher and St. Mellion Golf Club. Ideal for exploring Dartmoor and Bodmin Moor, and within easy reach of both the north and south coasts. A warm friendly welcome with service above and beyond expectations. Evening meals of home grown and local produce by arrangement.

Bed & Breakfast per night: single room from £17.00–£20.00; double room from £34.00–£40.00
Half board per person: £27.00–£32.00 daily
Evening meal 1830 (last orders 2030)

Bedrooms: 1 single, 2 double, 1 twin
Bathrooms: 3 en-suite, 1 public
Parking for 6
Open: March–November

---

291 Lydford House Hotel

 HIGHLY COMMENDED

Lydford, Okehampton, Devon EX20 4AU Tel (01822) 820347 Fax (01822) 820442

A country house hotel of considerable charm in a beautiful garden setting just on the edge of Dartmoor. There are delightful bedrooms with every facility, comfortable lounges and a well-stocked bar. The restaurant offers the finest traditional English fare and an interesting wine list. Service is by friendly, efficient staff and the resident proprietors are always on hand to ensure that guests receive personal attention. Riding stables in the grounds provide superb hacking over Dartmoor.

Bed & Breakfast per night: single room from £36.00; double room from £72.00
Half board per person: from £51.00 daily; from £290.00 weekly
Evening meal 1900 (last orders 2030)

Bedrooms: 2 single, 3 double, 3 twin, 1 triple, 3 family rooms
Bathrooms: 11 en-suite, 1 private
Parking for 30
Cards accepted: Mastercard, Visa

---

292 Boringdon Hall Hotel

HIGHLY COMMENDED

Colebrook, Plympton, Plymouth, Devon PL7 4DP Tel (01752) 344455 Fax (01752) 346578

Boringdon Hall Hotel is a Grade I Listed Elizabethan manor house where Queen Elizabeth may have stayed. Situated on the edge of Dartmoor – a place of tranquil calm in a world of hustle and bustle. The Hall and historic outbuildings have been tastefully restored to their former glory. The forty luxury bedrooms stand around a courtyard, along with the leisure facilities which include a swimming pool, sauna, nine-hole pitch and putt, and a tennis court.

Bed & Breakfast per night: single room from £70.00–£75.00; double room from £90.00–£95.00
Half board per person: £48.50–£65.00 daily; £291.00–£455.00 weekly
Lunch available: 1200–1400

Evening meal 1900 (last orders 2130)
Bedrooms: 1 single, 20 double, 15 twin, 4 triple
Bathrooms: 40 en-suite
Parking for 250
Cards accepted: Mastercard, Visa, Amex, Switch/Delta

Entries are cross referenced by number to the maps on pages 120–121

293 BOWLING GREEN HOTEL

HIGHLY COMMENDED

9-10 Osborne Place, Lockyer Street, Plymouth, Devon PL1 2PU Tel (01752) 209090 Fax (01752) 209092

Situated in the historic naval city of Plymouth opposite the world famous 'Drake's Bowling Green', this elegant Georgian hotel has superbly appointed bedrooms offering all the modern facilities the traveller requires. With a full breakfast menu and friendly and efficient family staff, you can be sure of a memorable visit to Plymouth. The Bowling Green Hotel is centrally situated for the Barbican, Theatre Royal, leisure/conference centre and ferry port, with Dartmoor only a few miles away.

Bed & Breakfast per night: single room from £34.00–£36.00; double room from £46.00–£49.00

Bedrooms: 1 single, 9 double, 1 twin, 1 triple
Bathrooms: 12 en-suite
Parking for 4
Cards accepted: Mastercard, Visa, Diners, Amex, Switch/Delta

294 HALFWAY HOUSE INN

HIGHLY COMMENDED

Fore Street, Kingsand, Torpoint, Cornwall PL10 1NA Tel (01752) 822279 Fax (01752) 823146 E-mail david.riggs@virgin.net

Situated on the Cornwall coastal path, just thirty yards from the beach. At the heart of the historical colour-washed villages of Kingsand and Cawsand, adjacent to Mount Edgcumbe Park and a ferry ride away from the great naval city of Plymouth. The intimate restaurant specialises in locally-caught sea food, complemented by a selection of fine wines and real ales. A haven of peace and tranquillity, your stay here will be a truly unforgettable experience.

Bed & Breakfast per night: single room from £22.00–£27.00; double room from £44.00–£50.00
Half board per person: £32.00–£37.00 daily; £200.00–£235.00 weekly
Lunch available: 1200–1430

Evening meal 1900 (last orders 2130)
Bedrooms: 1 single, 3 double, 1 family room
Bathrooms: 5 en-suite
Cards accepted: Mastercard, Visa, Diners, Amex, Switch/Delta

295 BUGLE ROCKS

Listed HIGHLY COMMENDED

The Old School, Battisborough, Holbeton, Plymouth, Devon PL8 1JX Tel (01752) 830422 Fax (01752) 830558

Bugle Rocks, situated in an area designated as one of outstanding natural beauty, was once the stable block and coach house of Battisborough House, the summer residence of the late Lord Mildmay, who died in 1951. Between then and 1985, it was part of Battisborough School. The property overlooks the coast and South Devon coast path and is just around the bay from Mothecombe, one of the most unspoilt and natural beaches in the area.

Bed & Breakfast per night: single occupancy maximum £22.00; double room maximum £44.00

Bedrooms: 2 double
Bathrooms: 1 public
Parking for 9

296 THURLESTONE HOTEL

HIGHLY COMMENDED

Thurlestone, Kingsbridge, Devon TQ7 3NN Tel (01548) 560382 Fax (01548) 561069

An intimate atmosphere, characteristic of grand establishments, distinguishes us from others due to our location on the Devon coast, in an area of outstanding natural beauty. Sixty five en-suite bedrooms (includes three suites), well furnished with every facility, including video in some rooms. A restaurant with a reputation for fine food, superb wine and long-serving staff. Leisure activities include indoor swimming pool, spa bath, sauna, solarium, 9-hole championship golf course and tennis, squash and badminton courts as well as opportunities for walks and fishing. Please telephone for brochure.

Bed & Breakfast per night: single room from £40.00–£90.00; double room from £80.00–£180.00
Half board per person: £45.00–£104.00 daily; £315.00–£728.00 weekly
Lunch available: 1230–1400

Evening meal 1930 (last orders 2100)
Bedrooms: 5 single, 18 double, 26 twin, 13 triple, 3 family rooms
Bathrooms: 65 en-suite Parking for 119
Cards accepted: Mastercard, Visa, Amex

297 HELLIERS FARM

HIGHLY COMMENDED

Ashford, Aveton Gifford, Kingsbridge, Devon TQ7 4ND Tel (01548) 550689 Fax (01548) 550689

Helliers Farm is a small sheep farm set on a hill overlooking a lovely valley in the South Hams. An ideal centre for touring the coasts, moors, golf courses (Bigbury, Thurlestone and Dartmouth), National Trust houses and walks, and the city of Plymouth. Tastefully appointed bedrooms and a comfortable lounge and dining room where excellent farmhouse breakfasts are served. Closed Christmas and New Year. No smoking.

Bed & Breakfast per night: single room from £17.00–£20.00; double room from £36.00–£44.00

Bedrooms: 1 single, 1 double, 1 twin, 1 family room
Bathrooms: 1 private, 1 public, 2 private showers
Parking for 6
Open all year except Christmas and New Year

298 BURTON FARM

HIGHLY COMMENDED

Galmpton, Kingsbridge, Devon TQ7 3EY Tel (01548) 561210 Fax (01548) 561210

A working South Hams farm, one mile from the fishing village of Hope Cove and just three miles from Salcombe. Once the property of the Duke of Devonshire, it is now owned by Mrs Anne Rossiter. She has extensively and lovingly restored the house, while the farm is expertly run by David, a traditional farmer who combines the wisdom of age-old husbandry with modern technology. Anne uses home-grown produce in her kitchen and local specialities are featured in her menus. Burton Farm is fully licensed with a world-wide selection of over forty red and white wines, as well as beers and ciders. Special diets catered for. Non-smoking.

Bed & Breakfast per night: single room from £25.00–£30.00; double room from £46.00–£56.00
Half board per person: £36.50–£41.50 daily
Evening meal 1930

Bedrooms: 2 single, 2 double, 2 twin, 3 family rooms
Bathrooms: 5 en-suite, 2 private, 1 public
Parking for 10
Cards accepted: Mastercard, Visa, Amex, Switch/Delta

Entries are cross referenced by number to the maps on pages 120–121

299 TIDES REACH HOTEL

HIGHLY COMMENDED

South Sands, Salcombe, Devon TQ8 8LJ Tel (01548) 843466 Fax (01548) 843954

Located in a tree-fringed sandy cove where country meets the sea, with a glorious view across the Salcombe Estuary, you can relax in style in this beautifully furnished and decorated hotel. Pamper yourself in the superb leisure complex, extensively-equipped and with a sunny tropical atmosphere. Award-winning creative cuisine served with courtesy and care in our garden-room restaurant.

Half board per person: £68.00–£105.00 daily;
£420.00–£644.00 weekly
Evening meal 1900 (last orders 2100)

Bedrooms: 18 double, 17 twin, 3 family rooms
Bathrooms: 38 en-suite, 2 public
Parking for 100
Open: February–December
Cards accepted: Mastercard, Visa, Diners, Amex, Switch/Delta

300 WHITE HOUSE HOTEL

HIGHLY COMMENDED

Chillington, Kingsbridge, Devon TQ7 2JX Tel (01548) 580580 Fax (01548) 581124

The White House is a lovely Grade II Listed building of great aesthetic and architectural appeal. Set in an acre of lawned and terraced gardens in one of the most beautiful corners of coastal England, the house has a special atmosphere reminiscent of a quieter and less hurried age. An elegant restaurant and cosy bar, comfortable lounges with log fires, interesting wines and home cooking from the kitchen range are all here for your delight.

Bed & Breakfast per night: single occupancy from £43.00–£60.00; double room from £68.00–£94.00
Half board per person: £47.00–£73.00 daily;
£280.00–£462.00 weekly
Evening meal 1900 (last orders 2005)

Bedrooms: 3 double, 5 twin
Bathrooms: 7 en-suite, 2 private, 1 public
Parking for 12
Open: April–December
Cards accepted: Mastercard, Visa, Amex

301 THE OLD FORGE AT TOTNES

HIGHLY COMMENDED

Seymour Place, Totnes, Devon TQ9 5AY Tel (01803) 862174 Fax (01803) 865385

This beautiful 600-year-old building is a haven of comfort and relaxation, not far from the town centre. Rooms are delightfully co-ordinated, offering hairdryer, radio alarm, telephone, central heating, colour TV, beverage tray and continental bedding. We also have ground floor rooms and a family cottage suite. Leisure lounge with whirlpool spa. Enjoy breakfast in the Tudor-style dining room which offers a wide choice of menu. Specialities: golf breaks (near 15 courses), adventure sport breaks, dance and painting holidays, 'hands on' pottery and blacksmithing. No smoking indoors. Extensive afternoon tea menu served in the walled tea garden or conservatory.

Bed & Breakfast per night: single room from £40.00–£50.00; double room from £50.00–£70.00

Bedrooms: 1 single, 5 double, 2 twin, 2 family rooms
Bathrooms: 9 en-suite, 2 private, 1 public
Parking for 10
Cards accepted: Mastercard, Visa, Switch/Delta

302 Follaton Farmhouse

HIGHLY COMMENDED

Plymouth Road, Totnes, Devon TQ9 5NA Tel (01803) 865441

In a peaceful setting on the edge of the historic town of Totnes, Follaton Farmhouse is an elegant former Georgian farmhouse offering high quality accommodation. The farmhouse has been sensitively restored and tastefully furnished to give you a memorable and relaxing stay. The house, which is deceptively large, has an impressive curved open stairway in the hall. The gardens, with the tranquil sounds of running water and bird song, create a very special atmosphere.

Bed & Breakfast per night: single occupancy from £35.00–£42.00; double room from £50.00–£54.00
Half board per person: £40.00–£57.00 daily; £280.00–£399.00 weekly
Evening meal 1800 (last orders 2000)

Bedrooms: 1 double, 2 twin
Bathrooms: 3 en-suite
Parking for 6

5 UL SP

303 Bel Alp House Country Hotel

HIGHLY COMMENDED

Haytor, Bovey Tracey, Newton Abbot, Devon TQ13 9XX Tel (01364) 661217 Fax (01364) 661292

The views from Bel Alp's spectacular setting on the edge of Dartmoor are simply breathtaking. Other great attractions are superb award-winning set dinners, beautiful furnishings, large comfortable bedrooms and the English country house atmosphere. Dartmoor, one of southern England's last great wildernesses, has its own magical beauty and is wonderful to explore. Bel Alp is ideally situated for discovering the heritage, beautiful countryside and coastline of Devon and into Cornwall. Excellent local golf, walking and riding.

Bed & Breakfast per night: single occupancy from £60.00–£70.00; double room from £120.00–£130.00
Half board per person: £90.00–£100.00 daily; £630.00–£700.00 weekly
Evening meal 1930 (last orders 2030)

Bedrooms: 4 double, 4 twin
Bathrooms: 8 en-suite
Parking for 20
Cards accepted: Mastercard, Visa, Diners, Amex, Switch/Delta

S SP

304 Edgemoor Hotel

HIGHLY COMMENDED

Haytor Road, Bovey Tracey, Devon TQ13 9LE Tel (01626) 832466 Fax (01626) 834760 E-mail Edgemoor@btinternet.com

'Loaded with charm', this wisteria-clad country house hotel is personally run by resident proprietors Rod and Pat Day. With its beautiful gardens and lovely en-suite bedrooms (including some four-posters) the Edgemoor provides the ideal setting in which to unwind from the cares of modern life. Friendly attentive staff, good food, fine wines and beautiful countryside combine to help make your stay memorable and enjoyable.

Bed & Breakfast per night: single room from £46.50–£52.50; double room from £75.95–£89.95
Half board per person: £47.99–£57.50 daily; £670.00–£700.00 weekly
Lunch available: 1200–1345

Evening meal 1900 (last orders 2100)
Bedrooms: 3 single, 9 double, 3 twin, 1 triple, 1 family room
Bathrooms: 17 en-suite
Parking for 50
Cards accepted: Mastercard, Visa, Diners, Amex, Switch/Delta

S SP

Entries are cross referenced by number to the maps on pages 120–121

305 Great Sloncombe Farm

HIGHLY COMMENDED

Moretonhampstead, Newton Abbot, Devon TQ13 8QF Tel (01647) 440595 Fax (01647) 440595

Share the magic of Dartmoor all year round while staying in our lovely rambling 13th-century farmhouse, which is full of interesting historical features. A working dairy farm set amongst peaceful meadows and woodland abundant in wild flowers and animals. A welcoming and informal place to relax and explore the countryside. Comfortable en-suite rooms, one with a four-poster bed, central heating, TVs and tea/coffee-making facilities. Delicious Devonshire suppers and breakfasts with new-baked bread.

Bed & Breakfast per night: double room from £40.00–£42.00
Half board per person: £32.00 daily
Evening meal 1830 (last bookings 1000)

Bedrooms: 2 double, 1 twin
Bathrooms: 3 en-suite
Parking for 3

306 Wooston Farm

HIGHLY COMMENDED

Moretonhampstead, Newton Abbot, Devon TQ13 8QA Tel (01647) 440367 Fax (01647) 440367

Wooston Farm is situated above the Teign Valley in the Dartmoor National Park, with views over open moorland. The farmhouse is surrounded by a delightful garden. There are plenty of walks to take on the moor and in the wooded Teign Valley. Good home cooking and cosy log fires await you at Wooston with two double (one four-poster) and one twin room. Mountain bikes available. Open all year except Christmas.

Bed & Breakfast per night: double room from £38.00–£42.00
Evening meal 1800 (last orders 1850)

Bedrooms: 2 double, 1 twin
Bathrooms: 2 en-suite, 2 private
Parking for 3
Open all year except Christmas

307 Lower Nichols Nymet Farm

HIGHLY COMMENDED

Lower Nichols Nymet, North Tawton, Devon EX20 2BW Tel (01363) 82510

We offer a haven of comfort and rest on our farm that is set in rolling countryside in the centre of Devon. On holiday, food becomes important – we serve hearty and healthy breakfasts and candle-lit dinners using local produce. Our elegantly furnished en-suite bedrooms have glorious views. There are many National Trust properties and other attractions to visit. This is a perfect base for exploring the beauties of the West Country. A no smoking establishment. Brochure available.

Bed & Breakfast per night: single occupancy maximum £20.00; double room from £34.00–£37.00
Half board per person: £27.00–£28.50 daily; £160.00–£170.00 weekly
Evening meal 1830

Bedrooms: 1 double, 1 family room
Bathrooms: 2 en-suite
Parking for 4
Open: March–October

308 PORLOCK VALE HOUSE

HIGHLY COMMENDED

Porlock Weir, Somerset TA24 8NY Tel (01643) 862338 Fax (01643) 862338

Formerly a hunting lodge, now a magnificent Edwardian country house hotel in a wonderful situation. Set in twenty five acres of grounds which sweep down to the sea, Porlock Vale House nestles at the foot of the ancient wooded fringe where Exmoor meets the coast. A friendly, unpretentious hotel where you can enjoy good food and fine wines served in a relaxed, informal atmosphere, with beautiful, uninterrupted views across Porlock Bay. Whether you enjoy the great outdoors, or sitting by a log fire, Porlock Vale is the perfect place for a short break at any time of the year.

Bed & Breakfast per night: single occupancy from £50.00–£65.00; double room from £80.00–£90.00
Half board per person: £60.00–£70.00 daily; £325.00–£350.00 weekly
Lunch available: 1200–1400

Evening meal 1900 (last orders 1930)
Bedrooms: 10 double, 5 twin
Bathrooms: 14 en-suite, 2 private, 2 public
Parking for 20
Cards accepted: Mastercard, Visa, Amex, Switch/Delta

309 SAVERY'S AT KARSLAKE HOUSE

HIGHLY COMMENDED

Halse Lane, Winsford, Minehead, Somerset TA24 7JE Tel (01643) 851242 Fax (01643) 851242

In this 15th-century malthouse, the emphasis is squarely placed on comfort, service and the cooking of John Savery. Sheltered by Winsford Hill and a few minutes from the moor. Walking, riding, shooting and fishing are the main pastimes here, and in this peaceful atmosphere commercial life seems light years away. With seven bedrooms, the house is perfect for private parties.

Bed & Breakfast per night: double room from £50.00–£80.00
Half board per person: £49.00–£64.00 daily; £322.00–£420.00 weekly
Lunch available: by arrangement
Evening meal 1930 (last orders 2000)

Bedrooms: 3 double, 4 twin
Bathrooms: 5 en-suite, 1 public, 2 private showers
Parking for 9
Open: January and March–December
Cards accepted: Mastercard, Visa, Switch/Delta

310 RALEIGH MANOR COUNTRY HOUSE HOTEL

HIGHLY COMMENDED

Wheddon Cross, Dunster, Somerset TA24 7BB Tel (01643) 841484

Raleigh Manor is a fine Victorian country house, totally secluded with beautiful far-reaching views set amidst the Exmoor National Park. Offering tea and home-made cakes on arrival, delicious freshly-prepared home-cooked dinners, fine wines and log fires, a relaxing atmosphere has been created and a warm welcome awaits. Ideally situated for exploring the moorland, wooded valleys and coastline of Exmoor. Close to Dunster, Dunkery Beacon and many National Trust properties. A no smoking house.

Bed & Breakfast per night: single room from £26.00–£30.00; double room from £52.00–£60.00
Half board per person: £40.50–£44.50 daily; £283.50–£311.50 weekly
Evening meal 1930 (last orders 2030)

Bedrooms: 1 single, 3 double, 2 twin
Bathrooms: 6 en-suite
Parking for 10
Open: March–November
Cards accepted: Mastercard, Visa, Switch/Delta

Entries are cross referenced by number to the maps on pages 120–121

311 LITTLE QUARME FARM

HIGHLY COMMENDED

Wheddon Cross, Exmoor National Park, Somerset TA24 7EA Tel (01643) 841249 Fax (01643) 841249 E-mail compuserve106425743

Originally mentioned in the Domesday Book, Little Quarme offers you an idyllic peaceful location in the heart of Exmoor. A beautifully furnished and decorated farmhouse with Sky TV and video lounge, dining room, two double en-suite bedrooms and one twin room with private bathroom. All bedrooms have hospitality trays. Maximum of six guests. Large gardens, ample parking and superb panoramic views from all rooms. Full central heating, non-smoking, log fires. A very warm welcome awaits you. Your host: Bob Cody-Boutcher.

Bed & Breakfast per night: single occupancy from £25.00–£30.00; double room from £38.00–£42.00
Half board per person: from £30.00 daily
Evening meal 1900

Bedrooms: 2 double, 1 twin
Bathrooms: 2 en-suite, 1 private
Parking for 6
Open: April–October

312 CHANNEL HOUSE HOTEL

HIGHLY COMMENDED

Church Path, Off Northfield Road, Minehead, Somerset TA24 5QG Tel (01643) 703229

An elegant Edwardian country house perfectly located for exploring the beauty of Exmoor and situated on the lower slopes of Minehead's picturesque North Hill where it nestles in two acres of award-winning gardens. The high standards of cuisine and accommodation will best suit those seeking superior quality and comfort. If you would like to experience smiling service in the tranquil elegance of this lovely hotel, we will be delighted to send you our brochure and sample menu.

Bed & Breakfast per night: single occupancy £62.00; double room £100.00
Half board per person: £60.00 daily; £339.50–£357.00 weekly
Evening meal 1900 (last orders 2030)

Bedrooms: 2 double, 5 twin, 1 triple
Bathrooms: 8 en-suite
Parking for 10
Open: March–November and Christmas
Cards accepted: Mastercard, Visa, Diners, Switch/Delta

313 COMBE HOUSE HOTEL

HIGHLY COMMENDED

Holford, Bridgwater, Somerset TA5 1RZ Tel (01278) 741382 Fax (01278) 741382

In the heart of the Quantock Hills (renowned as an area of outstanding natural beauty) lies this 17th-century house of great character. Once a tannery, this cottage-style hotel offers absolute peace and quiet in beautiful surroundings. Inside the beamed building, with its charming collection of pictures, porcelain and period furniture, the visitor will find the relaxed atmosphere and friendly service ideal to enjoy Combe House, the Quantocks and the many attractions in the area.

Bed & Breakfast per night: single room from £34.00–£39.00; double room from £68.00–£78.00
Half board per person: £52.50–£57.50 daily; £325.50–£410.00 weekly
Evening meal 1930 (last orders 2030)

Bedrooms: 4 single, 6 double, 8 twin
Bathrooms: 16 en-suite, 2 private, 2 public
Parking for 20
Open: March–October
Cards accepted: Mastercard, Visa, Amex, Switch/Delta

At-a-glance symbols are explained on the flap inside the back cover

314 BLACKMORE FARM

HIGHLY COMMENDED

Cannington, Bridgwater, Somerset TA5 2NE Tel (01278) 653442 Fax (01278) 653442

A rare Grade I Listed 14th-century manor house retaining many period features including oak beams, stone archways, log fires and its own private chapel. A traditional farmhouse breakfast is served in the Great Hall. All the bedrooms are en-suite, one with a four-poster bed. You can be assured of a warm welcome to this family home situated in a quiet, rural location, with views of the Quantock Hills. An ideal base for touring Bath, Somerset and Exmoor. Facilities for disabled guests. CATEGORY 2

Bed & Breakfast per night: single occupancy from £20.00–£28.00; double room from £38.00–£45.00

Bedrooms: 3 double, 1 triple
Bathrooms: 4 en-suite
Parking for 6

315 WEMBDON FARM

HIGHLY COMMENDED

Hollow Lane, Wembdon, Bridgwater, Somerset TA5 2BD Tel (01278) 453097 or 0402 272755 Fax (01278) 445856

Enjoy a refreshing change and a memorable stay at our homely Georgian farmhouse. Our working farm is situated near the Quantock Hills, an area of outstanding natural beauty. Conveniently central for all that Somerset has to offer. Elegant and romantic bedrooms – 2 double en-suite, 1 twin with private bathroom. Guests have their own lounge and dining room. Relax in our pretty garden. Off-road parking. Quietly tucked away, yet easy to find – a place for all seasons.

Bed & Breakfast per night: single occupancy from £20.00–£22.00; double room from £36.00–£40.00

Bedrooms: 2 double, 1 twin
Bathrooms: 2 en-suite, 1 private
Parking for 3
Open: February–November

10

316 WALNUT TREE HOTEL

HIGHLY COMMENDED

North Petherton, Bridgwater, Somerset TA6 6QA Tel (01278) 662255 Fax (01278) 663946

It is rare to find a delightful hotel with such easy access to the M5 as the Walnut Tree. This former 18th-century coaching inn has been tastefully designed with the accent on comfort. All bedrooms are individually designed with every facility for today's travellers. Good food is served in the pleasing surroundings of the Sedgemoor Restaurant, whilst with its four meeting rooms, cosy bar and friendly staff, the Walnut Tree is a popular venue for honeymooners, travellers and those seeking a relaxing break.

Bed & Breakfast per night: single room from £37.00–£57.00; double room from £52.00–£72.00
Half board per person: from £49.00 daily
Lunch available: 1200–1400
Evening meal 1900 (last orders 2200)

Bedrooms: 1 single, 23 double, 8 twin
Bathrooms: 32 en-suite
Parking for 74
Cards accepted: Mastercard, Visa, Diners, Amex, Switch/Delta

Entries are cross referenced by number to the maps on pages 120–121

317 ROYAL CASTLE HOTEL

HIGHLY COMMENDED

11 The Quay, Dartmouth, Devon TQ6 9PS Tel (01803) 833033 Fax (01803) 835445

An unusual 17th-century coaching hostelry in the heart of the historic port of Dartmouth – an unrivalled location ideal for short breaks at any time of year. Twenty five luxuriously appointed en-suite bedrooms are individually decorated and furnished, some with four-poster or brass beds and jacuzzis. The elegant restaurant on the first floor overlooks the estuary and specialises in select regional produce and locally-caught seafood. Two bars serve delicious food, traditional ales and a good choice of wines. We look forward to welcoming you.

Bed & Breakfast per night: single room from £46.95–£58.45; double room from £83.90–£96.90
Half board per person: £53.95–£76.95 daily
Lunch available: Bar meals 1100–1430
Evening meal 1845 (last orders 2200)

Bedrooms: 4 single, 10 double, 7 twin, 4 triple
Bathrooms: 25 en-suite
Parking for 4
Cards accepted: Mastercard, Visa, Switch/Delta

318 FORD HOUSE

HIGHLY COMMENDED

44 Victoria Road, Dartmouth, Devon TQ6 9DX Tel (01803) 834047 or 0378 771971 Fax (01803) 834047

Situated within walking distance from Dartmouth's historic quay and town centre. Ford House has a friendly, lived-in atmosphere with three attractively decorated and fully equipped en-suite rooms. Breakfast is served until noon around a large mahogany dining table, with smoked haddock, kippers, scrambled egg with smoked salmon, freshly squeezed orange juice, bacon and eggs. Special mid-week dinner, bed & breakfast packages have been arranged with the famous Carved Angel restaurant.

Bed & Breakfast per night: single occupancy from £35.00–£70.00; double room from £50.00–£70.00
Half board per person: £50.00–£60.00 daily; from £350.00 weekly
Evening meal 1900 (last bookings 1200)

Bedrooms: 3 double, 1 twin
Bathrooms: 3 en-suite, 1 private
Parking for 4
Open: March–October
Cards accepted: Mastercard, Visa, Amex

319 THE CAPTAINS HOUSE

HIGHLY COMMENDED

18 Clarence Street, Dartmouth, Devon TQ6 9NW Tel (01803) 832133

A charming small Grade II Listed house built c1730 and containing the original staircase and Adam-style fire surroundings. It is conveniently situated in a quiet street just off the River Dart, and a three minute walk from the harbour and historic town centre. Each bedroom is individually furnished and decorated but with every modern facility. Full English breakfast with a choice, served with home-made breads and preserves, can be taken either downstairs or upstairs.

Bed & Breakfast per night: single room from £30.00–£35.00; double room from £44.00–£55.00

Bedrooms: 1 single, 3 double, 1 twin
Bathrooms: 4 en-suite, 1 private

320 ROUNDHAM LODGE

HIGHLY COMMENDED

16 Roundham Road, Paignton, Devon TQ4 6DN Tel (01803) 558485 Fax (01803) 553090

Situated in the heart of the English Riviera, we are a family-run bed and breakfast with a warm and friendly atmosphere, offering fine English breakfasts. Close to Paignton Harbour, our lodge affords magnificent sea views from most rooms, and some have balconies. Roundham Lodge provides an ideal centre from which to explore the south west, visit the wide expanses of Dartmoor, take a boat trip from the harbour, or just relax on the many beaches.

Internet: http://www.zynet.co.uk/adnet/client/roundham.html

Bed & Breakfast per night: single room from £20.00–£27.00; double room from £40.00–£48.00

Bedrooms: 1 single, 4 double, 1 twin, 2 triple
Bathrooms: 8 en-suite
Parking for 9
Cards accepted: Mastercard, Visa, Switch/Delta

321 BLUE HAZE HOTEL

HIGHLY COMMENDED

Seaway Lane, Torquay, Devon TQ2 6PS Tel (01803) 607186 or (01803) 606205 Fax (01803) 607186

A small friendly hotel set in lovely grounds in a quiet country lane leading down to the sea. Spacious quality en-suite bedrooms which are sparklingly clean, pleasantly decorated, well appointed and all non-smoking. You are welcome to book bed and breakfast only, or you may wish to enjoy our traditional home cooking which is served straight from the oven and made from fresh local produce wherever possible. Parking is no problem in our large car park. Truly 'Somewhere Special'.

Bed & Breakfast per night: double room from £58.00–£62.00
Half board per person: £42.00–£44.00 daily; £249.00–£263.00 weekly
Evening meal 1900 (last orders 1900)

Bedrooms: 4 double, 2 twin, 2 triple, 1 family room
Bathrooms: 9 en-suite
Parking for 15
Open: April–October
Cards accepted: Mastercard, Visa, Amex

322 FAIRMOUNT HOUSE HOTEL

HIGHLY COMMENDED

Herbert Road, Chelston, Torquay, Devon TQ2 6RW Tel (01803) 605446 Fax (01803) 605446

Enjoy the best of both worlds – coast and country. In lovely gardens overlooking a quiet, residential valley close to Cockington and a few minutes from the sea, Fairmount is a lovingly restored Victorian family house with high ceilings, polished brass, beautifully appointed bedrooms, a cosy conservatory bar and log fires. Fairmount has won its reputation over the years for mouth-watering menu choices and delicious home cooking, complemented by fine international wines and friendly, personal service. Dogs welcome too.

Bed & Breakfast per night: single room from £26.00–£32.00; double room from £52.00–£64.00
Half board per person: £38.50–£44.50 daily; £249.50–£291.50 weekly
Lunch available: 1230–1330 (bar snacks)

Evening meal 1830 (last orders 1930)
Bedrooms: 2 single, 4 double, 2 triple
Bathrooms: 8 en-suite, 2 public
Parking for 8 Open: March–October
Cards accepted: Mastercard, Visa, Amex

Entries are cross referenced by number to the maps on pages 120–121

323 OSBORNE HOTEL & LANGTRY'S RESTAURANT

HIGHLY COMMENDED

Hesketh Crescent, Meadfoot Beach, Torquay, Devon TQ1 2LL Tel (01803) 213311 Fax (01803) 296788

This 29-bedroomed hotel, centrepiece of an elegant Regency crescent, overlooks the seclusion of Meadfoot Beach. The hotel offers the friendly ambience of a country home complemented by superior standards of comfort, five acres of gardens, indoor/outdoor pools, tennis court, gym, sauna, solarium, snooker room and putting green. Langtry's guide-acclaimed restaurant offers superlative food every evening and is one of the foremost restaurants on the English Riviera. The all-day Brasserie serves an international selection of food and drinks.

Bed & Breakfast per night: single room from £45.00–£70.00; double room from £70.00–£140.00
Half board per person: £50.00–£80.00 daily; £350.00–£550.00 weekly
Evening meal 1900 (last orders 2145)

Bedrooms: 1 single, 26 double, 2 family rooms
Bathrooms: 29 en-suite
Parking for 100
Cards accepted: Mastercard, Visa, Amex, Switch/Delta

324 THOMAS LUNY HOUSE

DE LUXE

Teign Street, Teignmouth, Devon TQ14 8EG Tel (01626) 772976

Thomas Luny House – built by the marine artist Thomas Luny around 1800 – is tucked away in a conservation area. It is now the home of Alison and John Allan and their young family. The house, which is surrounded by a secluded garden, is furnished tastefully with antiques and has four themed en-suite rooms, two with views to the river. Drive under an archway (beware: the entrance is narrow) and enjoy a warm welcome.

Bed & Breakfast per night: single occupancy from £30.00–£35.00; double room from £50.00–£70.00

Bedrooms: 2 double, 2 twin
Bathrooms: 4 en-suite
Parking for 6
Open: February–December

12

325 OAK COTTAGE

HIGHLY COMMENDED

Luscombe Hill, Dawlish, Devon EX7 0PX Tel (01626) 863120

Set in a peaceful woodland location with terrace views of the sea and close to Dartmoor, this 19th-century Tudor revival house is described as having a National Trust atmosphere and was used in the 'Miss Marple' TV series. Stone mullions, leaded lights, classically styled gardens with pools and woodland birdsong. Paintings, old prints, antiques, log fires and warm hospitality. Dinner is freshly prepared to a high standard using local produce. Ample private parking.

Bed & Breakfast per night: double room £54.00
Half board per person: £42.00 daily; £284.00 weekly
Evening meal 1930

Bedrooms: 1 double, 1 twin
Bathrooms: 2 en-suite
Parking for 3

326 HOTEL RIVIERA

DE LUXE

The Esplanade, Sidmouth, Devon EX10 8AY Tel (01395) 515201 Fax (01395) 577775 E-mail enquiries@hotelriviera.co.uk

Splendidly positioned at the centre of Sidmouth's Esplanade overlooking Lyme Bay. With its mild climate and the beach just on the doorstep, the setting echoes the south of France and is the choice for the discerning visitor in search of relaxation and quieter pleasures. Behind the fine Regency façade lies an alluring blend of old-fashioned service and present-day comforts. Glorious sea views can be enjoyed from the en-suite bedrooms, all of which are fully appointed. In the elegant bay-view dining room, guests are offered a fine choice of dishes from the extensive menus prepared by French and Swiss-trained chefs. Internet: http://www.hotelriviera.co.uk

Bed & Breakfast per night: single room from £66.00–£90.00; double room from £114.00–£162.00
Half board per person: £75.00–£99.00 daily
Lunch available: 1230–1400
Evening meal 1900 (last orders 2100)

Bedrooms: 7 single, 6 double, 14 twin
Bathrooms: 27 en-suite, 1 public
Parking for 24
Open: February–December
Cards accepted: Mastercard, Visa, Diners, Amex

Exeter Underground Passageways

There can be few city centres in England where it is possible to walk a distance of some half a mile without having to dodge the traffic or endure the roar of motor vehicles, but in Exeter such an experience is on offer – underground. Beneath the pavements and roads near the High Street is a network of subterranean passageways. Built in medieval times, these narrow, silent tunnels of mellow golden brick wind their way just below ground level. They have long exerted a fascination for the people of Exeter, and colourful tales abound of hidden treasure, secret escapes, and even a ghost on a bicycle. The real function of the tunnels was rather more prosaic: to bring clean drinking water from natural springs outside the city into the centre.

In the Middle Ages piped water was a luxury few could afford, and so its provision was usually undertaken by large institutions, especially the church. Exeter's cathedral had its own supply as early as the 12th century, but by the mid 14th century this supply was proving inadequate and another pipeline was laid. Then, as now, water pipes occasionally sprang leaks and the only way to repair them was to dig up the ground to reveal the fractured pipe. Worried about the disruption this could cause in the garden of St John's Hospital, the cathedral authorities ordered the construction of the first short section of passageway beneath the garden, designed to enable workers to repair the length of pipe which ran along its floor. Further passages followed; one of the longest sections was built in 1492–7 to service a pipe which supplied water to a grand new fountain in the heart of the city (now demolished). This section includes most of the extent now open to the public.

A visit to Exeter's underground passages (tel: 01392 265887) is a unique experience, for no other similar system of passageways can be explored by the public anywhere else in Britain. Upon entering the complex from Romansgate Passage, just off the High Street, the visitor passes through an interpretation centre consisting of a video and exhibition presentation, before being taken on a guided tour of the passageways. The tour (not suitable for people with disabilities or affected by claustrophobia) is rich in colourful anecdote and detailed historical fact, and bears testimony to a bold and remarkable piece of medieval civil engineering.

Entries are cross referenced by number to the maps on pages 120–121

327 BEACH END GUEST HOUSE

HIGHLY COMMENDED

8 Trevelyan Road, Seaton, Devon EX12 2NL Tel (01297) 23388 Fax (01297) 625604

We are situated at the mouth of the River Axe in unspoilt Seaton, from where you can enjoy unrivalled views over Axmouth Harbour and Seaton Bay. We offer you fine food and friendly, attentive service in our lovely Edwardian guesthouse. You can be sure that we will try our best to make your holiday really special.

Bed & Breakfast per night: double room maximum £43.00
Half board per person: maximum £31.50 daily; maximum £210.00 weekly
Evening meal 1900 (last bookings 1500)

Bedrooms: 4 double, 1 twin
Bathrooms: 5 en-suite
Parking for 5
Open: February–October

328 SWALLOWS EAVES HOTEL

HIGHLY COMMENDED

Colyford, Colyton, Devon EX13 6QJ Tel (01297) 553184

Enjoy the beauty and treasures of Devon and Dorset from this attractive wisteria-clad small hotel. In a village setting with spacious gardens and glorious views towards the heritage coast, between Lyme Regis and Sidmouth. An abundance of walks, gardens and National Trust properties nearby. Only eight delightful en-suite rooms and wonderful home-cooked meals. Ground floor room available, easy parking. No children, no dogs, no smoking rooms. Complimentary use of nearby private swimming club, heated indoor pool (88°F) and outdoor pool, sauna, solarium.

Bed & Breakfast per night: single room from £38.00–£48.00; double room from £56.00–£76.00
Half board per person: £42.00–£57.00 daily; £290.00–£350.00 weekly
Evening meal 1900 (last orders 2000)

Bedrooms: 1 single, 3 double, 4 twin
Bathrooms: 8 en-suite
Parking for 10
Open: February–November
Cards accepted: Mastercard, Visa, Amex, Switch/Delta

329 THE DOWER HOUSE HOTEL

HIGHLY COMMENDED

Rousdon, Lyme Regis, Dorset DT7 3RB Tel (01297) 21047 Fax (01297) 24748

Welcome to a world of tranquil charm! The Dower House, created in true country house hotel tradition, stands in its own lawned, wooded grounds ensuring safe easy parking. Rooms are en-suite and we also have an indoor heated swimming pool and sauna, central heating, colour television, radio, telephone, beverage tray, hairdryers, open fires, fine cuisine plus old fashioned courteous service. Enjoy the many nearby local walks, bracing coastal footpath walks, and golf. Special Winter and Spring breaks.

Bed & Breakfast per night: single room from £38.00–£48.00; double room from £60.00–£80.00
Half board per person: £45.00–£60.00 daily; £275.00–£341.00 weekly
Lunch available: 1200–1400

Evening meal 1900 (last orders 2100)
Bedrooms: 1 single, 3 double, 2 twin, 3 triple
Bathrooms: 9 en-suite, 1 public
Parking for 48
Cards accepted: Mastercard, Visa, Diners, Amex

330 THATCH LODGE HOTEL

HIGHLY COMMENDED

The Street, Charmouth, near Lyme Regis, Dorset DT6 6PQ Tel (01297) 560407 Fax (01297) 560407

'Picture postcard' 14th-century thatched hotel offering tranquillity, discerning quality and superb chef-inspired cuisine. The world famous fossil beach is just three minutes' walk away. Non-smoking throughout.

Bed & Breakfast per night: double room from £56.00–£90.00
Half board per person: £47.50–£64.50 daily
Evening meal 2000

Bedrooms: 6 double, 1 twin
Bathrooms: 6 en-suite, 1 private
Parking for 10
Open: All year except February
Cards accepted: Mastercard, Visa, Switch/Delta

331 HENSLEIGH HOTEL

Lower Sea Lane, Charmouth, Bridport, Dorset DT6 6LW Tel (01297) 560830

A family-run hotel with a reputation for friendly service, comfort, hospitality and delicious food, complemented by a relaxing atmosphere which has made it a favourite with visitors to Charmouth. Situated just three hundred metres from the beach, in an area of outstanding beauty, with spectacular cliff walks and fossil hunting, we have ample car parking within the grounds.

Bed & Breakfast per night: single room from £25.00–£27.00; double room from £50.00–£54.00
Half board per person: £39.00–£41.00 daily; £245.00–£260.00 weekly
Evening meal 1830 (last orders 1930)

Bedrooms: 2 single, 4 double, 4 twin, 1 triple
Bathrooms: 11 en-suite
Parking for 14
Open: March–October
Cards accepted: Mastercard, Visa, Amex

332 ROUNDHAM HOUSE HOTEL

HIGHLY COMMENDED

Roundham Gardens, West Bay Road, Bridport, Dorset DT6 4BD Tel (01308) 422753 Fax (01308) 421500

Owned and personally managed by Daphne and Jeremy Thomas, Roundham House is situated in an enviable position within an acre of feature gardens, with westerly views over the Dorset countryside and Lyme Bay. Built of local stone in 1903, the hotel offers every modern amenity for the discerning guest and is renowned for its excellent food, wine and hospitality. The table d'hôte and à la carte menus offer a wide choice, including vegetarian options, and feature local produce and fresh vegetables from the kitchen garden. The hotel is an ideal base for walking, touring or just relaxing in an area of outstanding beauty.

Bed & Breakfast per night: single room from £33.00–£35.00; double room from £55.00–£65.00
Half board per person: £47.00–£52.00 daily; £275.00–£280.00 weekly
Lunch available: 1230–1400 (Sunday only)

Evening meal 1900 (last orders 2030)
Bedrooms: 1 single, 3 double, 2 twin, 2 family rooms
Bathrooms: 7 en-suite, 1 private
Parking for 12 Open: March–December
Cards accepted: Mastercard, Visa

Entries are cross referenced by number to the maps on pages 120–121

333 BRITMEAD HOUSE

HIGHLY COMMENDED

West Bay Road, Bridport, Dorset DT6 4EG Tel (01308) 422941 Fax (01308) 422516

An elegant and spacious, recently refurbished detached house. Situated between Bridport and West Bay harbour with its beaches, Chesil Beach and the Dorset Coastal Path. An ideal base from which to discover Dorset. The spacious south-west facing dining room and lounge overlook an attractive garden and open countryside beyond. Well-appointed bedrooms, all with many thoughtful extras. Delicious meals, table d'hôte dinner. Quite simply everything, where possible, is tailored to suit your needs.

Bed & Breakfast per night: single occupancy from £25.00–£36.00; double room from £40.00–£58.00
Half board per person: £33.50–£42.50 daily; £206.50–£241.50 weekly
Evening meal 1900 (last bookings 1700)

Bedrooms: 4 double, 3 twin
Bathrooms: 6 en-suite, 1 private
Parking for 8
Cards accepted: Mastercard, Visa, Diners, Amex

5 S SP T

Chesil Beach

ONE OF THE STRANGER natural phenomena of the South Coast, Chesil Beach resembles a hawser tethering the 'Isle' of Portland to the mainland. From the map it seems to all the world to be man-made, but it is in reality the restless swell of the sea that has shaped this long, stony strand. Never quite satisfied with her creation however, Nature relentlessly refashions her pebbly breakwater, making one stretch steeply raked, only for a storm to flatten the shingle once again.

The bank begins a few miles west of the attractive Dorset village of Abbotsbury, renowned for centuries for its Swannery (tel: 01305 871684), and runs due south-east for about 16 miles (26km) until it hits the cliffs of Portland. For the latter half of its length the shingle forms a thin barrier between the Fleet, the largest lagoon in Britain, and the fury of the Channel. In fact the Fleet, barely disturbed by mankind, is as much an attraction as the beach itself. Glass-bottomed boats take visitors to the lagoon which is tidal for most of its 8 miles (13km). It supports as many as 150 species of seaweed, and the eagle-eyed may also make out sea anemones and sponges, as well as fish such as sea bass and the rare black-faced blenny. Above the water, waders and waterfowl such as oyster catchers, godwits, plovers and red-breasted mergansers all feed on the Fleet, especially in the winter months. You may even glimpse the increasingly rare little tern (tel: 01305 773396 for more details of boat trips). Otherwise the best way to discover the Fleet Nature Reserve is to walk along the coastal path, which follows the land shore of the lagoon, or to visit the Chesil Beach Centre (tel: 01305 760579).

Chesil Beach itself is also home to some hardy flora capable of withstanding salt spray. Sea pea and yellow-horned poppy are two unusual examples. The strong winds have often blasted shipping in the area and in 1824 the gales were so ferocious that the sloop Ebeneezer fetched up on top of the bank and could be refloated only on the other side of the 30–40ft (9–12m)-high ridge of shingle. The same storm swept most of East Fleet church out to sea. Smugglers often braved the dangers of the isolated shore to land their contraband. Even in the worst of weather, locals could determine their exact whereabouts by the size of the pebbles on the beach; one strange result of the sea's actions is that the stones west of Abbotsbury are the size of peas, while 16 miles (26km) to the south-east they are more like cobbles. Locals can place themselves to an accuracy of 300 yards (333m). A final word of caution; over the years the waves have wrecked countless vessels – and are just as dangerous for swimmers.

334 THE OLD RECTORY

HIGHLY COMMENDED

Winterbourne Steepleton, Dorchester, Dorset DT2 9LG Tel (01305) 889468 Fax (01305) 889737 E-mail TREES@ZYNET.CO.UK

Genuine Victorian rectory situated in a quiet hamlet, surrounded by breathtaking countryside. Close to historic Dorchester and Weymouth's sandy beaches. We specialise in providing a quiet comfortable night's sleep followed by a copious English, vegetarian or continental breakfast, with fresh organic home produce. The Crystal Dining Room is available for celebration dinners and cordon bleu cuisine. Enjoy our superbly appointed lounge, croquet lawn and putting green, or meander through country lanes with our mountain bikes.

Bed & Breakfast per night: single occupancy £30.00; double room from £38.00–£80.00

Bedrooms: 3 double, 1 twin, 1 family room
Bathrooms: 4 en-suite, 1 private
Parking for 10

335 ALMSHOUSE FARM

HIGHLY COMMENDED

Hermitage, Sherborne, Dorset DT9 6HA Tel (01963) 210296 Fax (01963) 210296

Visit this unspoilt part of Dorset whilst staying on our working dairy farm. The surrounding area lends itself to all types of outdoor pursuits, or maybe you would rather unwind in the spacious country garden. The listed farmhouse retains its original beauty in the exposed beams and the wonderful inglenook fireplace, whilst also boasting every modern convenience for your comfort. Good food and country air will make your stay here truly memorable.

Bed & Breakfast per night: double room from £38.00–£44.00

Bedrooms: 2 double, 1 twin
Bathrooms: 2 en-suite, 1 private
Parking for 4
Open: February–December

336 KINGS ARMS INN

HIGHLY COMMENDED

Montacute, Somerset TA15 6UU Tel (01935) 822513 Fax (01935) 826549

The historic village of Montacute boasts a real gem: a traditional English inn offering first-class cuisine and comfort – the ideal venue for the discerning guest. The Kings Arms is a handsome 16th-century building of local Ham stone, offering sixteen charming well-appointed en-suite bedrooms. Chef Mark Lysandrou's award-winning cuisine is establishing a reputation in the West Country – try a tasty snack by a roaring log fire in the Pickwick Bar or enjoy a more formal meal in the Abbey Restaurant. A central location for numerous National Trust properties and gardens.

Bed & Breakfast per night: single occupancy from £53.00–£59.00; double room from £69.00–£85.00
Half board per person: £74.00–£80.00 daily; £370.00–£440.00 weekly
Lunch available: 1200–1400

Evening meal 1900 (last orders 2200)
Bedrooms: 10 double, 6 twin
Bathrooms: 16 en-suite
Parking for 20
Cards accepted: Mastercard, Visa, Diners, Amex

Entries are cross referenced by number to the maps on pages 120–121

337 BROADVIEW GARDENS

DE LUXE

East Crewkerne, Crewkerne, Somerset TA18 7AG Tel (01460) 73424 Fax (01460) 73424

Unusual colonial bungalow with en-suite rooms overlooking an acre of beautiful secluded gardens with lawns and hundreds of unusual plants. Furnished in keeping with the Edwardian style. Extremely comfortable and relaxing in a friendly, informal atmosphere. We offer the very best quality traditional English home cooking. Stay awhile and explore this wonderful area for garden visits, antique enthusiasts, Dorset coast and quaint old villages. Our list provides fifty varied places. A completely no smoking house.

Bed & Breakfast per night: single occupancy from £25.00–£46.00; double room from £50.00–£56.00
Half board per person: £39.00–£42.00 daily; £273.00–£294.00 weekly
Evening meal 1830 (last bookings 1200)

Bedrooms: 1 double, 2 twin
Bathrooms: 2 en-suite, 1 private
Parking for 6
Cards accepted: Mastercard, Visa, Switch/Delta

338 THE PHEASANT

HIGHLY COMMENDED

Seavington St Mary, Ilminster, Somerset TA19 0QH Tel (01460) 240502 Fax (01460) 242388

The Pheasant Hotel is a beautifully converted 17th-century farmhouse with a wealth of olde-world charm nestling in the peaceful little village of Seavington St Mary, deep in the heart of Somerset. With its two sumptuous suites and six individually-designed and tastefully appointed en-suite bedrooms, the hotel provides the highest standards of luxury and comfort complemented by its cosy, welcoming bar with huge open inglenooks and beautiful oak-beamed restaurant.

Bed & Breakfast per night: single occupancy from £75.00–£105.00; double room from £95.00–£125.00
Evening meal 1930 (last orders 2130)

Bedrooms: 6 double, 2 twin
Bathrooms: 8 en-suite
Parking for 60
Cards accepted: Mastercard, Visa, Amex, Switch/Delta

339 HORNSBURY MILL

HIGHLY COMMENDED

Eleighwater, Chard, Somerset TA20 3AQ Tel (01460) 63317 Fax (01460) 63317

A working watermill set in a five-acre beauty spot with character en-suite bedrooms and a locally renowned restaurant and bar open to non-residents. Attractions include the lake with many breeds of duck, the curious and bygones museum and speciality cream teas. Hornsbury Mill is open all year and is conveniently situated on the borders of Dorset, Devon and Somerset between Chard and Ilminster. Please contact the owners, Keith and Sarah Jane Lewin, for brochure and further details.

Bed & Breakfast per night: single occupancy maximum £55.00; double room maximum £69.50
Half board per person: £54.00–£74.00 daily; £335.00–£435.00 weekly
Lunch available: 1200–1400

Evening meal 1900 (last orders 2100)
Bedrooms: 3 double, 1 twin, 1 triple
Bathrooms: 5 en-suite
Parking for 80
Cards accepted: Mastercard, Visa, Amex, Switch/Delta

340 LEA HILL HOTEL

HIGHLY COMMENDED

Membury, Axminster, Devon EX13 7AQ Tel (01404) 881881 or (01404) 881388

14th-century hotel set in eight acres of grounds overlooking a secluded valley in peaceful Devon countryside, only ten miles from the coast. Mellow stone, oak beams and inglenook fireplaces enhance the relaxed, informal and friendly atmosphere. The beamed restaurant offers superb cuisine which is freshly prepared using local produce such as Lyme Bay seafood and Devonshire lamb and game. Lea Hill is ideally situated for touring the West Country, walking, bird-watching, golfing or simply relaxing away from it all.

Bed & Breakfast per night: single occupancy from £48.00–£61.00; double room from £77.00–£106.00
Half board per person: £66.00–£80.00 daily; £485.00–£508.00 weekly
Lunch available: 1200–1400 (bar lunches)

Evening meal 1900 (last orders 2030)
Bedrooms: 6 double, 3 twin, 2 suites
Bathrooms: 11 en-suite
Parking for 50
Cards accepted: Mastercard, Visa, Amex, Switch/Delta

341 THE BELFRY COUNTRY HOTEL

HIGHLY COMMENDED

Yarcombe, Honiton, Devon EX14 9BD Tel (01404) 861234 Fax (01404) 861579

This small luxury hotel is tastefully converted from the Victorian village school. Each en-suite room is individually furnished, comprehensively equipped, and has lovely countryside views. The cosy candle-lit restaurant with log fire serves Jackie's scrumptious home cooking, using all fresh local produce. Ideally located for walking the countryside and coast, visiting the many National Trust properties, gardens and places of scenic beauty nearby, and a convenient stop-over en-route for Cornwall. Phone Jackie or Tony Rees for the hotel information package and brochure.

Bed & Breakfast per night: single occupancy from £39.00–£44.00; double room from £59.00–£68.00
Half board per person: £39.00–£52.95 daily; £273.00–£297.00 weekly
Evening meal 1900 (last orders 2100)

Bedrooms: 3 double, 2 twin, 1 triple
Bathrooms: 6 en-suite
Parking for 10
Cards accepted: Mastercard, Visa, Amex, Switch/Delta

342 FARTHINGS HOTEL AND RESTAURANT

HIGHLY COMMENDED

Hatch Beauchamp, Taunton, Somerset TA3 6SG Tel (01823) 480664 Fax (01823) 481118

Farthings is a charming Georgian hotel in the pretty Somerset village of Hatch Beauchamp. The hotel is ideally located and easily accessible from the M5 and A303, making it the perfect base for discovering the villages, National Trust properties and lovely countryside of Somerset, or as a stop over on journeys further west. With eight spacious guest rooms, elegant lounges and an excellent award-winning restaurant, all set in three acres of gardens. Our guests are assured of a warm welcome and a restful few days. Short breaks and golf packages are available all year.

Bed & Breakfast per night: single occupancy from £55.00–£65.00; double room from £80.00–£90.00
Half board per person: £47.50–£58.50 daily
Evening meal 1900 (last orders 2100)

Bedrooms: 4 double, 4 twin
Bathrooms: 8 en-suite
Parking for 27
Cards accepted: Mastercard, Visa, Amex, Switch/Delta

Entries are cross referenced by number to the maps on pages 120–121

343 BURNT HOUSE FARM

HIGHLY COMMENDED

Waterlip, West Cranmore, Shepton Mallet, Somerset BA4 4RN Tel (01749) 880280

Our charming refurbished period farmhouse offers character features, low beamed ceilings, pitch pine floors, and an inglenook fireplace (fires lit in the winter). Heated bedrooms have private showers or bathrooms, lace-canopied beds, colour TVs, complimentary refreshments/toiletries, clock radios, trouser presses and flowers. Morning newspapers can be ordered to accompany your plentiful, choice breakfast. Quality meals in nearby pub. Spacious parking or garage space available. Full sized snooker table. No smoking. A warm welcome and attentive service. Mendip Hill location.

Bed & Breakfast per night: single occupancy maximum £27.50; double room from £40.00–£44.00

Bedrooms: 2 double, 1 twin
Bathrooms: 1 en-suite, 2 private
Parking for 14

344 BOWLISH HOUSE

HIGHLY COMMENDED

Coombe Lane, Shepton Mallet, Somerset BA4 5JD Tel (01749) 342022 Fax (01749) 342022

An elegant Georgian restaurant with rooms, wonderfully counterbalanced by the relaxed atmosphere. The award-winning restaurant and wine list are famous for their range and eclectic mix of modern classics and local produce. Shepton Mallet is a market town on the south-west slopes of the Mendip Hills, just ten minutes from the cathedral city of Wells. It is an ideal centre for exploring nearby Bath, Stourhead, Longleat, Glastonbury and Cheddar.

Bed & Breakfast per night: single occupancy £48.00; double room £58.00
Half board per person: £46.50 daily; £325.50 weekly
Lunch available: by appointment
Evening meal 1900 (last orders 2130)

Bedrooms: 2 double, 1 twin
Bathrooms: 3 en-suite
Parking for 10
Cards accepted: Mastercard, Visa, Amex

345 BERYL

HIGHLY COMMENDED

Beryl, Wells, Somerset BA5 3JP Tel (01749) 678738 Fax (01749) 670508

'Beryl' – a precious gem in a perfect setting. Small 19th-century Gothic mansion, set in peaceful gardens, one mile from the centre of Wells. Well placed for touring the area. Offers comfortable, well-equipped bedrooms and relaxed use of the beautifully furnished reception rooms. Dinner is served with elegant style using fresh produce from the vegetable garden and local supplies. Children and pets are welcome. Outdoor heated pool, June-September. Open all year, except Christmas.

Bed & Breakfast per night: single occupancy from £50.00–£75.00; double room from £65.00–£85.00
Half board per person: £52.50–£62.50 daily; £367.50–£437.50 weekly
Evening meal 2000

Bedrooms: 3 double, 4 twin
Bathrooms: 7 en-suite
Parking for 14
Open all year except Christmas
Cards accepted: Mastercard, Visa

346 GLENCOT HOUSE

HIGHLY COMMENDED

Glencot Lane, Wookey Hole, near Wells, Somerset BA5 1BH Tel (01749) 677160 Fax (01749) 670210

Idyllically set in eighteen acres of gardens and parkland with river frontage, this elegantly furnished Victorian mansion offers high-class accommodation and excellent cuisine. Glencot has a homely atmosphere and friendly service. Facilities abound, with a small indoor pool, sauna, snooker, table-tennis, private fishing and more.

Bed & Breakfast per night: single room from £57.50–£60.00; double room from £80.00–£95.00
Half board per person: £65.00–£75.00 daily; £345.00–£370.00 weekly
Evening meal 1830 (last orders 2030)

Bedrooms: 3 single, 8 double, 2 twin
Bathrooms: 13 en-suite
Parking for 21
Cards accepted: Mastercard, Visa, Amex

347 TOR FARM

HIGHLY COMMENDED

Nyland, Cheddar, Somerset BS27 3UD Tel (01934) 743710 Fax (01934) 743710

Our working farm is situated on the beautiful Somerset levels, with open views from every window. The farmhouse is fully central-heated and has log fires on cold evenings in the guests' own lounge. En-suite and four-poster bedrooms available, some with private patios. Ideal base for visiting Bath, Wells, Glastonbury, Cheddar Gorge and the coast.

Bed & Breakfast per night: single room from £21.00–£27.00; double room from £35.00–£44.00

Bedrooms: 1 single, 5 double, 1 twin, 1 family room
Bathrooms: 5 en-suite, 2 public
Parking for 10
Cards accepted: Mastercard, Visa

348 APSLEY HOUSE HOTEL

HIGHLY COMMENDED

141 Newbridge Hill, Bath BA1 3PT Tel (01225) 336966 Fax (01225) 425462 E-mail apsleyhouse@easynet.co.uk

David and Annie Lanz warmly welcome guests into their elegant Georgian house. Beautifully proportioned reception rooms overlook the pretty garden. Fine antiques and oil paintings create a gracious but relaxed atmosphere. En-suite bedrooms are all individually decorated and furnished, offering TVs, direct dial telephones, and tea/coffee-making facilities. Breakfast is a delight, with full English breakfast and house specialities. Local information available. Just over one mile west of the city centre. Private car park. Licensed bar. Internet: http://www.gratton.co.uk/apsley

Bed & Breakfast per night: single occupancy from £50.00–£65.00; double room from £65.00–£95.00

Bedrooms: 5 double, 2 twin, 1 triple
Bathrooms: 8 en-suite
Parking for 10
Cards accepted: Mastercard, Visa, Amex, Switch/Delta

Entries are cross referenced by number to the maps on pages 120–121

349 HOLLY LODGE

DE LUXE

8 Upper Oldfield Park, Bath BA2 3JZ Tel (01225) 424042 Fax (01225) 481138

This charming Victorian town house commands panoramic views of the city and is delightfully furnished with individually-designed bedrooms, some with four-posters, and superb bathrooms. Elegant and stylish, it is owned and operated with meticulous attention to detail by George Hall. Superb breakfasts are enjoyed in the appealing breakfast room with yellow and green decor. Furnished with antiques, this immaculate establishment makes a pleasant base for touring Bath and the Cotswolds.

Bed & Breakfast per night: single room from £48.00–£55.00; double room from £75.00–£89.00

Bedrooms: 1 single, 4 double, 2 twin
Bathrooms: 7 en-suite
Parking for 8
Cards accepted: Mastercard, Visa, Diners, Amex, Switch/Delta

350 KENNARD HOTEL

HIGHLY COMMENDED

11 Henrietta Street, Bath BA2 6LL Tel (01225) 310472 Fax (01225) 460054 E-mail kennard@dircon.co.uk

The Kennard Hotel, a Georgian town house with its own charm and character, is quietly situated within minutes of the city centre, Abbey and Roman Baths. Built in 1794 for the grand era of Bath's elegance and prosperity, it has been thoughtfully restored to provide every modern comfort. Personally managed by the proprietors, Richard Ambler and Malcolm Wright, who extend to you 'a warm welcome'. It really is 'Somewhere Special' and the ideal setting to enjoy the delights of this famous city.

Bed & Breakfast per night: single room from £38.00–£45.00; double room from £65.00–£85.00

Bedrooms: 2 single, 9 double, 1 twin, 1 family room
Bathrooms: 11 en-suite, 1 public
Cards accepted: Mastercard, Visa, Diners, Amex, Switch/Delta

351 VILLA MAGDALA HOTEL

HIGHLY COMMENDED

Henrietta Road, Bath BA2 6LX Tel (01225) 466329 Fax (01225) 483207 E-mail villa@btinternet.com

Ideally situated, this charming Victorian town house hotel enjoys a peaceful location overlooking Henrietta Park, only five minutes' level walk to the city centre and the Roman Baths. The spacious rooms all have private bathrooms, TVs, direct dial telephones and refreshment trays. Private parking for guests is available in the hotel grounds. Special mid-week short breaks are available from November to March.

Bed & Breakfast per night: single room from £50.00–£65.00; double room from £60.00–£95.00

Bedrooms: 2 single, 9 double, 5 twin, 1 triple
Bathrooms: 17 en-suite
Parking for 17
Cards accepted: Mastercard, Visa, Amex, Switch/Delta

352 SIENA HOTEL

HIGHLY COMMENDED

24/25 Pulteney Road, Bath BA2 4EZ Tel (01225) 425495 Fax (01225) 469029

The Siena is one of the most attractive small hotels in Bath, situated within a few minutes' level walk from the centre. It is a fine example of early Victorian architecture, and is built within a walled garden, affording exceptional views of the city and the medieval Abbey. The interior combines elegant decoration with superb classical furnishings, creating an atmosphere of warmth and tranquillity. We pride ourselves on our quality accommodation, friendly approach and flexibility of service.

Bed & Breakfast per night: single room from £42.50–£57.50; double room from £57.50–£87.50

Bedrooms: 2 single, 6 double, 2 twin, 3 triple, 2 family rooms
Bathrooms: 15 en-suite
Parking for 15
Cards accepted: Mastercard, Visa, Diners, Amex, Switch/Delta

Claverton American Museum

THE CITY OF BATH, so quintessentially English, attracts American tourists like a magnet, so it is perhaps appropriate that just outside the city is a museum which offers a good measure of cultural exchange. Claverton Manor, a large 19th-century neo-classical mansion set in beautiful grounds overlooking the peaceful Avon valley, is now the American Museum in Britain (tel: 01225 460503) and is devoted entirely to the cultural history of the United States.

The museum has been based at Claverton since 1961 and was the brainchild of two Americans, Dallas Pratt and John Judkyn, whose desire it was to encourage greater mutual understanding between Britain and America. The bulk of the museum's collection takes the form of furnished rooms brought, often in their entirety, from houses in the United States, and representing different aspects of American society. Other galleries are devoted to specific crafts (pewter, silver, glass, textiles) or themes (North American Indians, maritime history, westward expansion).

The museum is something of a revelation in the sheer range and variety of cultural influences on display; it vividly demonstrates the enormous mixture of ethnic and social influences which were combined in the melting pot of American society, and the contrasts are immense. One room, for example, contains the austere furniture of the Shakers, a puritanical religious sect which settled in New England in the late 18th century. Utility and simplicity were the hallmarks of their plain, but beautiful, hand-made wooden furniture. Roughly contemporary, but a world apart, is the New Orleans bedroom. Its factory-made, dark mahogany furniture is heavily adorned with curly, baroque flourishes while curtains and carpets riot with elaborate patterns. Displays on American Indians and Spanish colonists compete for space with less well-known ethnic groups. The Pennsylvania Dutch, for example (actually 17th-century refugees from Germany and Switzerland) brought a colourful decorative tradition manifested in vividly painted furniture and kitchenware.

The large number of different styles and traditions demanding representation has meant that the exhibits have spilled out into the manor's immediate surroundings. While one part of the grounds is planted as a colonial herb garden, another is a replica of George Washington's garden at Mount Vernon. An 18th-century Dutch summerhouse is furnished as a 19th-century American milliner's shop, and a stable block is devoted to a delightful collection of American naive and folk art.

Entries are cross referenced by number to the maps on pages 120–121

353 THE BATH TASBURGH HOTEL

HIGHLY COMMENDED

Warminster Road, Bath BA2 6SH Tel (01225) 425096 Fax (01225) 463842

This beautiful Victorian mansion stands in lovely gardens with spectacular views, providing ideal country comfort in a city setting and convenient for the magnificent Georgian setting of Bath. All the bedrooms are en-suite and tastefully furnished, having all the many extras to ensure a comfortable stay. Four-poster and spacious family bedrooms. Elegant drawing room and stunning conservatory. Evening meals served. Ample car parking available. The adjacent canal towpath provides a scenic walk into the city centre.

Bed & Breakfast per night: single room from £48.00–£55.00; double room from £65.00–£78.00
Half board per person: £49.00–£55.50 daily; £336.00–£378.00 weekly
Evening meal 1930 (last orders 2000)

Bedrooms: 1 single, 7 double, 1 twin, 3 family rooms
Bathrooms: 12 en-suite
Parking for 15
Cards accepted: Mastercard, Visa, Amex, Switch/Delta

354 THE BATH SPA HOTEL

HIGHLY COMMENDED

Sydney Road, Bath BA2 6JF Tel (01225) 444424 Fax (01225) 444006

The award-winning Bath Spa Hotel, a former Georgian mansion, is set in seven acres of lovingly restored gardens just ten minutes' walk from the centre of Bath. The elegance of the city is recreated in a traditionally English style, combining exceptional comfort with attentive personal service and friendly informality. With a choice of restaurants – the cosmopolitan atmosphere of the Vellore, or the distinctive Alfresco in the Colonnade – and for relaxation, the Laurels Health and Leisure Spa.

Bed & Breakfast per night: double room from £79.00–£119.00
Lunch available: 1200–1400
Evening meal 1830 (last orders 2200)

Bedrooms: 7 single, 45 double, 46 twin
Bathrooms: 98 en-suite
Parking for 156
Cards accepted: Mastercard, Visa, Diners, Amex, Switch/Delta

355 BROMPTON HOUSE

HIGHLY COMMENDED

Saint Johns Road, Bath BA2 6PT Tel (01225) 420972 Fax (01225) 420505 E-mail BROMPTON_HOUSE@compuserve.com

A charming former Georgian rectory (1777) set in beautiful secluded gardens, Brompton House has been converted and extended with exquisite care and attractive furnishings and is only a few minutes' level walk from the city centre. All en-suite rooms are equipped with colour television, direct dial telephone, radio, hairdryer and tea/coffee-making facilities. A very friendly welcome is assured from the Selby family in a relaxing and informal atmosphere. Car park. Winter short breaks available. Strictly no smoking.

Bed & Breakfast per night: single room from £32.00–£55.00; double room from £55.00–£80.00

Bedrooms: 2 single, 9 double, 5 twin, 2 family rooms
Bathrooms: 18 en-suite
Parking for 18
Cards accepted: Mastercard, Visa, Amex, Switch/Delta

At-a-glance symbols are explained on the flap inside the back cover

356 COMBE GROVE MANOR HOTEL AND COUNTRY CLUB

HIGHLY COMMENDED

Brassknocker Hill, Monkton Combe, Bath BA2 7HS Tel (01225) 834644 Fax (01225) 834961

Set in 82 acres of gardens and woodlands with panoramic views, this 18th-century elegant manor house hotel, with its 21st-century sports and leisure amenities, hosts 40 individually-designed bedrooms, from modern de luxe to four-poster suites. There is a choice of two restaurants – the Georgian Restaurant offers superb cuisine and fine dining, while The Manor Vaults offers bistro fare in a more relaxed atmosphere.

Bed & Breakfast per night: single occupancy from £99.00–£270.00; double room from £99.00–£270.00
Half board per person: £130.00–£300.00 daily
Lunch available: 1200–1430 (bar snacks available all day)
Evening meal 1900 (last orders 2130)

Bedrooms: 27 double, 11 twin, 2 triple
Bathrooms: 40 en-suite
Parking for 200
Cards accepted: Mastercard, Visa, Diners, Amex, Switch/Delta

357 WIDBROOK GRANGE

HIGHLY COMMENDED

Trowbridge Road, Widbrook, Bradford-on-Avon, Wiltshire BA15 1UH Tel (01225) 864750 or (01225) 863173 Fax (01225) 862890

An elegant Georgian house with courtyard rooms, exquisitely decorated and furnished with antiques, and all rooms having baths and showers en-suite. Set in its own grounds of eleven acres, the emphasis is on peaceful comfort and relaxation. Widbrook Grange has its own magnificent heated indoor swimming pool with a small gymnasium area, and superb conference facilities in the Manvers Suite. Evening dinner is served Monday to Thursday and all is home-prepared, with an interesting wine list.

Bed & Breakfast per night: single occupancy from £55.00–£79.00; double room from £89.00–£99.00
Evening meal 1830 (last orders 2000)

Bedrooms: 13 double, 3 twin, 2 triple, 1 family room
Bathrooms: 19 en-suite, 1 public
Parking for 50
Cards accepted: Mastercard, Visa, Diners, Amex, Switch/Delta

358 THE OLD HOUSE

HIGHLY COMMENDED

Frome Road, Southwick, Trowbridge, Wiltshire BA14 9QF Tel (01225) 752761

An imposing Grade II Listed Queen Anne country house surrounded by a garden of magnificent trees, lawns and old fashioned roses. A romantic converted coach house provides unusual extra accommodation. The house dates from 1650 and has a very special atmosphere, with stone mullioned windows, a winding Jacobean oak staircase and inglenook fireplace. Its position in the village of Southwick, close to the Wiltshire/Somerset border, is ideal for exploring Bath, the West Country or the Cotswolds.

Bed & Breakfast per night: single occupancy from £20.00–£25.00; double room from £35.00–£44.00

Bedrooms: 3 double
Bathrooms: 2 en-suite, 1 private
Parking for 4

Entries are cross referenced by number to the maps on pages 120–121

359 HOWARDS HOUSE HOTEL

HIGHLY COMMENDED

Teffont Evias, Salisbury, Wiltshire SP3 5RJ Tel (01722) 716392 or (01722) 716821 Fax (01722) 716820

A 17th-century dower house in an idyllic rural setting. High-quality accommodation, an award-winning restaurant and an atmosphere of tranquillity and friendliness.

Bed & Breakfast per night: single occupancy from £75.00–£95.00; double room from £95.00–£135.00
Half board per person: £72.50–£100.00 daily
Lunch available: 1230–1400 (Sunday only)
Evening meal 1930 (last orders 2130)

Bedrooms: 8 double, 1 twin
Bathrooms: 9 en-suite
Parking for 12
Cards accepted: Mastercard, Visa, Diners, Amex, Switch/Delta

360 SPOUT COTTAGE

HIGHLY COMMENDED

Stert, Devizes, Wiltshire SN10 3JD Tel (01380) 724336

In an idyllic, peaceful retreat, Spout Cottage is located in the secluded and attractive valley of Stert and is well away from the road. This picturesque and unspoilt part of Wiltshire is a few minutes from Devizes, an historic and bustling market town, and an easy driving distance from places like Bath, Stonehenge and Avebury. The cottage is spacious, comfortable and tastefully furnished. Delicious and imaginative meals are served in the south-facing conservatory, overlooking the beautiful garden.

Bed & Breakfast per night: single room from £18.00–£20.00; double room from £32.00–£36.00
Evening meal 2000

Bedrooms: 1 single, 1 twin
Bathrooms: 2 public
Parking for 4

361 MARRIDGE HILL

HIGHLY COMMENDED

Ramsbury, Marlborough, Wiltshire SN8 2HG Tel (01672) 520237 Fax (01672) 520053 E-mail dando@impedaci.demon.co.uk

Our family home is set in glorious countryside, yet is only one hour's drive from Heathrow Airport. You will be warmly welcomed into a relaxed, informal atmosphere. There are three comfortable, attractive bedrooms, one with spacious en-suite facilities, and both bathrooms have power showers. Pleasant drawing and dining rooms, and an acre of well-kept garden. Good pubs and restaurants nearby. Ideal base for visiting Avebury, Bath, Oxford and the Cotswolds. A no smoking house.

Bed & Breakfast per night: single occupancy from £23.00–£28.00; double room from £36.00–£42.00

Bedrooms: 3 twin
Bathrooms: 1 en-suite, 1 public
Parking for 10
Cards accepted: Mastercard, Visa

362 Cricklade Hotel and Country Club — Highly Commended

Common Hill, Swindon, Wiltshire SN6 6HA Tel (01793) 750751 Fax (01793) 751767

This beautiful and dignified house is set in extensive grounds, offering a range of sporting activities including a golf course with an on-site golf professional. The luxurious lounge, warmed by open fires in winter, extends through to a magnificent Victorian conservatory, and all the bedrooms are smartly furnished and fully equipped. The first-class restaurant offers a varied and interesting menu with an emphasis on fresh local produce and careful presentation. Regular live entertainment, dinner dances and barbecues.

Bed & Breakfast per night: single room from £78.00–£94.00; double room from £96.00–£115.00
Lunch available: 1200–1400
Evening meal 1900 (last orders 2200)

Bedrooms: 6 single, 33 double, 7 twin
Bathrooms: 46 en-suite, 4 public
Parking for 100
Cards accepted: Mastercard, Visa, Amex, Switch/Delta

14 S SP

Swindon the railway town

IN THE MIDDLE of the 19th century Swindon underwent a rapid expansion. In 1831 the Wiltshire market town had only 1,742 inhabitants; by the end of the century the population stood at 40,000, and 30 years later 65,000. The reason for this dramatic growth was the advent of the railway. Not only did the newly founded Great Western Railway (GWR) route its London–Bristol line via Swindon, but it also chose to locate its Locomotive Carriage and Wagon Works here. This vast enterprise manufactured all the rolling stock and equipment for the company; at its height it covered 320 acres (129 hectares) and employed 12,000 people. As soon as it opened in 1843 it attracted a flood of prospective employees to the town and proceeded to dominate Swindon's life and commerce for the next hundred years. Its legacy in the town remains strong.

Close to Swindon's station are rows of pretty Victorian stone-built cottages, remarkable for their uniformity and their 'unimproved' state. These were built by the GWR in the 1840s to house its growing workforce, and were designed as a model village. No. 34 Farringdon Road is now a museum (tel: 01793 466553) furnished as it might have been in the late 19th century when it was home to an engine driver and his family.

Overcrowding was a continual problem in the village, as the provision of housing failed to meet demand. In one notorious example, a one-bedroomed house was occupied by eleven people: man, wife, five children and four lodgers. The GWR attempted to solve the problem by building an impressive, gothic-looking, three-storey building as a hostel for single men. Known as 'The Barracks', it was never a success, since the men preferred the relative freedom of lodging in the village. After being used as a Wesleyan chapel, it is now the GWR museum (tel: 01793 466555). Here the railway enthusiast will find an impressive permanent exhibition of locomotives and memorabilia dating from GWR's century of railway supremacy, including special exhibits on Isambard Kingdom Brunel (GWR's chief engineer) and the Swindon works.

In 1948 the GWR was absorbed into the nationalised British Railway network and the works were gradually wound down, finally closing in 1986. The site, accessible by subway from the village, contains 12 listed buildings and is currently being developed for commercial and recreational purposes.

Entries are cross referenced by number to the maps on pages 120–121

South & South East *England*

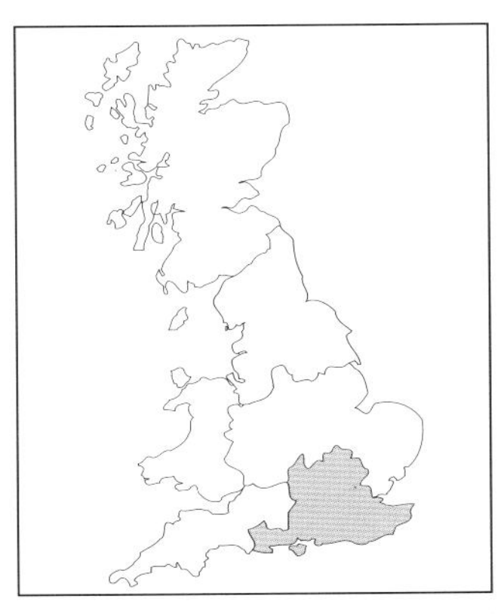

ENGLAND'S MOST populous region is also its leafiest corner. Much of Hampshire's chalk downland is covered in either beech or yew (known locally as the 'Hampshire weed') while in spring the Kentish orchards are thick with the heady aromas of apple, cherry and pear blossom. By autumn the squirrels of Sussex feast upon sweet chestnuts and acorns, though the poorer, sandy soils of neighbouring Surrey suit birch and pine. On the southern edge of this heathland, and thickly clad in broad-leaved forest, is Leith Hill, the highest point in the North Downs – and one of the finest viewpoints of the South-East.

Selborne, hiding amongst the trees a few miles south of Alton, is an attractive stone-built village in a region well supplied with attractive villages. Others in this part of the world include Chawton, forever linked with Jane Austen, and New Alresford, rebuilt in fine Georgian style after a devastating fire: to this day a bye-law forbids thatched roofs. If time runs slowly here, then across the Solent on the Isle of Wight the clocks seem to have stopped at some indeterminate period between the Wars. Three picturesque settlements to explore on lazy summer days are Newtown, Calbourne and Shorwell. Time may look benignly on the island's viticulturists, too, for some believe that climatic change will make these some of the best vineyards in Europe. From

The Tolpuddle Martyrs

In the Dorset of 1833 agricultural wages had fallen below the bread-line. When further reduction looked likely, six farmworkers joined – and swore loyalty to – a trade union. Landowners, desperate to prevent any return to the unrest of past years, secured conviction of the six under an obscure clause in the 1797 Mutiny Act in which administering false oaths was deemed a crime. Outcry greeted the sentence of seven years' transportation and after two years the six were fully pardoned. The Tolpuddle Martyrs Museum (tel: 01305 848237) tells their remarkable story.

Mad Jack Fuller

Nineteenth-century patron of the arts, bon viveur and local squire, 'Mad' Jack Fuller lives on thanks to his abiding passion for follies. His grave in the churchyard at Brightling, East Sussex, is a 25ft (7.5m)-high stone pyramid. Despite his wish to be interred at table, dressed for dinner and resplendent in top hat, he rests – in conventional repose – in the ground below. Nearby edifices include the 'Tower', a gothic-looking building with a battlemented top, and the Sugar Loaf, reputedly built in a night to enable Fuller to 'win' a bet that the spire of Dallington church was visible from his windows.

the jagged western tip of the island Poole Harbour, its captive Brownsea Island and the Purbeck Ridge all heave into sight. One of the rivers flowing into the huge natural harbour (almost a hundred miles (160km) round) is the delightfully named River Piddle. Following this upstream leads you first to Throop, then to Affpuddle and on to Tolpuddle, home to the renowned 19th-century martyrs. Should you prefer to stay on the coast, some of the South-East's least spoilt beaches, as at Studland, beckon.

Moving north and east to the meeting of Hampshire, Berkshire and Wiltshire you reach the highest chalk down in England. Inkpen Hill, despite being near the hamlet of Buttermere, offers beauty of a gentler nature than its Lakeland namesake. Those admiring the panorama a few centuries ago might also have seen the sombre sight of a hanged felon on Combe Gibbet. The road descending from these heights leads into Berkshire and the small market town of Hungerford, renowned for its High Street lined with handsome antique shops. The restored Kennet and Avon Canal runs through the town and is quite the best way to explore the area. For those with a nautical bent, leisure craft are also available for hire on the Thames. One of the most appealing stretches is at Goring Gap: to the south lie the Berkshire Downs, to the north and east the slopes of the Chilterns clad in the beech woods that still feed the local furniture industry. From here choosing which way to head is a problem: upstream to Oxford with its sublime architecture and welcoming pubs, downstream past the opulence of Henley and Cliveden, or into the Chilterns, whose sumptuous brick-built villages, once home to highwaymen, are now popular amongst discerning London commuters. There's always the longer westward detour to the unassuming Oxfordshire town of Faringdon, whose features number a magnificent 13th-century tithe barn and the intriguing Folly Hill.

Leaving the Chilterns behind and venturing north, you reach Buckingham, once the administrative town of the county that bears its name. However, local government abandoned Buckingham in favour of the busier Aylesbury in the 18th century, and not that much seems to have happened since, making it an excellent place for unhurried exploration. Fine Georgian townhouses in narrow streets reward visitors prepared to head off the beaten track. North once again are two contrasting attractions: within a couple of miles of one another are the sound and fury of Silverstone, home of the British Grand Prix each July, and the serenity of the gardens of Stowe.

Kent is divided literally and figuratively by its principal river, the Medway. Its eastern banks look across woods, hopfields and orchards towards the distant spire of Canterbury Cathedral and the busy port of Dover; the residents of this part of the county are traditionally known as 'Men of Kent'. The western banks of the Medway look up to the heights of the North Downs and beyond to the outskirts of London; those that live in this more urban portion are 'Kentish Men'. Known for its glorious castles (such as Hever, Leeds and Scotney), villages (Patrixbourne, Chilham and Chiddingstone) and stately homes (Knole, Ightham Mote and Penshurst), Kent also boasts lesser-known attractions such as Reculver's remarkable Norman church, the attractive city of Rochester and the Royal Military Canal near Appledore.

Indeed the strength of the South Coast fortifications – of which the Military Canal is part – testifies to the fact that Kent and Sussex have, from Roman times until the Battle of Britain, seen more than their fair share of would-be invaders. A total of 74 Martello Towers, running from Folkestone to Seaford in East Sussex, were built to protect Britain from the threat of invasion by Napoleon. Once the threat of attack diminished 19th-century engineers turned their skills to constructions dedicated to pleasure rather than defence. Brighton, playground for London and the South and currently enjoying something of a renaissance, acquired two piers (one under restoration) and the Promenade. Present-day visitors are just as likely to pass the time in the Lanes (twisting alleyways full of unusual shops and cafés) or in one of the town's lively clubs. Inland, small, characterful towns such as Arundel, set amid unspoilt Sussex scenery, provide peaceful alternatives. The South Downs Way stretches from Eastbourne in the east over the Hampshire border towards Winchester. The views are consistently superb.

The South-East's other chalk ridge, the North Downs, contains countryside of a splendour that belies its proximity to London. Sleepy villages with intriguing names such as Abinger Hammer and Friday Street complete a picture of English rural beauty. Surrey's busy towns, such as Dorking, Farnham and Guildford, all have equally busy histories – and the architecture to match.

Left: Shaftesbury, Dorset; inset: Bodiam Castle, East Sussex

Selborne's natural history

Selborne, in a Hampshire backwater south of Alton, is largely synonymous with the work of late 18th-century clergyman-turned-naturalist, Gilbert White. Through a deep love of nature – and profound coach-sickness – White spent much of his time in the village of his birth. He eventually recorded his minute observation of natural phenomena in his masterpiece, The Natural History of Selborne, which has never been out of print since publication in 1789. His attractive home, The Wakes, is now a museum dedicated to his memory (tel: 01420 511275).

The Gardens of Stowe

Perhaps the finest statement of the art of the 18th-century garden lives on at Stowe, near Buckingham. John Vanbrugh, William Kent, James Gibbs and 'Capability' Brown – the most talented gardeners and architects of their day – went to great lengths to create a landscape remodelled and replanted to look as natural as possible, in order to match the aesthetic blueprint of ancient Rome. To this end, grottoes were built, lakes dug, columns erected and monuments – thirty, all told – sited with consummate care. The National Trust is now restoring these majestic gardens.

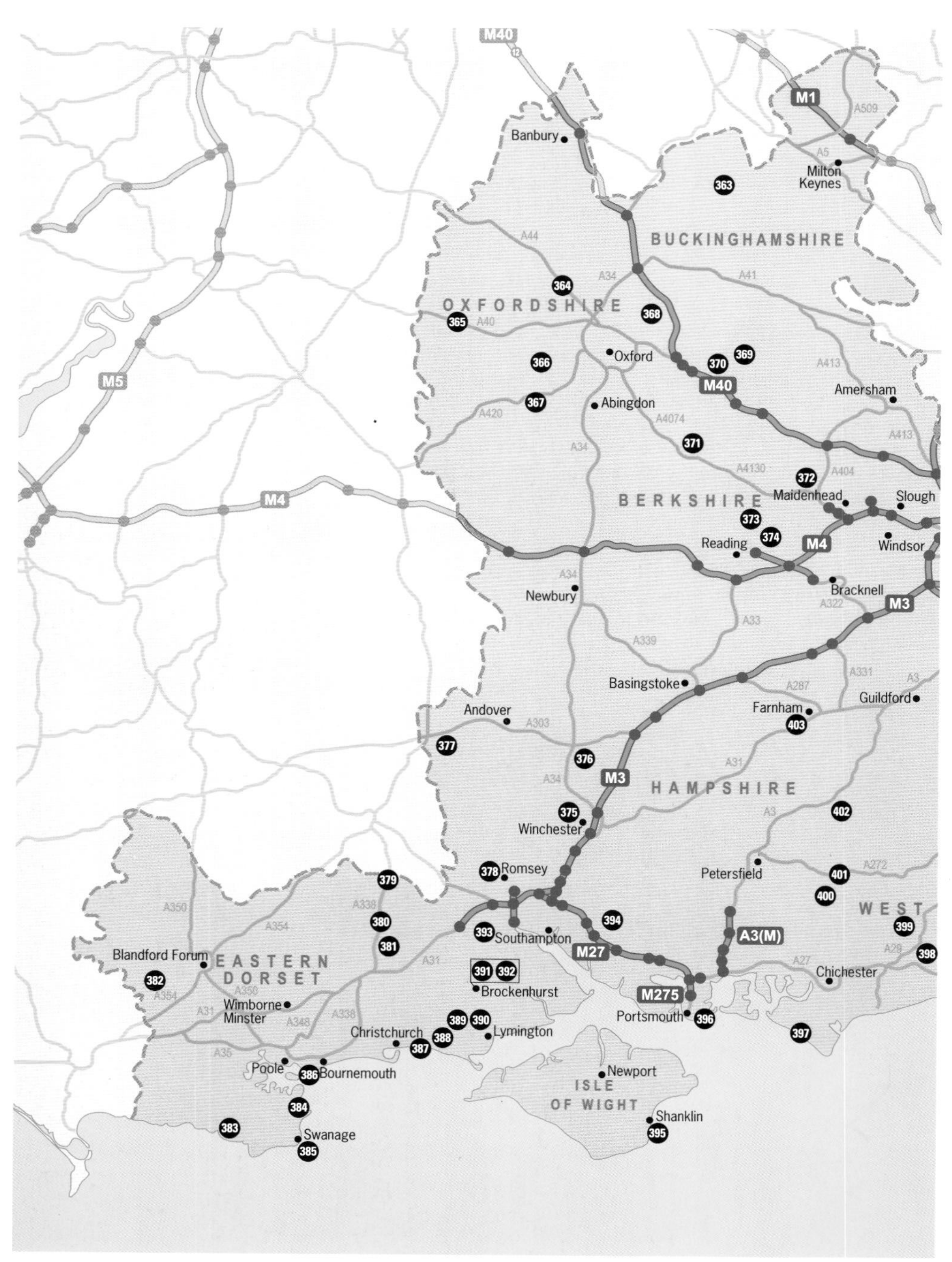
M40
M1
A509
Banbury
A5
Milton Keynes
363
BUCKINGHAMSHIRE
A44
A34
A41
364
OXFORDSHIRE
368
365
A40
Oxford
369
370
366
M40
A413
Amersham
M5
367
Abingdon
A420
A4074
A34
371
A413
A4130
372
A404
Maidenhead
Slough
M4
BERKSHIRE
373
374
Reading
M4
Windsor
A34
Newbury
Bracknell
A322
M3
A33
A339
Basingstoke
A331
A287
A3
Guildford
Andover
Farnham
A303
403
377
376
A31
A34
M3
HAMPSHIRE
375
A3
402
Winchester
A272
Petersfield
378
Romsey
401
379
400
WEST
A338
A350
A354
380
394
399
393
Southampton
A3(M)
381
A29
398
Blandford Forum
EASTERN DORSET
A31
M27
A27
382
391
392
Chichester
A354
A350
Brockenhurst
M275
A31
Wimborne Minster
A348
A338
Portsmouth
396
389
390
Christchurch
Lymington
388
397
387
A35
Newport
Poole
386
Bournemouth
ISLE OF WIGHT
384
Shanklin
383
Swanage
395
385

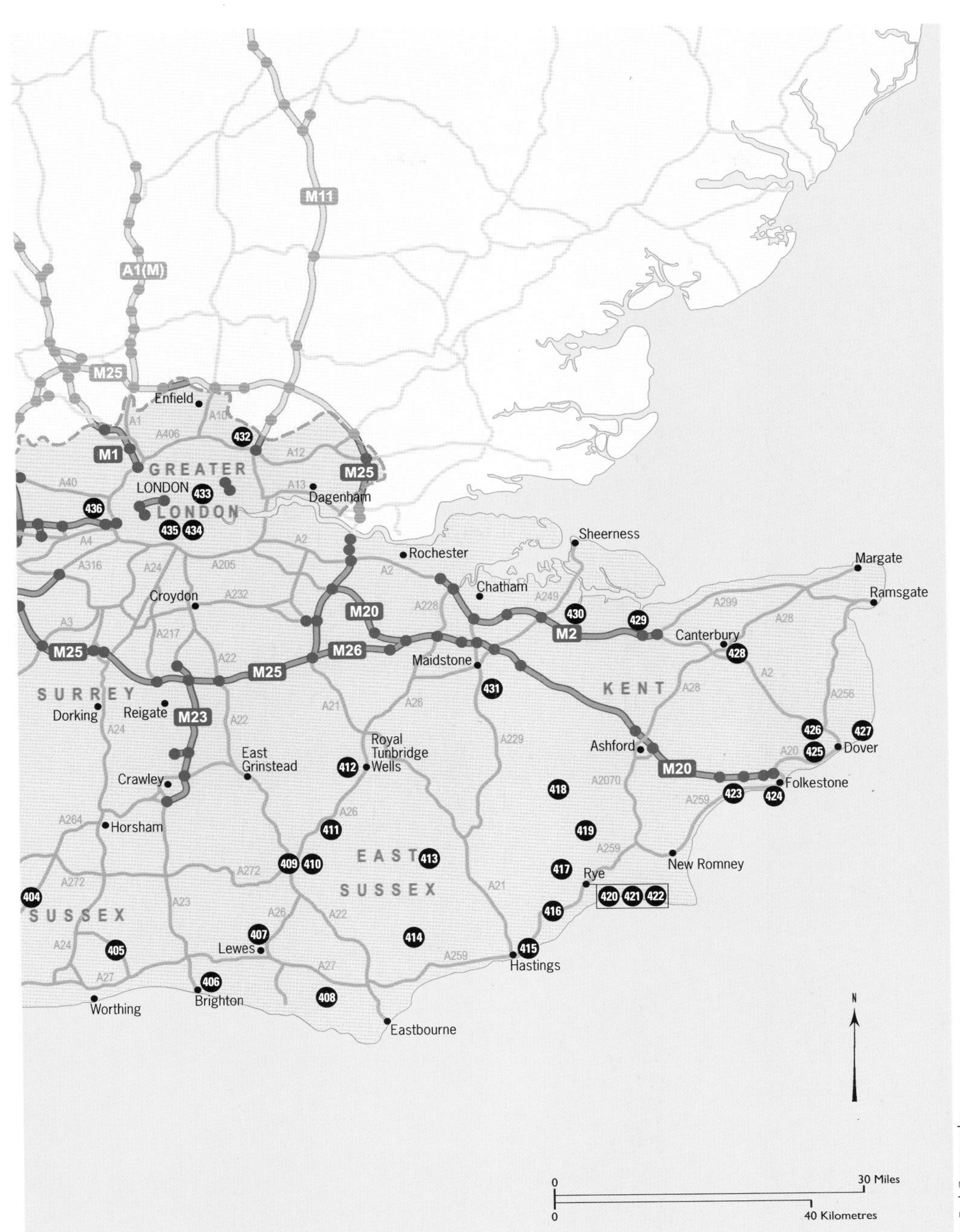

Colin Earl Cartography

363 VILLIERS HOTEL

HIGHLY COMMENDED

3 Castle Street, Buckingham, Buckinghamshire MK18 1BS Tel (01280) 822444 Fax (01280) 822113

When we created Villiers Hotel from the old Swan and Castle Inn, we set out to build a very special and individual hotel. Drawing upon the character of the four-hundred-year-old hostelry we included the highest quality facilities and services, with comfort a priority for you, our guest – a home away from home.

Bed & Breakfast per night: single room from £59.00–£80.00; double room from £79.00–£120.00
Half board per person: £77.75–£97.75 daily
Lunch available: 1230–1400
Evening meal 1900 (last orders 2230)

Bedrooms: 3 single, 18 double, 17 twin
Bathrooms: 38 en-suite
Parking for 36
Cards accepted: Mastercard, Visa, Diners, Amex, Switch/Delta

364 SHIPTON GLEBE

HIGHLY COMMENDED

Woodstock, Oxford, Oxfordshire OX20 1QQ Tel (01993) 812688 Fax (01993) 813142 E-mail phase@patrol.i-way.co.uk

This lovely country house, set in nine acres of garden/parkland, is situated on the edge of historic Woodstock, close to Blenheim Palace. All the rooms are en-suite, luxuriously furnished, and incorporate sitting room facilities. Breakfasts are served in the conservatory overlooking the gardens, and evening meals – available by prior arrangement – can be served in the elegant dining room. You will find that Shipton Glebe is the perfect setting for that special and relaxing few days away.

Bed & Breakfast per night: double room from £60.00–£70.00
Half board per person: £85.00–£95.00 daily
Evening meal 1930 (last orders 2030)

Bedrooms: 1 double, 1 twin, 1 family room
Bathrooms: 3 en-suite, 1 public
Parking for 6
Open: April–October
Cards accepted: Mastercard, Visa, Switch/Delta

365 BURFORD HOUSE HOTEL

HIGHLY COMMENDED

99 High Street, Burford, Oxford, Oxfordshire OX18 4QA Tel (01993) 823151 Fax (01993) 823240

Situated in one of the Cotswold's most historic towns, Burford House is perfectly placed for exploring this lovely area. Run with care by owners Jane and Simon Henty, importance is placed on comfort, a relaxed atmosphere and attention to detail, and the house is cosy and intimate with a wealth of personal touches. Wonderful breakfasts are served and guests can return to traditional afternoon tea in the sitting rooms or delightful courtyard garden. A warm welcome awaits.

Bed & Breakfast per night: single occupancy from £65.00–£115.00; double room from £75.00–£115.00
Lunch available: 1200–1415

Bedrooms: 6 double, 1 twin
Bathrooms: 7 en-suite
Cards accepted: Mastercard, Visa, Amex, Switch/Delta

Entries are cross referenced by number to the maps on pages 170–171

366 Pinkhill Cottage

HIGHLY COMMENDED

45 Rack End, Standlake, Witney, Oxfordshire OX8 7SA Tel (01865) 300544

A charming 17th-century thatched cottage in half-acre gardens fronting the River Windrush in a quiet Oxfordshire village, offering exclusive, private bed & breakfast accommodation for two. The old stable has been transformed into a sitting room with its own external door and staircase to the hayloft – now an airy double bedroom with en-suite shower room. Many original beams are a feature of our cottage. Standlake is ideal for touring Oxford and the Cotswolds.

Bed & Breakfast per night: single occupancy from £29.00–£30.00; double room from £40.00–£42.00

Bedrooms: 1 double
Bathrooms: 1 en-suite
Parking for 1
Open: February–December

UL TV

367 Fallowfields Country House Hotel

HIGHLY COMMENDED

Kingston Bagpuize with Southmoor, Oxford, Oxfordshire OX13 5BH Tel (01865) 820416 Fax (01865) 821275

The Fallowfields' recipe – take near-organic garden produce, add meticulously chosen meat and fish, mix in a three-hundred-year-old (in parts) manor farmhouse, add interesting company, personal care of the owners, and serve in a candle-lit dining room, preferably by a log fire – leave with your bank manager still talking to you and you have the perfect recipe for a stay on business or pleasure. 'The next step is heaven' said one guest.

Bed & Breakfast per night: single occupancy from £85.00; double room from £95.00
Half board per person: from £76.00 daily; from £532.00 weekly
Evening meal 2000 (last orders 2100)

Bedrooms: 6 double, 2 twin, 2 triple
Bathrooms: 10 en-suite, 1 public
Parking for 23
Cards accepted: Mastercard, Visa, Amex, Switch/Delta

10 S TV SP T

368 Studley Priory Hotel

HIGHLY COMMENDED

Horton cum Studley, Oxford, Oxfordshire OX33 1AZ Tel (01865) 351203 or (01865) 351254 Fax (01865) 351613

Timeless seclusion characterises the wooded setting of Studley Priory, whose exterior has scarcely altered since Elizabethan times. Enjoy fine views of the Chilterns and surrounding countryside. Our restaurant offers modern English cooking complemented by our outstanding wine list. A short drive away are the dreaming spires of Oxford and magnificent Blenheim Palace at Woodstock. Public rooms and master bedrooms contain antique furniture. Log fires in public rooms in the winter months.

Bed & Breakfast per night: single room from £105.00–£145.00; double room from £125.00–£185.00
Half board per person: £55.00–£80.00 daily
Lunch available: 12.00–13.45
Evening meal 1930 (last orders 2130)

Bedrooms: 6 single, 8 double, 5 twin
Bathrooms: 19 en-suite
Parking for 101
Cards accepted: Mastercard, Visa, Diners, Amex

S SP T

369 THE OXFORD BELFRY

♕♕♕♕ HIGHLY COMMENDED

Milton Common, Thame, Oxfordshire OX9 2JW Tel (01844) 279381 Fax (01844) 279624

A privately-owned and extended Tudor-style hotel, situated on the A40 near junctions 7 and 8 of the M40, ten minutes from historic Oxford. The hotel is an ideal location for touring the Thames, the Chilterns, Oxford and the Cotswolds. One hour from London and Birmingham, with Heathrow a 45-minute drive away. Leisure facilities include a heated indoor pool, sauna, sunbed, mini-gym and relaxation area. Charming oak-panelled restaurant.

Bed & Breakfast per night: single room £98.50; double room £124.00
Half board per person: £69.00–£89.00 daily; £390.00–£510.00 weekly
Lunch available: 1230–1400

Evening meal 1930 (last orders 2130)
Bedrooms: 11 single, 54 double, 32 twin
Bathrooms: 97 en-suite
Parking for 200
Cards accepted: Mastercard, Visa, Diners, Amex, Switch/Delta

---

370 THE DAIRY

♕ HIGHLY COMMENDED

Moreton, Thame, Oxfordshire OX9 2HX Tel (01844) 214075 Fax (01844) 214075

This former milking parlour, set in over four acres, provides a beautiful, peaceful and comfortable stay. All bedrooms are bright and airy and include hairdryers, writing tables, fresh flowers, biscuits and comfortable sofas and chairs. There is a large open plan lounge with views of the Chilterns. The property is very convenient for London, either by train (50 minutes from local station), coach or car. Oxford is 20 minutes by car.

Bed & Breakfast per night: single occupancy from £50.00; double room from £60.00

Bedrooms: 3 double
Bathrooms: 3 en-suite
Parking for 6

---

371 MAYS FARM

♕ HIGHLY COMMENDED

Ewelme, Wallingford, Oxfordshire OX10 6QF Tel (01491) 641294 Fax (01491) 641697

A very comfortable bungalow with wonderful views and typically English garden. We are half a mile off the main Henley-on-Thames to Oxford road, up a private drive of chestnut trees. The farm is near the Ridgeway path, Huntercombe golf course, historic Wallingford and the delightful village of Ewelme. A full farmhouse breakfast is provided. Enjoy a restful stay for a night, a weekend, or longer. Forty minutes from Heathrow airport, 8 miles from the M40. Good pubs locally.

Bed & Breakfast per night: single occupancy from £25.00–£30.00; double room from £40.00–£42.00

Bedrooms: 1 twin
Bathrooms: 1 en-suite
Parking for 2

Entries are cross referenced by number to the maps on pages 170–171

372 DANESFIELD HOUSE

HIGHLY COMMENDED

Medmenham, Marlow-on-Thames, Buckinghamshire SL7 2EY Tel (01628) 891010 Fax (01628) 890408

Danesfield House offers one of England's finest award-winning country house hotels, ideally set within the Chiltern Hills in an area of outstanding natural beauty, and yet within only one hour of London. Your stay will be enhanced by fresh flowers from the 65 acres of landscaped gardens. Panoramic views of the River Thames from luxurious bedrooms and a beautiful terrace brasserie have helped establish Danesfield as a very popular destination.

Bed & Breakfast per night: single room from £115.00–£149.00; double room from £130.00–£195.00
Half board per person: £150.00–£185.00 daily
Lunch available: 1200–1400
Evening meal 1830 (last orders 2200)

Bedrooms: 7 single, 61 double, 16 twin, 3 family rooms
Bathrooms: 87 en-suite
Parking for 300
Cards accepted: Mastercard, Visa, Diners, Amex

Lord Berners and Folly Hill

WHEN GERALD TYRWHITT-WILSON, 14th Baron Berners first opened his 140ft (42m) folly to a select gathering of friends in 1935 he displayed the following notice above the entrance: 'Members of the public committing suicide from this tower do so at their own risk'. Most people who ascend the twisting staircase to the tower's splendid octagonal lantern do so for the view, a magnificent panorama of several counties with views to the Berkshire Downs and the White Horse of Uffington. The folly, standing high on a hilltop near Faringdon in Berkshire, is now a much loved local landmark, but plans for its construction were greeted by a storm of protest and the determination of the local council to withhold planning permission. Lord Berners, who had friends in high places, was not to be thwarted however. 'The great point of the tower,' he commented with characteristic insouciance, 'is that it will be entirely useless'. The folly was built and Berners held a dazzling party to celebrate.

Berners' flippant remarks and disregard of public opinion were hallmarks of the eccentric man who bought Faringdon House and its estate in 1920. A neat and dapper man with a clipped moustache, his appearance gave few clues to his character. He was a member of England's artistic and aristocratic elite, and entertained extravagantly at homes in London and Rome, as well as Faringdon. Here, at his country home, a flock of doves, each dyed a different vivid colour, fluttered over the lawns while whippets with diamond collars roamed the house. A contemporary photograph shows Lord Berners entertaining friends to tea, amongst them Penelope Chetwode – and her horse.

Yet he was also a man of many serious pursuits. Not only an accomplished painter whose works were well received by public and critics alike, he was also a writer with two volumes of autobiography and six novels, mostly satirical, to his name. Furthermore he was a talented composer who studied under Stravinsky and Vaughan Williams and was commissioned by Diaghilev to compose the music for his ballet *The Triumph of Neptune*.

Talented though he was, however, Berners, who died in 1950, will not be remembered for his paintings, his writing or his music. His memory lives on in his magnificent folly, open the first Sunday of every month and occasional bank holidays. Phone Faringdon Tourist Information Centre (tel: 01367 242191) for more details.

373 HOLMWOOD

HIGHLY COMMENDED

Shiplake Row, Binfield Heath, Henley-on-Thames, Oxfordshire RG9 4DP Tel (0118) 947 8747 Fax (0118) 947 8637

Holmwood is an elegant Georgian country house with a galleried hall, mahogany doors and marble fireplaces. The house is set in three acres of beautiful gardens with extensive views over the Thames valley. The large bedrooms are furnished with antique and period furniture – all have bathrooms en-suite, colour TV and tea/coffee-making facilities. Holmwood is convenient for Windsor, Oxford, London and Heathrow. Nearby are several pubs offering excellent evening meals. CATEGORY 3

Bed & Breakfast per night: single room from £30.00; double room from £50.00

Bedrooms: 1 single, 2 double, 2 twin
Bathrooms: 5 en-suite
Parking for 8
Cards accepted: Visa

12

374 THE GREAT HOUSE AT SONNING

HIGHLY COMMENDED

Thames Street, Sonning-on-Thames, Reading, Berkshire RG4 6UT Tel (0118) 969 2277 Fax (0118) 944 1296

Situated in the beautiful conservation village of Sonning, parts of The Great House date back to pre-Elizabethan times. With a four-acre estate and positioned on one of the loveliest stretches of the Thames, the hotel offers accommodation in five different areas. The elegant Moorings Restaurant overlooks the gardens and offers a choice of menu at luncheon and dinner. The cosy Ferryman's Bar serves a selection of real ales and is open all day.

Bed & Breakfast per night: single room from £114.00; double room from £155.00
Half board per person: from £62.00 daily
Lunch available: 1230–1430 (1500 on Sunday)
Evening meal 1900 (last orders 2215)

Bedrooms: 6 single, 30 double, 10 twin, 3 triple
Bathrooms: 49 en-suite
Parking for 100
Cards accepted: Mastercard, Visa, Switch/Delta

375 ACACIA

HIGHLY COMMENDED

44 Kilham Lane, Winchester, Hampshire SO22 5PT Tel (01962) 852259 or (0585) 462993

Our friendly home is set in beautiful gardens, five minutes' drive from the city centre, offering you a peaceful stay. Excellent and easy access to road and rail communications for many tourist areas all within one hour, including London (by rail), Portsmouth, New Forest, Salisbury, Stonehenge etc. Off-street parking. Double and twin bedrooms with en-suite bathrooms and tea/coffee-making facilities. Good choice of food for breakfast. Guests' private sitting room. A no-smoking house. Highly recommended for quality accommodation.

Bed & Breakfast per night: double room from £40.00–£44.00

Bedrooms: 1 double, 2 twin
Bathrooms: 2 en-suite, 1 private
Parking for 4
Open: March–October

10

Entries are cross referenced by number to the maps on pages 170–171

376 KNOLL HOUSE

HIGHLY COMMENDED

Wonston, Sutton Scotney, Winchester, Hampshire SO21 3LR Tel (01962) 760273

Knoll House is a ranch-type house set in the rural hamlet of Wonston, six miles from the city of Winchester, the former capital of Wessex. We have two rooms: one double-bedded room on the ground floor, with a bathroom en-suite, together with a sitting/dining-room including colour TV for our guests' personal use; and one twin-bedded room, also on the ground floor, but with a private bathroom and sitting room on the first floor, also including a colour TV. This is a family home, but we are delighted to welcome our guests and hope you will be very comfortable whilst you are with us.

Bed & Breakfast per night: single occupancy from £19.00; double room from £38.00
Half board per person: from £28.00 daily; from £190.00 weekly
Evening meal 1830 (last orders 2030)

Bedrooms: 1 double, 1 twin
Bathrooms: 1 en-suite, 1 private
Parking for 2

377 LAINS COTTAGE

HIGHLY COMMENDED

Quarley, Andover, Hampshire SP11 8PX Tel (01264) 889697 Fax (01264) 889697

Lains Cottage is a charming thatched house combining modern comforts with traditional cottage style. An ideal base from which to explore Stonehenge, Salisbury, the New Forest, Winchester and the south coast. The house is set in a quiet situation, yet only half a mile from the A303, giving access to London and the West Country.

Bed & Breakfast per night: single occupancy from £26.00–£35.00; double room from £42.00–£46.00

Bedrooms: 2 double, 1 twin
Bathrooms: 3 en-suite
Parking for 10

8

378 HIGHFIELD HOUSE

HIGHLY COMMENDED

Newtown Road, Awbridge, Romsey, Hampshire SO51 0GG Tel (01794) 340727 Fax (01794) 341450

Set in an unspoilt rural village in a delightful position with charming gardens. Home cooking a speciality. Close to Mottisfont Abbey (National Trust) and Hillier Arboretum. Twelve miles from Winchester and Salisbury. Fishing, golf and horse-riding can be arranged. On-site parking.

Bed & Breakfast per night: double room from £45.00–£50.00
Evening meal 1900

Bedrooms: 1 double, 2 twin
Bathrooms: 3 en-suite, 1 public
Parking for 10

12

379 THE WOODFALLS INN

HIGHLY COMMENDED

The Ridge, Woodfalls, Salisbury, Wiltshire SP5 2LN Tel (01725) 513222 Fax (01725) 513220

Nestling on the northern edge of the New Forest on an old coaching route to the city of Salisbury, the award-winning Woodfalls Inn has provided hospitality to travellers since 1870. An ideal base for a relaxing break, when you can visit the New Forest, Salisbury, Stonehenge, Romsey or a number of stately homes nearby. All bedrooms are individually decorated with en-suite facilities (some four-posters). Prize-winning restaurant, bar food and real ales. A warm welcome assured.

Bed & Breakfast per night: single occupancy from £49.95–£57.50; double room from £65.00–£95.00
Half board per person: £52.50–£65.00 daily; £325.00–£400.00 weekly
Lunch available: 1200–1430

Evening meal 1830 (last orders 2130)
Bedrooms: 7 double, 1 triple, 2 family rooms
Bathrooms: 10 en-suite
Parking for 30
Cards accepted: Mastercard, Visa, Switch/Delta

S SC SP T

380 A GREEN PATCH

HIGHLY COMMENDED

Furze Hill, Fordingbridge, Hampshire SP6 2PS Tel (01425) 652387 Fax (01425) 656594

An elegant house in a beautiful setting of eight acres which is very secluded and quiet, with direct access on to the New Forest. Wonderful views. Spacious bedrooms with bathrooms, TVs and tea/coffee-making facilities. Wide choice of breakfasts in a lovely oak-panelled dining room or on the terrace. Huge conservatory and garden for guests to use. Within easy reach of Bournemouth, Southampton, Salisbury, Winchester and Portsmouth. Plenty to see and do, good eating places nearby. Dogs welcome.

Bed & Breakfast per night: single occupancy from £25.00–£30.00; double room from £42.00–£45.00

Bedrooms: 2 double
Bathrooms: 1 en-suite, 1 private

UL S

381 PLANTATION COTTAGE

HIGHLY COMMENDED

Mockbeggar, Ringwood, Hampshire BH24 3NL Tel (01425) 477443

A charming two-hundred-year-old Grade II Listed cottage set in three acres of gardens and paddocks in the beautiful New Forest between Ringwood and Fordingbridge. Mockbeggar is a peaceful hamlet where wild ponies graze by the roadside, and is also within easy reach of Bournemouth, Poole and Salisbury. There are many excellent pubs and restaurants in the area, which is ideal for walking and cycling, and riding at stables close by. The guest lounge and garden are available all day.

Bed & Breakfast per night: single occupancy from £25.00–£30.00; double room from £45.00–£50.00

Bedrooms: 1 double, 1 twin
Bathrooms: 2 en-suite
Parking for 5
Cards accepted: Mastercard, Visa

UL S TV SP T

Entries are cross referenced by number to the maps on pages 170–171

382 STOCKLANDS HOUSE

HIGHLY COMMENDED

Hilton, Blandford Forum, Dorset DT11 0DE Tel (01258) 880580 or (01258) 881188 Fax (01258) 881188

With wonderful views over the Dorset countryside, this secluded house is superbly located for the coast, sightseeing, walking or riding (paddock and stable for your horse, if required). The delightfully appointed, ground floor en-suite bedrooms have all facilities, an accomplished chef provides delicious meals, and picnics are available. The heated pool is open from June to September and golf and tennis are nearby. We specialise in pampering our guests, and a warm welcome awaits you.

Bed & Breakfast per night: single occupancy from £30.00–£42.00; double room from £40.00–£52.00

Bedrooms: 2 double, 1 twin
Bathrooms: 2 en-suite, 1 private
Parking for 15

383 KIMMERIDGE FARMHOUSE

HIGHLY COMMENDED

Kimmeridge, Wareham, Dorset BH20 5PE Tel (01929) 480990

Enjoy a relaxing holiday in our picturesque farmhouse, with views of Kimmeridge Bay across 700 acres of farmland. Spectacular walks along the coastal paths, or inland across the Purbeck Hills surrounding the ruins of Corfe Castle. Nearby are Lulworth Cove and Castle, Studland Bay, Poole, Bournemouth and a wide choice of excellent places to eat. Spacious and attractively furnished rooms overlooking a peaceful garden. Home-cooked breakfast of your choice. A warm welcome assured.

Bed & Breakfast per night: single occupancy from £25.00–£30.00; double room from £38.00–£40.00

Bedrooms: 2 double, 1 twin
Bathrooms: 3 en-suite
Parking for 3

10

384 FAIRFIELDS HOTEL

HIGHLY COMMENDED

Studland Bay, Dorset BH19 3AE Tel (01929) 450224 Fax (01929) 450224

A small family-run hotel situated in a National Trust village, with magnificent views over Studland Bay to the Isle of Wight. A perfect place to relax in all seasons for those who appreciate good food, friendly service and an award-winning wine list. We use the very best of local produce, and herbs and vegetables from our garden. We welcome and cater for the needs of children, as well as discerning adults.

Bed & Breakfast per night: single room from £27.50–£39.50; double room from £55.00–£79.00
Half board per person: £40.00–£52.00 daily; £240.00–£312.00 weekly
Evening meal 1900 (last orders 1945)

Bedrooms: 2 single, 5 double, 1 triple, 4 family rooms
Bathrooms: 12 en-suite, 1 public
Parking for 16
Open: January and March–December
Cards accepted: Mastercard, Visa, Switch/Delta

385 PURBECK HOUSE HOTEL

HIGHLY COMMENDED

91 High Street, Swanage, Dorset BH19 2LZ Tel (01929) 422872 Fax (01929) 421194 E-mail purbeckhouse@easynet.co.uk

Our enchanting country house style hotel, which nestles in two acres of Victorian gardens, is close to the town centre and safe, sandy beaches. The hotel, which is steeped in history, boasts tessellated mosaic floors, original painted ceilings and Carrara marble fireplaces sculpted by Italian craftsmen. Our aim is to provide an oasis of relaxation and enjoyment reminiscent of a bygone era, with all of the requirements of a modern hotel.

Bed & Breakfast per night: single room from £40.00–£50.00; double room from £80.00–£100.00
Half board per person: £55.00–£65.00 daily; £364.00–£434.00 weekly
Lunch available: 1200–1430

Evening meal 1830 (last orders 2130)
Bedrooms: 2 single, 9 double, 2 twin, 1 triple, 4 family rooms
Bathrooms: 18 en-suite Parking for 23
Cards accepted: Mastercard, Visa, Diners, Amex, Switch/Delta

Brownsea Island

A SHORT TRIP FROM POOLE QUAY across the sheltered waters of Poole Harbour leads to Brownsea Island. At just over 500 acres (202 hectares) this is the largest of the five islands in the harbour. Brownsea's recorded history begins before the Norman Conquest when Bruno, Lord of Studland, owned the island; his name lives on, in corrupt form, in the word Brownsea.

In 1722 William Benson bought Brownsea for £300. Dubbed 'Mad' Benson by locals, he was briefly certified insane amidst accusations of satanic worship and child sacrifice. Whatever the truth, Benson introduced many rare plants and trees and was instrumental in making the island the wildlife haven it is today. By 1852, when Colonel William Petrie Waugh purchased Brownsea, the price was £13,000. He and his wife were convinced that the island had all the raw materials necessary for a china clay business. A persuasive pair, the Waughs talked a London bank into investing £237,000 in Brownsea. When the clay proved good enough only for items such as drain pipes (remnants can be seen on much of the southern shore) the enterprise failed. As the Waughs fled to Spain so the island's economy – and the bank – collapsed.

Successive private owners stamped their mark on Brownsea: one briefly resurrected the pottery business; another turned the castle – originally one of Henry VIII's South Coast fortifications – into a luxurious dwelling; a third cut the island off from all outside influence between 1925 and 1961, so allowing a range of rare fauna and flora to flourish away from the destructive habits of mankind. The National Trust, who inherited something of a jungle in 1961, has restored parts of the island to order, while leaving much to nature.

Today's visitors landing at Town Quay have plenty to discover. The northern shores and small lagoon now form a nature reserve populated by countless species of waders, gulls and waterfowl. There is a viewing hide not far from the quay and guided tours are available by arrangement. Look up into the pine trees and you may see red squirrels, for this is one of their last retreats in England; look down and you may glimpse the secretive sika deer. Come in late May or early June and two natural displays you cannot miss are the peacocks and the rhododendrons, the former flamboyantly and noisily strutting their stuff in front of the drab peahens, the latter creating huge splashes of purple in the sun. There are miles of glorious paths to explore, long sandy (if also a little muddy) beaches and an attractive little church. The castle is not open to the public. Further details from The National Trust on 01202 707744.

Entries are cross referenced by number to the maps on pages 170–171

386 HAVEN HOTEL

HIGHLY COMMENDED

Banks Road, Sandbanks, Poole, Dorset BH13 7QL Tel (01202) 707333 Fax (01202) 708796

Located at the water's edge, at the entrance to Poole Harbour, the Haven is a traditional hotel, constantly being improved and refurbished to a luxurious standard. The high level of friendly and reliable service, coupled with award-winning cuisine, makes the Haven an ideal hotel for every occasion. A wide range of facilities is offered, including a leisure centre.

CATEGORY 3

Bed & Breakfast per night: single room from £75.00–£115.00; double room from £150.00–£230.00
Half board per person: £85.00–£125.00 daily; £510.00–£750.00 weekly
Lunch available: 1230–1400

Evening meal 1900 (last orders 2130)
Bedrooms: 18 single, 41 double, 27 twin, 6 triple, 2 suites
Bathrooms: 94 en-suite
Parking for 160
Cards accepted: Mastercard, Visa, Diners, Amex, Switch/Delta

S SP T

387 THE BEECH TREE

HIGHLY COMMENDED

2 Stuart Road, Highcliffe, Christchurch, Dorset BH23 5JS Tel (01425) 272038

A superb value guest house, offering above average accommodation, quality home cooking and a welcome which is second to none. Just five minutes' walk through the woods by the stream is the unspoilt coastline of Highcliffe-on-Sea, with outstanding views of the Isle of Wight, the Needles and Christchurch Harbour. The nearby New Forest has unlimited potential for exploring and the ancient borough of Christchurch is but a short drive away. Highcliffe and Barton-on-Sea Golf Clubs nearby.

Bed & Breakfast per night: single occupancy from £18.00–£21.00; double room from £36.00–£42.00
Half board per person: £27.00–£30.00 daily; £181.00–£210.00 weekly
Evening meal 1800 (last orders 1800)

Bedrooms: 5 double, 1 twin
Bathrooms: 6 en-suite
Parking for 7

10 UL S TV

388 CHEWTON GLEN HOTEL, HEALTH & COUNTRY CLUB

DE LUXE

Christchurch Road, New Milton, Hampshire BH25 6QS Tel (01425) 275341 Fax (01425) 272310 E-mail reservations@chewtonglen.com

A very warm welcome awaits you here. Great emphasis is placed on service, with the restaurant being renowned for the quality of its food and wines. All bedrooms are individually decorated, and most have a balcony or terrace with a beautiful view. The health club offers a full range of health and fitness facilities, including an indoor pool and gymnasium. Beauty therapy appointments also available. Nine-hole golf course within grounds.

Bed & Breakfast per night: single occupancy from £210.00–£400.00; double room from £210.00–£400.00
Half board per person: £161.50–£256.50 daily; £1,043.00–£1,627.50 weekly
Lunch available: 1230–1345

Evening meal 1930 (last orders 2130)
Bedrooms: 52 double
Bathrooms: 52 en-suite
Parking for 125
Cards accepted: Mastercard, Visa, Diners, Amex, Switch/Delta

7 S SP

389 The Nurse's Cottage

HIGHLY COMMENDED

Station Road, Sway, Lymington, Hampshire SO41 6BA Tel (01590) 683402 Fax (01590) 683402

Formerly home to the village's successive District Nurses, this cosy cottage has been lovingly refurbished in recent years by chef/proprietor Tony Barnfield to provide every possible creature comfort. The enterprising dinner menu comprises thoughtfully-prepared dishes from fresh local produce wherever possible, and the wine list (unrivalled in an establishment of this size) contains over 70 worldwide selections. Ideal touring centre for the New Forest and surrounding area, with good connections to London and elsewhere.

Half board per person: £45.00–£50.00 daily;
£260.00–£295.00 weekly
Lunch available by arrangement
Evening meal 1830 (last orders 1930)

Bedrooms: 1 single, 1 double, 1 twin
Bathrooms: 3 en-suite
Parking for 4
Cards accepted: Mastercard, Visa, Amex, Switch/Delta

10

390 String of Horses

HIGHLY COMMENDED

Mead End Road, Sway, Lymington, Hampshire SO41 6EH Tel (01590) 682631 Fax (01590) 682631

A secluded hotel set in four acres of grounds. Experience the luxury of individually-designed bedrooms – several with four-poster beds – each with its own fantasy bathroom and offering every facility. Intimate, award-winning candle-lit restaurant. The perfect setting for newly-weds, second honeymooners and couples. Heated outdoor swimming pool. Excellent location for horse-riding, yachting, golfing and exploring the New Forest. Regrettably, we are unable to accommodate children.

Bed & Breakfast per night: single occupancy from £52.50–£55.00; double room from £40.00–£55.00
Half board per person: £59.95–£72.45 daily;
£377.00–£425.00 weekly
Lunch available: 1230–1330 (Sunday only)

Evening meal 1900 (last orders 2030)
Bedrooms: 7 double
Bathrooms: 7 en-suite
Parking for 24
Cards accepted: Mastercard, Visa, Diners, Amex, Switch/Delta

391 Whitley Ridge Country House Hotel

HIGHLY COMMENDED

Beaulieu Road, Brockenhurst, Hampshire SO42 7QL Tel (01590) 622354 Fax (01590) 622856

A charming Georgian house, formerly a royal hunting lodge, situated in New Forest parkland. The restaurant has a good reputation for serving food in elegant surroundings. All bedrooms are individually designed and prettily furnished, with forest views. We are conveniently placed, well off the road, with plenty of walks directly accessible from the hotel. Special midweek dinner, bed and breakfast rates are available. We look forward to welcoming you to Whitley Ridge.

Bed & Breakfast per night: single room from £56.00–£60.00; double room from £90.00–£126.00
Half board per person: £65.00–£75.00 daily;
£320.00–£413.00 weekly
Lunch available: 1200–1400 (Sunday only)

Evening meal 1900 (last orders 2030)
Bedrooms: 2 single, 9 double, 3 twin
Bathrooms: 14 en-suite
Parking for 24
Cards accepted: Mastercard, Visa, Diners, Amex, Switch/Delta

Entries are cross referenced by number to the maps on pages 170–171

392 NEW PARK MANOR HOTEL

HIGHLY COMMENDED

Lyndhurst Road, Brockenhurst, Hampshire SO42 7QH Tel (01590) 623467 Fax (01590) 622268

The New Park Manor is a prestigious and romantic country house hotel, dating back to the 16th century, in a wonderful setting of gardens, lawns and beautiful parkland in the heart of the New Forest. The award-winning Stag Head restaurant offers excellent French-influenced cuisine. Log-fire ambience, quality and service with a smile. Charmingly designed en-suite bedrooms. Own equestrian centre, seasonal heated swimming pool and tennis court. Wedding receptions, conferences and all other celebrations.

Bed & Breakfast per night: single occupancy £85.00; double room from £110.00–£160.00
Half board per person: £65.00–£90.00 daily
Evening meal 1930 (last orders 2145)

Bedrooms: 16 double, 5 twin
Bathrooms: 21 en-suite
Parking for 40
Cards accepted: Mastercard, Visa, Diners, Amex, Switch/Delta

7 S SP T

393 WOODLANDS LODGE HOTEL

HIGHLY COMMENDED

Bartley Road, Woodlands, New Forest, Hampshire SO4 2GN Tel (01703) 292257 Fax (01703) 293090

Luxuriously restored Georgian country house hotel. Our gardens have direct access to the New Forest. The peaceful and relaxing setting enables you to enjoy luxury without ostentation and unwind from the stress that is all too common today. The beautiful well-equipped bedrooms are all en-suite with showers and baths, all with whirlpool.

Bed & Breakfast per night: double room from £118.00–£170.00
Evening meal 1900 (last orders 2100)

Bedrooms: 16 double, 1 twin
Bathrooms: 17 en-suite
Parking for 25
Cards accepted: Access, Visa

S SP T

394 BOTLEY PARK HOTEL, GOLF & COUNTRY CLUB

HIGHLY COMMENDED

Winchester Road, Boorley Green, Botley, Southampton, Hampshire SO32 2UA Tel (01489) 780888 Fax (01489) 789242

Set in 176 acres of parkland golf course, within easy reach of motorways and 60 minutes from London, Botley Park offers 100 well appointed bedrooms with en-suite facilities. Enjoy our 18-hole golf course, driving range and putting green, squash and tennis courts, large gymnasium, aerobics dance studio, sauna and steam rooms, indoor heated swimming pool and spa pool. We also have a croquet lawn and petanque terrain, snooker room, and hair and beauty salon. A choice of two bars, or dine in our award-winning restaurant. ♿ CATEGORY 1

Bed & Breakfast per night: single occupancy from £70.00–£110.00; double room from £90.00–£140.00
Half board per person: £75.00–£95.00 daily
Evening meal 1900 (last orders 2145)

Bedrooms: 44 double, 56 twin
Bathrooms: 100 en-suite
Parking for 250
Cards accepted: Mastercard, Visa, Diners, Amex, Switch/Delta

S SP T

395 CHINE COURT HOTEL

HIGHLY COMMENDED

Popham Road, Shanklin, Isle of Wight PO37 6RG Tel (01983) 862732 Fax (01983) 862732

Welcome to Chine Court. A truly elegant Victorian residence, lavishly furnished and decorated throughout. Standing in large grounds, it commands magnificent sea views from its elevated cliff-top position. Beautifully appointed public rooms include a large luxurious bar lounge, dry lounges and an elegant Victorian dining room offering a sumptuous five course dinner with a full choice of traditional and continental dishes. The hotel offers peace and tranquillity and a high degree of comfort and Victorian grace and charm.

Bed & Breakfast per night: single room from £24.00–£31.00; double room from £48.00–£62.00
Half board per person: £33.00–£40.00 daily; £205.00–£264.00 weekly
Evening meal 1830 (last orders 1915)

Bedrooms: 3 single, 8 double, 6 twin, 5 triple, 4 family rooms
Bathrooms: 25 en-suite, 1 public
Parking for 24
Open: April–October

3 S SC SP T

Isle of Wight Geology

NO PART OF THE Isle of Wight's complex geology is unaffected by the action of the waves. The sea has periodically inundated the land and then retreated, laying down sediments and battering away at them, carving out dramatic cliffs and steep-sided valleys and creating some of the most spectacular coastal scenery in southern England.

The island is bisected by a high chalk ridge running east–west and rising to a height of some 650ft (198m). At its western end this chalk band forms a narrow headland pointing out to sea, shaped by the waves into the spectacular snow-white cliffs of Freshwater Bay and, at its furthest extremity, eroded into a series of jagged, white teeth poking from the sea: the famous Needles (shown below).

The character of the landscape north and south of the band of chalk differs markedly. The soils of the northern half of the island were laid down about 60 million years ago, in sedimentary layers of sand (crushed quartz) and clay. At Alum Bay, just north of the Needles, some of these layers have been exposed by the sea to create an extraordinary phenomenon. Mineral impurities have changed the colour of the usually white quartz, creating an amazing variety of coloured sands: white, black, green, red and yellow.

On the southern side of the island, ancient earth movements have exposed sedimentary layers laid down between 120 and 65 million years ago. Of these, the Wealden group, Wight's oldest rocks, meet the sea in just two places, one north of Sandown, the other along the south west coast. They were deposited when dinosaurs roamed the area and now yield some of the richest sources of dinosaur bones in Europe. On the beach at Hanover Point is Pine Raft, the fossilised remains of tree-trunks, some beautifully preserved, with annular growth rings still visible.

The southernmost region of the island is a complex arrangement of soft gault clay sandwiched between harder layers of sandstone. The gault, known as 'blue slipper', creates a highly unstable lubricant layer, causing the hard strata above to collapse periodically in giant landslips. Between Shanklin and Chale, each of the distinctive terraces falling down to the sea represents a different landslip. Known as the Undercliff, this picturesque terrain is the largest area of coastal landslip in north-western Europe.

The Museum of Isle of Wight Geology at Sandown (tel: 01983 404344) records the island's geological history and displays some spectacular fossil remains.

Entries are cross referenced by number to the maps on pages 170–171

396 BEAUFORT HOTEL

HIGHLY COMMENDED

71 Festing Road, Southsea, Hampshire PO4 0NQ Tel (01705) 823707 or 0800 919237 Fax (01705) 870270

The Beaufort Hotel is situated in a quiet part of Southsea, overlooking the canoe lake, with the seafront just a one-minute walk away. All the bedrooms have recently been refurbished and individually designed to a very high standard, each with en-suite bath and shower. Delightful restaurant offering both à la carte and table d'hôte menus. Satellite TV. Licensed bar. Car park. For reservations freephone 0800 919237.

Bed & Breakfast per night: single room from £48.00–£55.00; double room from £56.00–£70.00
Half board per person: £56.00–£60.00 daily; £220.00–£270.00 weekly
Evening meal 1830 (last orders 2030)

Bedrooms: 3 single, 11 double, 2 twin, 2 triple, 1 family room
Bathrooms: 19 en-suite
Parking for 10
Cards accepted: Mastercard, Visa, Amex, Switch/Delta

397 BROADWATER

HIGHLY COMMENDED

West Bracklesham Drive, Bracklesham Bay, Chichester, West Sussex PO20 8PH Tel (01243) 670059

Our completely self-contained ground-floor apartment is only 50 yards from a gently shelving beach, and its outlook is a delightful secret garden where total peace and privacy have been achieved. Yet we are within a short walk of comprehensive local amenities. A truly comfortable and welcoming base from which to explore the host of attractions the beautiful Chichester area has to offer. Minimum stay of two nights.

Bed & Breakfast per night: double room from £50.00–£70.00

Bedrooms: 1 twin
Bathrooms: 1 private

398 BURPHAM COUNTRY HOUSE HOTEL

HIGHLY COMMENDED

Burpham, Arundel, West Sussex BN18 9RJ Tel (01903) 882160 Fax (01903) 884627

Nestling in a fold of the famous Sussex South Downs, the hotel offers the most perfect location for a 'Stress Remedy Break'! The hamlet of Burpham is totally peaceful and unspoilt and the walks are truly spectacular. The dining room offers a regularly changing menu using only the best ingredients. Swiss-born Marianne Walker and husband George – the resident owners – are justly proud of their award-winning cuisine. The comfort offered here is truly memorable. Please mention this guide when booking.

Bed & Breakfast per night: single room £37.00; double room from £78.00–£95.00
Half board per person: £61.00–£69.50 daily; £385.00–£448.00 weekly
Evening meal 1930 (last orders 2045)

Bedrooms: 1 single, 6 double, 3 twin
Bathrooms: 10 en-suite
Parking for 12
Cards accepted: Mastercard, Visa, Amex

399 WHITE HORSE INN

HIGHLY COMMENDED

The Street, Sutton, Pulborough, West Sussex RH20 1PS Tel (01798) 869221 Fax (01798) 869291

Sutton is a picture-postcard village tucked away at the foot of the South Downs. Great sensitivity has been used to bring our charming Georgian inn up to the standards expected by the discerning traveller, whilst retaining its essential character. The bedrooms are elegantly furnished, each with its own spacious bathroom. The food has a strong emphasis on traditional country cooking, enhanced by a selection of other well-chosen dishes. Log fires in the winter!

Bed & Breakfast per night: single occupancy £48.00; double room from £58.00–£68.00
Lunch available: 1200–1400
Evening meal 1900 (last orders 2145)

Bedrooms: 4 double, 2 twin
Bathrooms: 5 en-suite, 1 private shower
Parking for 10
Cards accepted: Mastercard, Visa, Diners, Amex

---

400 PARK HOUSE HOTEL

HIGHLY COMMENDED

Bepton, Midhurst, West Sussex GU29 0JB Tel (01730) 812880 Fax (01730) 815643

Beautifully situated country house hotel nestling in the South Downs, but close to Goodwood racecourse and Chichester Festival Theatre. A quiet village location and beautifully furnished accommodation, with fourteen en-suite bedrooms, make this hotel the perfect retreat. Home-cooked food is served in the elegant dining room. Set in nine acres of grounds with two grass tennis courts, putting and croquet lawns, 9-hole pitch and putt course and heated swimming pool. Conference facilities available.

Bed & Breakfast per night: single room from £49.00–£70.00; double room from £90.00–£120.00
Evening meal 2000

Bedrooms: 1 single, 6 double, 6 twin, 1 triple
Bathrooms: 14 en-suite, 1 public
Parking for 40
Cards accepted: Mastercard, Visa, Amex, Switch/Delta

---

401 THE ANGEL HOTEL

HIGHLY COMMENDED

North Street, Midhurst, West Sussex GU29 9DN Tel (01730) 812421 Fax (01730) 815928

The Angel Hotel is a large 16th-century coaching inn located in the historic market town of Midhurst. Sympathetically restored by owners Peter Crawford-Rolt and Nicholas Davies, the hotel retains many features from its Tudor origins. Each of the bedrooms and suites have been individually designed and four-poster beds grace the larger suites. Many of the bedrooms have wonderful views over the Elizabethan rose gardens and Cowdray Castle beyond. Good food, impeccably presented and served, is central to the hotel's approach and has won many awards.

Bed & Breakfast per night: single room from £80.00–£110.00; double room from £90.00–£155.00
Half board per person: £148.00 daily; £554.50 weekly
Lunch available: 1200–1430

Evening meal 1800 (last orders 2200)
Bedrooms: 4 single, 12 double, 11 twin, 1 triple
Bathrooms: 28 en-suite
Parking for 40
Cards accepted: Mastercard, Visa, Diners, Amex, Switch/Delta

Entries are cross referenced by number to the maps on pages 170–171

402 LYTHE HILL HOTEL

HIGHLY COMMENDED

Petworth Road, Haslemere, Surrey GU27 3BQ Tel (01428) 651251 Fax (01428) 644131 E-mail lythe@lythehill.co.uk

A village of buildings set in twenty acres of parkland, only one hour from London, make up Lythe Hill Hotel. The 14th-century house has five rooms, including one with an antique four-poster bed, and a large brass-bedded suite with an 'old time' clawed-feet bath. Across the courtyard, more modern bedrooms include luxury doubles with jacuzzi bathrooms, and two glorious garden suites with their own patios overlooking the lake. Two restaurants include the Auberge de France, which is oak-panelled and beamed.

Bed & Breakfast per night: single room from £103.00–£143.00; double room from £133.00–£193.00
Half board per person: £83.00–£103.00 daily; £539.00–£619.00 weekly
Lunch available: 1215–1415

Evening meal 1915 (last orders 2115)
Bedrooms: 4 single, 20 double, 8 twin, 8 family rooms
Bathrooms: 40 en-suite
Parking for 150
Cards accepted: Mastercard, Visa, Diners, Amex, Switch/Delta

403 THE BISHOP'S TABLE HOTEL & RESTAURANT

HIGHLY COMMENDED

27 West Street, Farnham, Surrey GU9 7DR Tel (01252) 710222 Fax (01252) 733494

An elegant, award-winning hotel where hospitality is at its best. All bedrooms are individually decorated. The walled garden is a walk into another world. The restaurant is well known and offers an excellent cuisine, including a full vegetarian menu.

Bed & Breakfast per night: single room from £78.00–£86.00; double room from £86.00–£95.00
Half board per person: £96.00–£113.00 daily
Lunch available: 1230–1345
Evening meal 1900 (last orders 2145)

Bedrooms: 6 single, 9 double, 2 twin
Bathrooms: 17 en-suite
Cards accepted: Mastercard, Visa, Diners, Amex

404 CHEQUERS HOTEL

HIGHLY COMMENDED

Church Place, Pulborough, West Sussex RH20 1AD Tel (01798) 872486 Fax (01798) 872715

Situated in the heart of the local conservation area and facing out over the Arun Valley towards the South Downs, we pride ourselves upon being the quintessential small English country hotel. Built in 1548 and carefully extended and refurbished, we offer luxury en-suite bedrooms, fine food in our award-winning restaurant, a conservatory coffee shop, and ample parking. Right outside is our 9-acre meadow for walks for you and your dog.

Bed & Breakfast per night: single room from £54.50–£59.50; double room from £79.00–£89.00
Half board per person: £48.00–£53.00 daily; £309.00–£344.00 weekly
Lunch available: 1200–1345

Evening meal 1930 (last orders 2045)
Bedrooms: 1 single, 5 double, 2 twin, 3 triple
Bathrooms: 10 en-suite, 1 private
Parking for 16
Cards accepted: Mastercard, Visa, Diners, Amex

405 ASCOTT HOUSE HOTEL

HIGHLY COMMENDED

21 New Steine, Marine Parade, Brighton, East Sussex BN2 1PD Tel (01273) 688085 Fax (01273) 623733

Located in one of the most convenient central positions in Brighton, this Grade II Listed building is situated in a seafront garden square close to the Palace Pier, Royal Pavilion, Theatre Royal, famous Lanes and the Brighton Conference Centre. Whether your visit is for business or pleasure, enjoy a delicious, individually-prepared English breakfast served in the elegant dining room. This excellent well-established, licensed hotel offers all the home comforts in a relaxed and welcoming atmosphere.

Bed & Breakfast per night: single room from £25.00–£40.00; double room from £40.00–£80.00
Evening meal 1830

Bedrooms: 4 single, 6 triple, 2 family rooms
Bathrooms: 10 en-suite, 1 public, 1 private shower
Cards accepted: Mastercard, Visa, Diners, Amex

Leith Hill

NOWHERE IN SOUTH-EAST ENGLAND does the landscape ever quite stretch its fingertips to the 1,000ft (304m) notch. However, thanks to the efforts of Richard Hull, an 18th-century Surrey man, it is quite possible to stand and admire the views from such an altitude. Hull's solution was to build a grandiose folly on the very top of 965ft (289m) Leith Hill, the highest point in the North Downs. Standing behind the battlements of his Leith Hill Tower and looking south you may catch sight of the gleam of the English Channel; looking north the dome of St Paul's and the pyramid on top of Canary Wharf are landmarks of historic and modern London. But whichever way you look the views are incomparable. It is said that thirteen counties are visible on the clearest of days.

The National Trust now manages the 860 acres (348 hectares) of heath and woodland that comprise the Leith Hill estate, and although the tower is the literal and figurative high point of a visit, there is much else to admire. Numerous paths lead through the broadleaved woods and past the ponds that characterise the southern slopes, on which there stands a fine avenue of mature lime trees, planned as a feature of a formal garden. To the west are the azalea and rhododendron woods, bursting with colour and rich with scent from mid-April until early June.

The composer and lover of English countryside Sir Ralph Vaughan Williams gave the estate to the National Trust at the end of the Second World War. Peaceful though it now is, it has seen bloodier times. In 851 Ethelwulf, father of the future King Alfred and leader of the West Saxons, inflicted a heavy defeat upon the invading Danes. Rivers of blood are said to have flowed from the battleground on the top of the hill. Leith Hill, with its commanding views, was clearly a place of great strategic importance and finds of flint tools suggest that there may have been settlements here as long ago as 1000–2000BC.

Leith Hill lies amidst the most attractive scenery of the North Downs a few miles south of Dorking. The tower is open at weekends throughout the year and also on Wednesdays in summer. Out of season last admission to the tower is at 3pm. Ring 01306 711777 for more details.

Entries are cross referenced by number to the maps on pages 170–171

406 THE OLD TOLLGATE RESTAURANT & HOTEL — HIGHLY COMMENDED

The Street, Bramber, Steyning, West Sussex BN44 3WE Tel (01903) 879494 Fax (01903) 813399

In a lovely old Sussex village nestling at the foot of the South Downs, standing on the original Tollhouse site, a perfect blending of the old with the new. Award-winning, carvery-style restaurant – a well-known and popular eating spot – offers a magnificent hors d'oeuvres display followed by a vast selection of roasts, pies and casseroles, with delicious sweets and cheeses to add the final touch. Luxuriously-appointed bedrooms, including two four-posters with jacuzzi baths, and two suites.

Bed & Breakfast per night: single occupancy from £67.95–£89.95; double room from £74.90–£96.90
Half board per person: £55.95–£66.95 daily
Lunch available: 1200–1345
Evening meal 1900 (last orders 2130)

Bedrooms: 21 double, 10 twin
Bathrooms: 31 en-suite
Parking for 60
Cards accepted: Mastercard, Visa, Diners, Amex, Switch/Delta

SP T

407 SHELLEYS HOTEL — HIGHLY COMMENDED

High Street, Lewes, East Sussex BN7 1XS Tel (01273) 472361 Fax (01273) 483152

The town of Lewes, which is well known to opera lovers who attend the celebrated annual Glyndebourne Opera Festival, is nestled among the picturesque South Downs. Recently refurbished, Shelleys offers the highest standard of comfort. A short break can offer you the chance to explore some beautiful scenery, shop for antiques and visit the attractions of Brighton – about twenty minutes away – before returning to a peaceful country house hotel, renowned for its service and cuisine.

Bed & Breakfast per night: single room from £53.00–£111.50; double room from £106.00–£120.00
Half board per person: £73.00–£80.00 daily; £511.00–£560.00 weekly
Lunch available: 1215–1415

Evening meal 1900 (last orders 2115)
Bedrooms: 1 single, 9 double, 9 twin
Bathrooms: 19 en-suite
Parking for 25
Cards accepted: Mastercard, Visa, Diners, Amex, Switch/Delta

SP T

408 WHITE LODGE COUNTRY HOUSE HOTEL — HIGHLY COMMENDED

Sloe Lane, Alfriston, Polegate, East Sussex BN26 5UR Tel (01323) 870265 Fax (01323) 870284

An Edwardian building set in five acres overlooking Alfriston village. All bedrooms are individually decorated with every facility, the majority having either extensive downland or village views. We have three lounges (one non-smoking) and our Orchid Restaurant, with views over the Cuckmere valley, offers freshly-prepared daily and à la carte menus accompanied by an extensive wine list. Alfriston village is a particularly attractive oasis of calm in the glorious South Downs and our welcome really makes the White Lodge 'Somewhere Special'.

Bed & Breakfast per night: single room £55.00; double room from £95.00–£135.00
Half board per person: £65.50–£85.50 daily
Lunch available: 1215–1330
Evening meal 1915 (last orders 2130)

Bedrooms: 3 single, 7 double, 6 twin, 1 triple
Bathrooms: 16 en-suite, 3 private
Parking for 25
Cards accepted: Mastercard, Visa, Amex, Switch/Delta

SP T

409 South Paddock

HIGHLY COMMENDED

Maresfield Park, Uckfield, East Sussex TN22 2HA Tel (01825) 762335

A comfortable country house, beautifully furnished with an atmosphere of warmth and elegance. All rooms face south, overlooking three and a half acres of mature gardens, landscaped for attractive colouring throughout the year. A peaceful setting for relaxing on the terrace, beside the fishpond and fountain or in spacious drawing rooms with log fires. Centrally located, 41 miles from London and within easy reach of Gatwick, the channel ports, Glyndebourne, Nymans, Sissinghurst and Chartwell. Good restaurants locally.

Bed & Breakfast per night: single occupancy from £34.00–£38.00; double room from £52.00–£56.00

Bedrooms: 1 double, 2 twin
Bathrooms: 2 private, 1 public
Parking for 6

10

410 Hooke Hall

HIGHLY COMMENDED

250 High Street, Uckfield, East Sussex TN22 1EN Tel (01825) 761578 Fax (01825) 768025

Hooke Hall is an elegant Queen Anne townhouse that has been fully restored by its owners (whose home it is) to give a blend of comfort with informality. All the rooms are individually decorated to very high standards. In the panelled study, guests can relax by the open fire before dining at La Scaletta, well known for its high-quality Italian regional food.

Bed & Breakfast per night: single occupancy from £47.50–£75.00; double room from £75.00–£130.00
Lunch available: 1200–1400
Evening meal 1930 (last orders 2100)

Bedrooms: 5 double, 4 twin
Bathrooms: 9 en-suite
Parking for 7
Cards accepted: Mastercard, Visa, Amex

12

411 Lye Green House

DE LUXE

Lye Green, Crowborough, East Sussex TN6 1UU Tel (01892) 652018 Fax (01892) 652018

An elegant Sussex country house offering spacious, tastefully decorated accommodation. The en-suite rooms are large and luxurious, with king-size beds for comfort. The beautiful six-acre garden was laid out in Edwardian times, with clipped yew hedges dividing the nine gardens – each with its own style, including a potager kitchen garden and some magnificent herbaceous borders. A lime walk leads to the natural ponds set in woodland. A rowing boat and fishing rods are available for relaxation.

Bed & Breakfast per night: single occupancy £45.00; double room £55.00

Bedrooms: 1 double, 2 twin
Bathrooms: 2 en-suite, 1 private
Parking for 3

Entries are cross referenced by number to the maps on pages 170–171

412 DANEHURST

HIGHLY COMMENDED

41 Lower Green Road, Rusthall, Tunbridge Wells, Kent TN4 8TW Tel (01892) 527739 Fax (01892) 514804

Danehurst is a charming gabled house in a village setting in the heart of Kent. Our tastefully furnished bedrooms afford you excellent accommodation and breakfast is served in our Victorian conservatory. You can also enjoy a candle-lit dinner in our elegant dining room between November and March. We would be delighted to welcome you to our home – we like to feel that once you are in our care you can relax and enjoy everything we have to offer you. Private parking is available.

Bed & Breakfast per night: single occupancy from £39.50–£45.00; double room from £59.50–£69.50

Bedrooms: 3 double, 2 twin
Bathrooms: 4 en-suite, 1 private
Parking for 5
Cards accepted: Mastercard, Visa, Amex

8 SP T

413 GLYDWISH PLACE

Listed HIGHLY COMMENDED

Fontridge Lane, Burwash, East Sussex TN19 7DG Tel (01435) 882869 or 0860 624197 Fax (01435) 882749

Beautiful, split-level house on a lovely wooded site, with far-reaching views for your relaxation. Large gardens with lawns and ponds on different levels, a summer house and putting green. Many different breeds of ducks, geese and pheasants. The surrounding countryside is delightful, with lovely walks and excellent pubs in the local villages. A sauna, solarium, gymnasium and games room are also available and free of charge when staying for two nights or more.

Bed & Breakfast per night: single room from £20.00–£30.00; double room from £45.00–£55.00

Bedrooms: 1 single, 3 double
Bathrooms: 2 en-suite, 2 private, 4 public
Parking for 14

UL TV SC SP

414 CONQUERORS

HIGHLY COMMENDED

Stunts Green, Herstmonceux, Hailsham, East Sussex BN27 4PR Tel (01323) 832446

With its commanding views over 1066 country, Conquerors was built, to the highest standards, in the 1930s. Peaceful and secluded in its parkland setting of outstanding natural beauty, Conquerors is only one mile from several old village inns and restaurants. Famous houses, castles and gardens are within easy touring distance, as are the historic towns of Hastings, Battle, Royal Tunbridge Wells, Brighton and Eastbourne. Conquerors aims to offer complete comfort in total tranquillity. CATEGORY 3

Bed & Breakfast per night: single occupancy from £22.00–£26.00; double room from £42.00–£50.00

Bedrooms: 1 double, 2 twin
Bathrooms: 2 en-suite, 1 private
Parking for 5

10 UL TV T

415 Beauport Park Hotel

👑👑👑👑 HIGHLY COMMENDED

Battle Road, Hastings, East Sussex TN38 8EA Tel (01424) 851222 Fax (01424) 852465

Our Georgian Country House is the jewel in a 1500-acre parkland estate, three miles from the village of Battle and a short drive to Rye. Our acclaimed restaurant offers the best of English and continental cuisine. Each bedroom overlooks our gardens and Sussex cream teas can be served in the Italian sunken garden. A 9 and 18-hole golf course and riding stables are adjacent to the hotel.

Bed & Breakfast per night: single room from £69.00–£75.00; double room from £95.00–£110.00
Half board per person: £71.00–£75.00 daily; £497.00–£525.00 weekly
Lunch available: 1230–1400

Evening meal 1900 (last orders 2130)
Bedrooms: 4 single, 10 double, 7 twin, 2 triple
Bathrooms: 23 en-suite
Parking for 64
Cards accepted: Mastercard, Visa, Diners, Amex, Switch/Delta

---

416 Manor Farm Oast

👑👑 HIGHLY COMMENDED

Windmill Orchard, Main Road, Icklesham, Winchelsea, East Sussex TN36 4AJ Tel (01424) 813787 Fax (01424) 813787

A three roundel oast house built in the 19th century and nestling in acres of apple and cherry orchards. A truly peaceful haven of luxury, ideally situated for country walks or coastal visits. Set in 1066 Country, within easy reach of Rye, Winchelsea, Battle and Hastings. Christmas house parties catered for – solve the murder mystery in front of open log fires whilst enjoying traditional fare. Most major credit cards accepted.

Bed & Breakfast per night: single occupancy from £38.00–£42.00; double room from £50.00–£60.00
Half board per person: £40.00–£45.00 daily; £280.00–£315.00 weekly

Bedrooms: 2 double, 1 twin
Bathrooms: 2 en-suite, 1 private
Parking for 10
Open: February–December
Cards accepted: Mastercard, Visa, Switch/Delta

12

---

417 Flackley Ash Hotel & Restaurant

👑👑👑👑 HIGHLY COMMENDED

London Road, Peasmarsh, Rye, East Sussex TN31 6YH Tel (01797) 230651 Fax (01797) 230510

A Georgian country house hotel, set in beautiful gardens with croquet and putting lawns. Indoor swimming pool and leisure centre with gym, saunas, whirlpool spa, steam room and flotation tank. Beauty salon offering aromatherapy massage. Warm, friendly atmosphere, fine wines and good food. Well situated for visiting the castles and gardens of East Sussex and Kent and the ancient Cinque port of Rye. Golf, bird-watching, country or seaside walks, potteries and steam trains are some of the attractions in the area.

Bed & Breakfast per night: single occupancy from £69.00–£85.00; double room from £108.00–£128.00
Half board per person: £49.50–£69.00 daily; £325.00–£415.00 weekly
Lunch available: 1230–1345

Evening meal 1900 (last orders 2130)
Bedrooms: 21 double, 9 twin, 1 triple, 1 family room
Bathrooms: 32 en-suite
Parking for 60
Cards accepted: Mastercard, Visa, Diners, Amex, Switch/Delta

Entries are cross referenced by number to the maps on pages 170–171

418 LITTLE SILVER COUNTRY HOTEL

HIGHLY COMMENDED

Ashford Road, St Michaels, Tenterden, Kent TN30 6SP Tel (01233) 850321 Fax (01233) 850647

Little Silver Country Hotel is set in its own landscaped gardens. The restaurant provides an intimate, tranquil atmosphere where local produce is enjoyed, pre-dinner drinks and after dinner coffee are offered in the beamed sitting room with its log fire. Breakfast is served in a Victorian conservatory overlooking the waterfall rockery. Luxury bedrooms, tastefully and individually designed, some with four-posters and jacuzzi baths, others with brass beds. Facilities for disabled. Personal attention, care for detail, warmth and friendliness create a truly memorable experience. CATEGORY 3

Bed & Breakfast per night: single occupancy from £60.00–£85.00; double room from £85.00–£110.00
Half board per person: £80.00–£110.00 daily; £378.00–£441.00 weekly
Lunch available: 1200–1400 (pre–booked only)

Evening meal 1830 (last orders 2200)
Bedrooms: 5 double, 3 twin, 1 triple, 1 family room
Bathrooms: 10 en-suite
Parking for 50
Cards accepted: Mastercard, Visa, Amex, Switch/Delta

419 ISLE OF OXNEY SHETLAND CENTRE

HIGHLY COMMENDED

Oxney Farm, Moons Green, Wittersham, near Tenterden, Kent TN30 7PS Tel (01797) 270558 or 0850 219830 Fax (01797) 270558

A warm 'home from home' welcome from Eve and Brian Burnett, together with excellent food, await you at Oxney Farm. Convenient for the Channel Tunnel and ports, the spacious well-furnished comfortable farmhouse, with luxurious indoor pool, lies midway between Tenterden and Rye in peaceful rural surroundings. The area is steeped in history, scenery and culture. Our miniature Shetland ponies add their charm to the friendly country house atmosphere. A no smoking house. Directions: from Tenterden or Rye, B2082 to Wittersham, at Swan Inn turn into Swan Street, Oxney Farm is 1.3 miles along on left.

Bed & Breakfast per night: single occupancy £25.00–£27.50; double room £50.00–£55.00
Evening meal by prior arrangement only

Bedrooms: 2 double, 1 twin
Bathrooms: 2 en-suite, 1 private
Parking for 6

420 PLAYDEN COTTAGE GUESTHOUSE

HIGHLY COMMENDED

Military Road, Rye, East Sussex TN31 7NY Tel (01797) 222234

On the old Saxon shore, less than a mile from Rye town and on what was once a busy fishing harbour, there is now only a pretty cottage with lovely gardens, a pond and an ancient right of way. The sea has long receded and, sheltered by its own informal gardens, Playden Cottage looks over the River Rother and across the sheep-studded Romney Marsh. It offers comfort, peace, a care for detail – and a very warm welcome.

Bed & Breakfast per night: double room from £50.00–£66.00
Half board per person: £37.00–£45.00 daily; £241.50–£291.90 weekly
Evening meal 1800 (last orders 2030)

Bedrooms: 1 double, 2 twin
Bathrooms: 3 en-suite, 1 public
Parking for 7
Cards accepted: Mastercard, Visa

12

421 JEAKE'S HOUSE

HIGHLY COMMENDED

Mermaid Street, Rye, East Sussex TN31 7ET Tel (01797) 222828 Fax (01797) 222623 E-mail jeakeshouse@btinternet.com

Jeake's House stands on the most famous cobbled street in medieval Rye. Bedrooms have been individually restored to create a very special atmosphere, combining traditional elegance and luxury with modern amenities. Oak-beamed and panelled bedrooms with brass, mahogany or four-poster beds overlook the marsh and rooftops to the sea. Vegetarian or traditional breakfast is served in the galleried former chapel where soft chamber music and a roaring fire will make your stay a truly memorable experience.

Bed & Breakfast per night: single room from £24.50–£58.00; double room from £45.00–£63.00

Bedrooms: 1 single, 7 double, 1 twin, 2 triple, 1 family room
Bathrooms: 9 en-suite, 2 private, 2 public
Cards accepted: Mastercard, Visa, Amex

422 RYE LODGE HOTEL

HIGHLY COMMENDED

Hilders Cliff, Rye, East Sussex TN31 7LD Tel (01797) 223838 Fax (01797) 223585

Premier position on East Cliff, close to the historic 14th-century Landgate, High Street shops and restaurants. De luxe rooms, all en-suite with luxurious bathrooms, remote control colour TVs, direct-dial telephones and hospitality trays. Room service with breakfast in bed as late as you like. Candle-lit dinners in the elegant Terrace Room, with delicious food and an extensive, well-chosen wine list. Tastefully furnished, where elegance is the keynote in a relaxed atmosphere with really caring service. Own car park.

Bed & Breakfast per night: single room from £47.50–£65.00; double room from £65.00–£105.00
Half board per person: £47.50–£65.00 daily; £299.50–£410.00 weekly
Evening meal 1930 (last orders 2130)

Bedrooms: 2 single, 11 double, 7 twin
Bathrooms: 20 en-suite
Parking for 20
Cards accepted: Mastercard, Visa, Diners, Amex, Switch/Delta

423 THE HYTHE IMPERIAL HOTEL

HIGHLY COMMENDED

Princes Parade, Hythe, Kent CT21 6AE Tel (01303) 267441 Fax (01303) 264610

An impressive sea-front resort hotel set within fifty acres in the historic Cinque port of Hythe. All the rooms enjoy sea or garden views with executive, four-poster, half-tester or jacuzzi rooms and suites available. Conference facilities available for up to two hundred, as well as superb leisure facilities, including 9-hole golf course, indoor swimming pool, luxurious spa bath, steam room, sauna, gym, sunbed, tennis, croquet, karting, beauty salon and hairdressing.

Bed & Breakfast per night: single room from £98.50–£118.50; double room from £124.00–£144.00
Half board per person: £72.50–£92.50 daily; £435.00–£555.00 weekly
Lunch available: 1300–1400

Evening meal 1900 (last orders 2100)
Bedrooms: 17 single, 43 double, 40 twin
Bathrooms: 100 en-suite
Parking for 202
Cards accepted: Mastercard, Visa, Diners, Amex, Switch/Delta

Entries are cross referenced by number to the maps on pages 170–171

424 HARBOURSIDE BED AND BREAKFAST HOTEL

HIGHLY COMMENDED

13/14 Wear Bay Road, Folkestone, Kent CT19 6AT Tel (01303) 256528 or 0468 123884 Fax (01303) 241299 E-mail r.j.pye@dial.pipex.com

Two beautifully restored Victorian houses on the East Cliff, overlooking sea and harbour, provide luxury en-suite accommodation. The quality, hospitality, service, and value for money are truly special. We can be your perfect base from which to tour South East England, the best stop-over when crossing the channel, or the centre point for a relaxing holiday. Phone, fax or e-mail us to reserve your room, ask for a colour brochure or just for more details.

Bed & Breakfast per night: single occupancy from £35.00–£60.00; double room from £50.00–£70.00

Bedrooms: 4 double, 2 twin
Bathrooms: 5 en-suite, 1 private
Parking for 1
Cards accepted: Mastercard, Visa, Amex, Switch/Delta

12

Martello Towers

ONE OF THE ECCENTRICITIES inherited from the Georgian era is the chain of strange-looking gun towers constructed early in the 1800s along England's south-east coast. At war with France and faced with the greatest threat of invasion since 1066, the British government decided to fend off Napoleon's massing armies by strengthening coastal defences. Several military engineers had been impressed, ironically, by a French-built fortified tower at Mortella Point on Corsica, which with just three guns had repelled two heavily armed British warships in 1794. A proposal was put forward that a chain of similar forts be built between Suffolk and Sussex. Prime Minister William Pitt backed the plan with characteristic vigour and work started in 1804 on what became known as the Martello Towers.

By 1808, 73 towers, numbered from east to west, had been built between Dover in Kent and Eastbourne in Sussex. Work then started on another 29 towers along the coasts of Suffolk and Essex, plus one more at Seaford in Sussex, bringing the total to 103 by 1812. Resembling upturned flower pots in shape, the towers were built on three levels. A ladder, retractable in case of siege, gave entrance to the first floor, which was divided into three areas – living quarters for the officer and his 24 men, and a storeroom. Ammunition and provisions were kept on the ground floor, approached through a trap-door. The top floor was a gun platform, where a 2½-ton cannon was mounted on a revolving pivot. From here a 24lb (11kg) shot could be fired a mile out to sea, and even the French acknowledged that, especially where the towers were just 600ft (182m) apart and their ships would be within range of 15 towers, the damage inflicted would be devastating.

However, the invasion never happened, Napoleon was defeated at Waterloo in 1815 and the most extensive defence system in the country's history stood like a string of follies. The towers were subsequently put to use by the Coastguard in its battle against the smuggling trade and a century later, in 1940, when Hitler threatened invasion, the War Department again prepared the towers for action – but once more the invasion never materialised. Now the number of towers has fallen to 43, many having sunk beneath the sea. Some are abandoned and in disrepair, some privately owned and converted to dwellings, others restored and open to the public. The following have a visitor centre or museum: No. 3 at East Cliff, Folkestone; No. 73, the Wish Tower, on Eastbourne seafront; No. 74, Seaford. Phone the Tourist Information Centre at Folkestone (tel: 01303 258594) for further details on No.3, at Eastbourne (tel: 01323 411400) for Nos. 73 and 74.

425 THE OLD VICARAGE

 DE LUXE

Chilverton Elms, Hougham, Dover, Kent CT15 7AS Tel (01304) 210668 Fax (01304) 225118

South East England Tourist Board 'Bed & Breakfast of the Year' 1997. Guests are welcomed in a warm and relaxed style at this Victorian country house, elegantly furnished with lovely antiques and pictures. Situated in the peaceful Elms Vale with outstanding views, yet only minutes from Dover, The Old Vicarage provides everything for your stay to the highest standards and in spacious comfort. Large informal gardens. Log fires in winter. Secure parking. An ideal base for touring East Kent.

Bed & Breakfast per night: single occupancy £40.00; double room from £55.00–£60.00
Evening meal by arrangement

Bedrooms: 2 double, 1 double/twin, 1 double/family
Bathrooms: 2 en-suite, 2 private
Parking for 10
Cards accepted: Mastercard, Visa

426 THE WOODVILLE HALL HOTEL

 DE LUXE

London Road, Temple Ewell, Dover, Kent CT16 3DJ Tel (01304) 825256 Fax (01304) 825256

The Woodville Hall was built for Henry Colman (of mustard fame) in 1820. A short drive from the port of Dover and the Channel Tunnel, this superb example of a Georgian country house is set amid some 25 acres of beautiful parkland – an oasis of timeless elegance and tranquillity. The magnificent decor of our spacious suites reflects the splendour of a bygone age and a sense of gracious calm pervades throughout.

Bed & Breakfast per night: double room from £95.00–£125.00
Half board per person: £72.50–£87.50 daily
Evening meal 2000

Bedrooms: 1 double, 2 suites
Bathrooms: 3 en-suite
Parking for 27
Cards accepted: Mastercard, Visa, Amex

427 WALLETTS COURT HOTEL & RESTAURANT

HIGHLY COMMENDED

Westcliffe, St-Margarets-at-Cliffe, Dover, Kent CT15 6EW Tel (01304) 852424 Fax (01304) 853430

Walletts Court is an 'historic building of Kent' – a restored 17th-century manor house with a truly authentic sense of history. In a lovely rural setting with far-reaching views towards St. Margaret's Bay, Dover and the famous White Cliffs. The restaurant, highly acclaimed in major guides, is under the personal supervision of Chris Oakley and his family. Fresh seasonal ingredients are used in a menu with a Jacobean flavour which, together with a fine selection of wines, makes your stay a memorable experience.

Bed & Breakfast per night: single room from £55.00–£75.00; double room from £65.00–£90.00
Half board per person: £60.00–£80.00 daily; £400.00–£500.00 weekly
Evening meal 1900 (last orders 2130)

Bedrooms: 1 single, 7 double, 2 twin, 2 triple
Bathrooms: 11 en-suite, 1 private
Parking for 20
Cards accepted: Mastercard, Visa, Diners, Amex, Switch/Delta

Entries are cross referenced by number to the maps on pages 170–171

428 THANINGTON HOTEL

HIGHLY COMMENDED

140 Wincheap, Canterbury, Kent CT1 3RY Tel (01227) 453227 Fax (01227) 453225

A spacious Georgian bed and breakfast hotel, ideally situated ten minutes' stroll from the city centre. En-suite bedrooms, beautifully decorated and furnished, all in immaculate condition with modern-day extras. King-size four-poster beds, antique bedsteads and two large family rooms. Walled garden with patio, indoor heated swimming pool, intimate bar, guest lounge and snooker/games room. A delicious breakfast, to suit all tastes, is served in the elegant dining room. Secure private car park. An oasis in a busy tourist city. Convenient for the channel ports, tunnel and historic houses and gardens of Kent.

Bed & Breakfast per night: single occupancy from £45.00–£50.00; double room from £65.00–£85.00

Bedrooms: 5 double, 3 twin, 2 family rooms
Bathrooms: 10 en-suite, 2 public
Parking for 12
Cards accepted: Mastercard, Visa, Diners, Amex

429 PRESTON LEA

HIGHLY COMMENDED

Canterbury Road, Faversham, Kent ME13 8XA Tel (01795) 535266 or 0421 329442 Fax (01795) 533388

This beautiful spacious house, built a century ago, was designed by a French architect and has many unique and interesting features, including two turrets, an oak-panelled hall, staircase, dining room and guest drawing room. Situated in lovely secluded gardens but by the A2, it is convenient for Canterbury, all the Channel ports, the M2 to London and beautiful countryside. Each bedroom is individually designed and all are large and sunny. A warm welcome is assured by caring hosts.

Bed & Breakfast per night: single occupancy £35.00; double room from £45.00–£48.00

Bedrooms: 2 double, 1 twin
Bathrooms: 2 en-suite, 1 private
Parking for 10
Cards accepted: Mastercard, Visa

430 HEMPSTEAD HOUSE

HIGHLY COMMENDED

London Road, Bapchild, Sittingbourne, Kent ME9 9PP Tel (01795) 428020 Fax (01795) 428020

Exclusive private Victorian country house hotel, set in three acres of beautifully landscaped gardens. We extend exceptional warmth and hospitality to all our guests, offering luxurious en-suite accommodation and elegant surroundings. You can spend a memorable evening in our licensed dining room and relax in our spacious drawing rooms and conservatory. In the daytime, wander around our peaceful grounds or relax by our outdoor heated swimming pool.

Bed & Breakfast per night: single occupancy £62.00; double room £72.00
Half board per person: £55.50–£81.50 daily; £350.00–£550.00 weekly
Evening meal 1800 (last orders 2200)

Bedrooms: 11 double, 2 twin
Bathrooms: 13 en-suite
Parking for 22
Cards accepted: Mastercard, Visa, Diners, Amex, Switch/Delta

431 TANYARD

HIGHLY COMMENDED

Wierton Hill, Boughton Monchelsea, Maidstone, Kent ME17 4JT Tel (01622) 744705 Fax (01622) 741998

Tanyard is a medieval country house hotel perched on a ridge with far-reaching views across the weald of Kent. All six bedrooms have en-suite facilities and are furnished with antiques combined with modern comforts. The top-floor suite, which is heavily beamed, has a spa bath and is particularly popular. The no smoking restaurant seats twenty eight and is in the oldest part of the building, dating from 1350. The modern English cuisine uses only fresh local produce.

Bed & Breakfast per night: single room from £65.00–£85.00; double room from £100.00–£140.00
Half board per person: £77.50–£112.50 daily; £542.50–£787.50 weekly
Lunch available: 1230–1345 (Sunday & Wednesday–Friday)

Evening meal 1900 (last orders 2100)
Bedrooms: 1 single, 3 double, 2 twin
Bathrooms: 6 en-suite
Parking for 20
Cards accepted: Mastercard, Visa, Diners, Amex, Switch/Delta

Dickens' Kent

FOR EIGHT DAYS IN LATE JUNE Broadstairs, on Kent's eastern coast, is thronged with characters in Victorian dress, parading the streets and participating in period cricket matches, bathing parties and other amusements. They are here for the Dickens festival, a literary event first staged in 1937 to mark the centenary of Dickens' first visit, and held annually ever since.

When Dickens came to Broadstairs he was 25 years old and on the point of achieving nationwide fame with the publication of *The Pickwick Papers*. He had spent part of his childhood in the Kent town of Chatham and had become well-acquainted with the county from accompanying his father on long country walks. For 14 years he frequently spent summer and autumn months in Broadstairs, eventually leasing Fort House, a fine residence overlooking Viking Bay. Now called Bleak House and open to the public as a museum (tel: 01843 862224), it is thought to have inspired its namesake in Dickens' famous novel, for it stands, tall and solitary, on the cliffs far above Broadstairs. Visitors may see rooms inhabited by the author, including the study where he completed *David Copperfield* and planned *Bleak House*. Also in Broadstairs is the Dickens House Museum (tel: 01843 862853) once the home of Miss Mary Strong, an eccentric woman who was probably the inspiration for one of Dickens' most colourful creations, Miss Betsey Trotwood, David Copperfield's aunt.

In 1856, Dickens purchased Gad's Hill Place, near Rochester, which he had admired as a boy, and always dreamed of owning. This substantial house, now a private school, is occasionally open to the public (details from Rochester's tourist information centre, tel: 01634 843666). The town also provided inspiration for many places in Dickens's works. Eastgate House was both Nun's House School in *The Mystery of Edwin Drood* and Westgate House in *The Pickwick Papers*. Now the Rochester Dickens Centre (tel: 01634 844176), it recreates scenes and characters from the author's best-known works. In its gardens an elaborately carved Swiss chalet was a gift to Dickens from an actor friend who sent it to Higham station in 58 packing cases. It once stood in the shrubbery at Gad's Hill and in it Dickens wrote his last words before his death in 1870. Further Dickensian associations may be followed up using *The Dickens Trail*, available from local tourist information centres.

Entries are cross referenced by number to the maps on pages 170–171

432 AUCKLANDS

Listed HIGHLY COMMENDED

25 Eglington Road, North Chingford, London E4 7AN Tel (0181) 529 1140 Fax (0181) 508 3837

Comfortable Edwardian family home on the edge of London, where an open fire and caring owners welcome guests as friends. We are within easy reach of Stansted and London City airports, just five minutes' walk to the station (lifts offered), 25 minutes to Liverpool Street station, and 35 minutes to Oxford Circus. We are right on the edge of Epping Forest, where you can enjoy relaxing walks or play a game of golf at the local course. We have one king-size double room and one twin, with a super bathroom! Enjoy our secluded garden with its small swimming pool (May to September). We serve good food and offer lunches by arrangement. The resident cat will tolerate guide-dogs only!

Bed & Breakfast per night: single occupancy from £30.00–£35.00; double room from £50.00–£70.00
Half board per person: £40.00–£55.00 daily; £240.00–£300.00 weekly
Lunch available: by arrangement

Evening meal 1700 (last orders 2300)
Bedrooms: 1 double, 1 twin
Bathrooms: 1 public

12 UL S TV T

433 THE LEONARD

HIGHLY COMMENDED

15 Seymour Street, London W1H 5AA Tel (0171) 935 2010 Fax (0171) 935 6700

Conveniently located off Portman Square, London's latest townhouse hotel has, in its short time of being open, received critical acclaim and awards. Each of the twenty suites and six bedrooms are air-conditioned and beautifully decorated with a combination of traditional furniture, both contemporary and antique, elegant fabrics and distinctive objets d'art. The bathrooms are bright and bedrooms contain everything from mini bars to satellite televisions. Professional, friendly house staff are around to provide service from concierge to 24-hour room service.

Bed & Breakfast per night: double room from £218.00–£288.00
Lunch available: 1200–1430

Bedrooms: 22 double, 1 triple, 3 family rooms
Bathrooms: 26 en-suite
Cards accepted: Mastercard, Visa, Diners, Amex, Switch/Delta

TV SP T

434 HOTEL NUMBER SIXTEEN

HIGHLY COMMENDED

16 Sumner Place, London SW7 3EG Tel (0171) 589 5232 Fax (0171) 584 8615 U.S. TOLL FREE 1800 592 5387

Situated in South Kensington, Number Sixteen has been created from four Victorian town houses. Offering style, elegance and seclusion, guests are encouraged to make themselves at home. There is a relaxed informality about the drawing room and the library, where everyone is invited to pour themselves a drink from the honour bar. The conservatory opens onto an award-winning garden. The comfortable well-appointed bedrooms are individually decorated with a combination of antique and traditional furnishings.

Bed & Breakfast per night: single room from £80.00–£115.00; double room from £150.00–£180.00

Bedrooms: 9 single, 23 double, 4 triple
Bathrooms: 32 en-suite, 2 private, 2 public
Cards accepted: Mastercard, Visa, Diners, Amex, Switch/Delta

T

435 FIVE SUMNER PLACE HOTEL

Listed HIGHLY COMMENDED

South Kensington, London SW7 3EE Tel (0171) 584 7586 Fax (0171) 823 9962 E-mail no.5@dial.pipex.com

This delightful award-winning hotel is situated in South Kensington, one of the most fashionable areas of London. The hotel itself has been sympathetically restored to recreate the ambience and style of a bygone era. Family-owned and run, it offers excellent service and personal attention. All rooms are luxuriously appointed and come with private en-suite facilities, telephone, colour television, trouser press and full buffet breakfast.

Bed & Breakfast per night: single room from £75.00–£90.00; double room from £110.00–£140.00

Bedrooms: 3 single, 5 double, 5 twin
Bathrooms: 13 en-suite, 1 public
Cards accepted: Mastercard, Visa, Amex

436 WELLMEADOW LODGE HOTEL

HIGHLY COMMENDED

24 Wellmeadow Road, London W7 2AL Tel (0181) 567 7294 Fax (0181) 566 3468

Winner of London Tourist Board 'Best Bed & Breakfast' Award 1997. This charming lodge combines the highest hotel standards with the atmosphere of a private home. Luxurious en-suite facilities and delicious breakfasts that are second to none, with various home-made items. Easy access to central London and Heathrow. One minute's walk from Boston Manor underground station.

Bed & Breakfast per night: single room from £65.00–£110.00; double room from £90.00–£120.00
Half board per person: £62.00–£130.00 daily; £434.00–£910.00 weekly
Evening meal 1800 (last orders 1900)

Bedrooms: 3 single, 4 double, 3 twin
Bathrooms: 10 en-suite
Cards accepted: Mastercard, Visa, Amex, Switch/Delta

Entries are cross referenced by number to the maps on pages 170–171

Symbols

For ease of use, the key to symbols appears on the back of the cover flap and can be folded out while consulting individual entries. The symbols which appear at the end of each entry are designed to enable you to see at a glance what's on offer, and whether any particular requirements you have can be met. Most of the symbols are clear, simple icons and few require any further explanation, but the following points may be useful:

Alcoholic drinks

Alcoholic drinks are available at all types of accommodation listed in the guide unless the symbol UL (unlicensed) appears. However, even in licensed premises there may be some restrictions on the serving of drinks, such as being available to diners only. You may wish to check this in advance.

Smoking

Many establishments offer facilities for non-smokers, indicated by the symbol ⚟. These may include no-smoking bedrooms and parts of communal rooms set aside for non-smokers. Some establishments prefer not to accommodate smokers at all, and if this is the case it will be made clear in the establishment description in the guide entry.

Pets

The symbol 🐕 is used to show that dogs are not accepted in any circumstances. Some establishments will accept pets, but we advise you to check this at the time of booking and to enquire as to whether any additional charge will be made to accommodate them.

Booking checklist

When enquiring about accommodation remember to state your requirements clearly and precisely. It may be necessary or helpful to discuss some or all of the following points:

- Your intended arrival and departure dates.
- The type of accommodation you require. For example, a twin-bedded room, a private bath and WC, whether the room has a view or not.
- The terms you require, such as room only; bed & breakfast; bed, breakfast and evening meal (half board); bed, breakfast, lunch and evening meal (full board).
- If you have any children travelling with you, say how old they are and state their accommodation requirements, such as a cot, and whether they will share your room.
- Any particular requirements, such as a special diet or a ground-floor room.
- If you think you are likely to arrive late in the evening, mention this when you book. Similarly, if you are delayed on your journey

a telephone call to inform the management may well help avoid any problems on your arrival.

- If you are asked for a deposit or the number of your credit card, find out what the proprietor's policy is if, for whatever reason, you can't turn up as planned – see 'cancellations' opposite.
- Exactly how the establishment's charges are levied – see below.

Misunderstandings can easily occur over the telephone, so it is advisable to confirm in writing all bookings, together with special requirements. Please mention that you learnt of the establishment through *Somewhere Special*. Remember to include your name and address, and please enclose a stamped, addressed envelope – or an international reply coupon if writing from outside Britain. Please note that the English Tourist Board does not make reservations; you should address your enquiry directly to the establishment.

Prices

The prices given throughout this publication will serve as a general guide, but you should always check them at the time of booking. The following information may prove useful when determining how much a trip may cost:

- Prices were supplied during the autumn of 1997 and changes may have occurred since publication.
- Prices include VAT where applicable.
- You should check whether or not a service charge is included in the published price.
- Prices for double rooms assume occupancy by two people; you will need to check whether there is a single person supplement.
- Half board means the price for the room, breakfast and evening meal per person per day or per person per week.
- A full English breakfast is not always included in the quoted price; you may be given a continental breakfast unless you are prepared to pay more.
- Establishments with at least four bedrooms or eight beds are obliged to display in the reception area or at the entrance overnight accommodation charges.
- Reduced prices may apply for children; check exactly how these reductions are calculated, including the maximum age for the child.
- Prices are often much cheaper for off-peak holidays; check to see whether special off-season packages are available.

Deposits and advance payments

For reservations made weeks or months ahead a deposit is usually payable which will be deducted from the total bill at the end of your stay.

Some establishments, particularly the larger hotels in big towns, now require payment for the room upon arrival if a prior reservation has not been made. Regrettably this practice has become necessary because of the number of guests who have left without settling their bills. If you are asked to pay in advance, it is sensible to see your room before payment is made to ensure that it meets your requirements.

If you book by telephone and are asked for your credit card number, you should note that the proprietor may charge your credit card account even if you subsequently cancel the booking. Ask the owner what his or her usual practice is.

Credit/charge cards

Any credit/charge cards that are accepted by the establishment are indicated at the end of the written description. The abbreviations used in this guide are:

Mastercard – Mastercard/Eurocard
Visa – Visa/Barclaycard
Diners – Diners
Amex – American Express
Switch/Delta – Direct debit card

If you intend to pay by either credit or charge card you are advised to confirm this at the time of booking. Please note that when paying by credit card, you may sometimes be charged a higher rate for your accommodation in order to cover the percentage paid by the proprietor to the credit card company. Again find this out in advance.

When making a booking, you may be asked for your credit card number as 'confirmation'. The proprietor may then charge your credit card account if you have to cancel the booking, but if this is the policy, it must be made clear to you at the time of booking – see below.

Cancellations

When you accept offered accommodation, including over the telephone, you are entering into a legally binding contract with the proprietor. This means that if you cancel a reservation or fail to take up all or part of the accommodation booked, the proprietor may be entitled to compensation if the accommodation cannot be re-let for all or a good part of the booked period. If you have paid a deposit, you will probably forfeit this, and further payment may well be asked for.

However, no such claim can be made by the proprietor until after the booked period, during which time every effort should be made to re-let the accommodation. It is therefore in your interests to advise the management immediately in writing if you have to cancel or curtail a booking. Travel or holiday insurance, available quite cheaply from travel agents and some hotels, will safeguard you if you have to cancel or curtail your stay.

And remember, if you book by telephone and are asked for your credit card number, you should check whether the proprietor intends charging your account should you later cancel your reservation. A

proprietor should not be able to charge for a cancellation unless he or she has made this clear at the time of your booking and you have agreed. However, to avoid later disputes, we suggest you check whether he or she intends to make such a charge.

Service charges and tipping

Some establishments levy a service charge automatically, and, if so, must state this clearly in the offer of accommodation at the time of booking. If the offer is accepted by you, the service charge becomes part of the contract. If service is included in your bill, there is no need for you to give tips to the staff unless some particular or exceptional service has been rendered. In the case of meals, the usual tip is 10% of the total bill.

Telephone call charges

There is no restriction on the charges that can be made by hotels for telephone calls made from their premises. Unit charges are frequently considerably higher than telephone companies' standard charges in order to defray the costs of providing the service. It is a condition of being awarded a national Crown classification that the telephone unit charges are displayed alongside the telephone. However, it may not always be clear how these compare with the standard unit charge. Before using a hotel telephone, particularly for long-distance calls, you should enquire how much extra you will be paying per unit.

Security of valuables

It is advisable to deposit any valuables for safe-keeping with the management of the establishment in which you are staying. If the management accept custody of your property they become wholly liable for its loss or damage. They can however restrict their liability for items brought on to the premises and not placed in their special custody to the minimum amounts imposed by the Hotel Proprietors Act, 1956. These are the sum of £50 in respect of one article and a total of £100 in the case of one guest. In order to restrict their liability the management must display a notice in the form required by the Act in a prominent position in the reception area or main entrance of the premises. Without this notice, the proprietor is liable for the full value of the loss or damage to any property (other than a motor car or its contents) of a guest who has booked overnight accommodation.

Feedback

Let us know about your holiday. We welcome suggestions about how the guide itself may be improved.

Most establishments welcome feedback. Please let the proprietor know if you particularly enjoyed your stay. We sincerely hope that you have no cause for complaint, but should you be dissatisfied or have any problems, make your complaint to the management at the time of the incident so that immediate action may be taken.

The English Tourist Board, Jarrold Publishing and Celsius cannot guarantee the accuracy of the information in this guide and accept no responsibility for any error or misrepresentation. All liability for any loss, disappointment or damage caused by reliance upon the information contained in this guide, or in the event of bankruptcy or liquidation or cessation of trade of any company, individual or firm mentioned, is hereby excluded. All establishments listed are bound by the Trades Description Acts of 1968 and 1972 when describing and offering accommodation and facilities, but we strongly recommend that prices and other details should be confirmed at the time of booking.

Details listed were believed correct at time of going to press. It is advisable to telephone in advance to check the details have not altered and to discuss any specific requirements.

Code of Conduct

All establishments appearing in this guide have agreed to observe the following Code of Conduct:

1. To ensure high standards of courtesy and cleanliness; catering and service appropriate to the type of establishment.
2. To describe fairly to all visitors and prospective visitors the amenities, facilities and services provided by the establishment, whether by advertisement, brochure, word of mouth or any other means. To allow visitors to see accommodation, if requested, before booking.
3. To make clear to visitors exactly what is included in all prices quoted for accommodation, meals and refreshments, including service charges, taxes and other surcharges. details of charges, if any, for heating or for additional services or facilities available should also be made clear.
4. To adhere to, and not to exceed, prices current at time of occupation for accommodation or other services.
5. To advise visitors at the time of booking, and subsequently, of any change, if the accommodation offered is in an unconnected annexe, or similar, or by boarding out, and to indicate the location of such accommodation and any difference in comfort and amenities from accommodation in the main establishment.
6. To give each visitor, on request, details of payments due and a receipt if required.
7. To deal promptly and courteously with all enquiries, requests, reservations, correspondence and complaints from visitors.
8. To allow an English Tourist Board representative reasonable access to the establishment, on request, to confirm that the Code of Conduct is being observed.